SOMEBODY'S
KNOCKING

*Lessons Learned from
a Quarter Century
of TV Reporting*

JASON PEDERSON

Oak Ridge Media Group
Little Rock, Arkansas

Somebody's Knocking:
Lessons Learned from a Quarter Century of TV Reporting

© 2024, Jason Pederson. All rights reserved.

Published by Oak Ridge Media Group, Little Rock, Arkansas

ISBN 979-8-218-38816-4 (paperback)
Library of Congress Control Number: 2024905891

Publication managed by AuthorImprints.com

"For 20 years, Jason Pederson was the award-winning broadcast journalist and host of KATV's 7 On Your Side. His new book, *Somebody's Knocking*, brings back memories of his intriguing stories as a consumer advocate, confronting and bringing to justice the crooks and scammers who conned Arkansas consumers. An interesting and satisfying read."

— **Mike Beebe, former Arkansas attorney general and former governor of Arkansas**

"Want an inside look at TV reporting from a truly honest and humble man defending the public from scoundrels and rip-offs? Jason Pederson will entertain and uplift you."

— **Jeff Kemp, author, speaker, and former NFL quarterback**

"Judging by your cover photograph, I would not want you knocking on my door. You look like a serious dude. Including the QR codes is an interesting way of bringing your subject to life. I wish you good luck on the book."

— **Ted Koppel, British-born American broadcast journalist**

"The lessons that Jason Pederson shares from his decades as a television reporter are evergreen and apply to every aspect of life:
- Those who love you the most tend to offer the best advice.
- Anchor your identity in something other than your work.
- Allow criticism to improve you, not define you.
- The vulnerable need advocates.

And as a bonus, his use of QR codes throughout this book add an enjoyable aspect for the reader: instant access to video clips that bring the written words to life!

— **Anne Jansen Broadwater, former KTHV-TV news anchor**

"Candid, readable, entertaining, vulnerable, revealing, and compelling. I loved it! I particularly liked the behind-the-scenes approach Jason takes on his experiences as a reporter and with the stories. Very enlightening. Honest and straightforward and fair, just as I remembered him to be as a reporter."

— **Dan McDonald, former director of the Arkansas Office of Child Support Enforcement**

In *Somebody's Knocking*, our intrepid reporter tells the tales of his pursuits in hilarious and eye-opening detail (the story of one victim's "indecent disposal" will leave you eternally grateful for your own indoor plumbing). One man who found himself on the wrong side of the door when Pederson came knocking declared, "The devil sent you here!" But this book leaves no doubt that the author was sent by a higher, divine power to do good—and to be "On Your Side."
> — Chris May, KATV-TV anchor

"Jason Pederson's book, *Somebody's Knocking, Lessons Learned from a Quarter Century of TV Reporting*, should be a "must-read" for any young journalist hoping to do meaningful work in an industry that requires a great deal from its practitioners. As a longtime college teacher, preparing students to work in the TV news business, I'm not sure there is a better handbook to follow."
> — Larry Foley, professor, School of Journalism and Strategic Media, University of Arkansas

"A very personal and entertaining 'inside look' at television news reporting. Jason's great stories and adventures will quickly draw you in. And the 'see it in real-time' QR codes and practical takeaways bring a creative bonus. I highly recommend this book."
> — Dr. Robert Lewis, author of *Raising a Modern Day Knight and Rocking the Roles: Building a Win-Win Marriage*

"Jason delivers a product that matches his days as a television consumer reporter by combining accuracy with empathy, which is what makes him a superior storyteller. Plus, Jason is able to weave his own life lessons into this book that shows his earnest desire to do the right thing at work and in marriage."
> — Lisa Fischer, journalist/podcaster

CONTENTS

Introduction: Somebody's Knockin' i

Chapter One: The History [How 7OYS started] 1

Chapter Two: The Racetrack [St. Croix Meadows]................................... 15

Chapter Three: The Internship [WCCO] 23

Chapter Four: The Start [From KTVE to KATV].. 33

Chapter Five: The Scoundrels [The Dishonest Eight]............................... 49

   MORE SCOUNDRELS [Scam Letter] 89

Chapter Six: The Money [Drew Co. Burial Association] 93

   MORE MONEY [SEWCO] 100

Chapter Seven: The Maddening [Tenant Rights]................................... 109

   MORE MADDENING [Restitution, Reputation, Rehabilitation]............... 121

Chapter Eight: The Unsolved [East End Bombing] 135

   MORE UNSOLVED [The Boys on the Tracks, Janie Ward]..................... 150

Chapter 9: The Impactful [Child Support Checks] 153

   MORE IMPACT [Wrongfully Jailed]... 160

Chapter 10: The Mistakes [#karma] 167

   MORE MISTAKES [Capitol Bump Shot, Ashley County Fatalities]........... 178

Chapter 11: The Vulnerable [Wiley Ballow] 183

   MORE VULNERABLE [Ronald Todd, Norman Butler, Mike Herman] 194

Chapter 12: The Incredulous [Lyme Disease]...................................... 207

   MORE INCREDULOUS STORIES [Big Fish, From Vows to Victories]......... 215

Chapter 13: The Heartbreak [Paul Eells/Anne Pressly]......................... 223

   MORE HEARTBREAK [Black Friday].. 235

Chapter 14: The Random [Do It Yourself Divorce] 239

   MORE RANDOMNESS [Pontiac Parisienne, Black Farmers, Medical Marijuana, Haley Zega]...248

Chapter 15: The Entertaining [Spencer and Shelby Visit Sat. DB, WTIBYBI] 255

   MORE ENTERTAINMENT [Christmas Celebrity Karaoke]...............................262

Epilogue: The Goodbye [undelivered] 281

Acknowledgments 285

About the Author 289

AUTHOR'S NOTE

I'VE DECIDED IT IS POINTLESS to try and convince people to put down their smart phones. In fact, I don't want you to! Keep your phone handy while you read: throughout the book, I've included QR codes that link to video clips discussed in the text.

To scan them, simply open your smartphone camera and hold it over the QR code until you see a clickable link. It will redirect you to the video.

You can also access the video/audio clips at www.jasonpedersonbook.com.

I hope you find the ability to watch the dozens of related video clips as cool as I do!

INTRODUCTION

SOMEBODY'S KNOCKIN'

KNOCKING ON DOORS WHERE YOU'RE not welcome produces an adrenaline rush.

And later, the experience can result in some entertaining messages left on your voicemail.

Because of my high-profile position on Arkansas television as a consumer reporter, I was asked to be a guest on a weekly radio segment. *The Show with No Name* (now *Morning Mayhem*) on 103.7 "The Buzz" in Little Rock was and remains a top-rated morning radio program. I combined the opening lyrics to Terri Gibbs's 1981 hit song "Somebody's Knockin" with actual voicemails left by viewers on the 7 On Your Side Helpline. It resulted in an amusing opening for my segment:

Throughout this book, you will have the opportunity to scan QR codes like the one above with your smartphone so you can hear and watch the events being described. QR codes became somewhat of a necessity during the pandemic when restaurants used them in place of menus. They are especially handy for someone writing a book about a career in television. You can also access the video/audio clips at www.jasonpedersonbook.com.

Back in the late '90s, Ted Koppel wrote a memoir called *Nightline: History in the Making and the Making of Television*. At the time, I was an avid viewer of the ABC late night news program, and I relished reading Koppel's behind-the-scenes accounts of his most famous interviews. What the book lacked, however, was a way to rewatch those moments as Koppel pelted his guests with questions they didn't always want to answer. That idea stayed with me, and I am thankful KATV has given me permission to use selected news clips that I believe will help make the words on these pages spring to life.

"Somebody's Knockin" was a natural fit for my radio intro, but not because I have blue eyes and blue jeans and not because I'm the devil (although some of the scoundrels you'll meet in Chapter Five might argue otherwise). It fits because during my twenty-year run as KATV's consumer reporter for "7 On Your Side," some of the most talked about and remembered segments involved me knocking on doors. Sometimes, someone answered; oftentimes, no one did. But just the act of going after the people who had done somebody wrong and trying to hold them accountable was appreciated and celebrated by viewers—whether or not I found the people I hoped to confront.

A police officer friend of mine watched one such segment and offered me advice: when knocking on a door where you might not be welcome, stand to the side rather than right in front of the door. That way, if a shot is fired through the door from inside the home, there will be a greater likelihood that it misses you. Some wise, albeit unsettling, counsel that I employed from that day forward.

Thankfully, no one ever fired a shot or assaulted me, but there were a few scares with dogs.

Sometimes, I never made it to the door.

Shortly after the arrest of Robert Todd Burmingham in 1997, photojournalist Marcus McDonald and I drove to a rural area near Colt, Arkansas, searching for people who could tell us more about the "Blue Light Rapist." Investigators suspected Burmingham of using a blue light to pull over female motorists and then attack them.

This was before GPS and cell phones. I'd received a tip and directions to a home where Burmingham reportedly lived. When we arrived, we saw a small, solitary white house about a quarter mile up a gravel driveway off the paved county road. It was a home that was impossible to sneak up on, with open fields on all four sides. We parked along the county road and walked up the driveway.

When we were about halfway to the house, a man walked out onto the porch holding a long gun. I hollered, "Hello!" I'm not sure what I was thinking ... other than we came a long way, and I might as well try and talk to him. He stood there unresponsive. "I'm Jason Pederson with Channel 7!" I yelled across the field. "We're looking for the home where Robert Todd Burmingham lives!" Again, no response. He just stood there stock still, gun in hand, staring at us.

Well, staring at me. Because when I turned around to ask Marcus what he thought we should do, I discovered Marcus had run back to our news vehicle.

"OK! Thanks! We're going to head out now!" I yelled, as I turned around and started back toward the paved road, looking back every few steps. The man never moved.

"What! Are! You! Doing?! He has a GUN!" Marcus exclaimed as soon as I joined him in the vehicle.

Chalk it up to stupidity, the invincibility of youth, or Divine protection, but I am thankful that in all my years of confrontin' and door knockin,' much of which is recounted in the following chapters, I am still in good health with all my original parts.

I covered Burmingham's trial in 1998 and a jury convicted him of rape, aggravated robbery, and kidnapping. It was one of the few stories I covered where cameras were allowed in the courtroom. Burmingham died in prison in 2020 at the age of fifty-four after contracting COVID-19.

Three years before his death, the Arkansas State Legislature passed Shannon's Law, named after Shannon Woods, one of Burmingham's victims. It makes it illegal to possess, purchase, sell, or transfer a blue light or a blue lens cap as well as any other police equipment or insignia (like a badge).

While there were no happy endings in this case, there was justice. Many of the stories you're about to read have neither, despite my efforts to hold people accountable. Some have both. Each features a 7 On Your Side reporter, a producer, and a team of volunteers behind him (or in the case of my successor, Marine Glisovic, behind her), born out of a vision developed decades ago, working to serve the citizens of Arkansas. Here is a KATV promotional spot from 2012 that captures the essence of being a 7 On Your Side reporter:

I hope you enjoy the read as much as I've enjoyed the ride.

CHAPTER ONE

THE HISTORY
(HOW 7OYS STARTED)

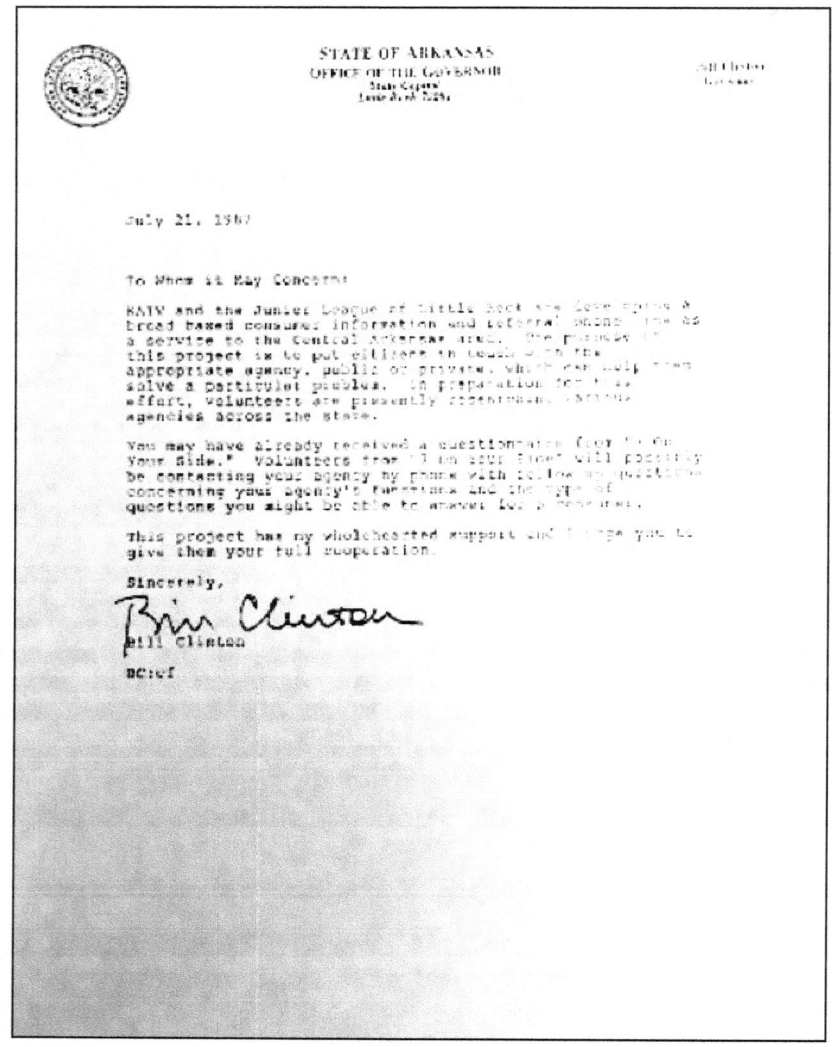

Copy of the original letter signed by Arkansas Governor Bill
Clinton, used to generate support for a new television segment.

KATV DEBUTED 7 ON YOUR Side in October 1987. Sportscaster
Paul Eels recorded a promotional spot to help educate Channel 7
viewers about what to expect from this new franchise—a segment
of the newscast aimed at helping everyday Arkansans. It would
work to expose scams and scoundrels but also provide education

about product recalls and ways to save money. Earlier that summer, then-Governor Bill Clinton and other elected leaders in central Arkansas signed letters of support as the station began planning and recruiting volunteers.

While the names Clinton and Eells are household names in Arkansas, it's doubtful you've heard the name of the woman most responsible for bringing a regular, televised consumer-reporting segment to the state: Ann Stargardter.

Stargardter would go on to help set up national hotlines for programs like Fox's "America's Most Wanted" and NBC's "Unsolved Mysteries." But in the early '80s, the California native was helping to launch hotline programs or consumer franchises for local TV stations all over the country, including Arkansas.

Stargardter wasn't yet thirty years old when she began testing her ideas and methods in 1973, first at KCRA-TV in Sacramento. She called the segment in Sacramento "Call-3." Over the course of a decade, Stargardter developed a model that she put into a 130-page how-to manual, a sixty-eight-page volunteer training manual, and a 110-page booklet of sample cases and scripts. Who knew so much thought went into the two-minute news stories Arkansans would grow to love?

In 1982, Stargardter expanded beyond Sacramento and offered her help to other stations interested in starting up a consumer segment. She had to first convince news directors, a group of largely older white men not accustomed to taking direction or suggestions from a woman, that the public exposure and goodwill generated by such an addition would benefit their station. If she got that far, she then needed to show them how to make it happen. As more stations signed on and launched consumer-help franchises, Stargardter amassed testimonials that she brought with her to the next news director pitch.

Jim Hart, general manager, WBIR/Knoxville: "If it's done properly, it puts the station in a position of protecting our viewers' interests and adds to our image as an organization that truly cares about its viewers."

Paul Paolicelli, news director, WESH/Orlando: "The most amazing thing to me is the response of the audience to the program—the [phone] lines were busy from the first day. This fills an obvious need in our community."

Bill Mitchell, news director, KDBS/El Paso: "The volunteers are what makes it work. This has been an established idea for a long time and Ann has done a great job putting it together; we're glad she came to us first."

Stargardter usually only worked with one station in each television market (Miami was an exception, where she helped launch franchises at both WCIX and WPLG). She helped bring consumer helplines to some of the biggest TV markets in the nation: New York (WCBS), Los Angeles (KCBS), Houston (KPRC), Washington DC (WJLA), San Francisco (KRON), and Baltimore (WMAR). Ultimately, she worked with 38 stations, including KATV in Little Rock.

Stargardter didn't have to convince KATV News Director Jim Pitcock to add a consumer franchise to his news product. Pitcock knew of her work in other markets and reached out to her. KATV Assistant News Director Bill Rogers recalls that it was likewise not hard to convince Stargardter to come to Arkansas.

"Ann had a special interest in being in Arkansas," recalls Rogers, "since it was the state where Joe Kleine played college basketball for the Arkansas Razorbacks. Joe later became a first-round pick of the Sacramento Kings, and Ann was a huge fan."

"We had been thinking about it for a while, and I approached Ann Stargardter about coming to Little Rock for a discussion about how we could get underway," says Pitcock. "She came in from

California for a visit with Dale (Nicholson, KATV general manager) and myself. She was here for about a day and brought up the subject of the Junior League. After Ann went back after the first meeting, I called the Junior League and set up a meeting for discussion. A week or so later, they gave me a conditional OK but wanted more details."

Stargardter's system relied on unpaid volunteers to answer the phones and to refer callers to organizations and agencies that could help them with their problems. So, in each city in which she arrived, her first goal was to pair the television station with a local volunteer group. In many cases, it would be a Junior League. Since 1901, Junior Leagues have been private, nonprofit organizations that serve their communities and develop social connections among their female members. In the case of KATV, it would be the Junior League of Little Rock. With a banquet hall and headquarters directly across from the station on Scott Street, it was a logical pick.

KATV paid to fly Stargardter back to Little Rock for a second and third meeting that included a committee of six Junior League of Little Rock members (Allison Holland, Terri Erwin, Betsy Robben, Luraette Tucker, Cathy Crass, and Ellon Cockrill) as well as Pitcock and Rogers. The meetings went so well that an optimistic Pitcock reserved the phone number that remains in use to this day: 501-324-HELP. Two weeks later, the Junior League of Little Rock officially said yes, calling it "…a worthwhile project and a positive marketing tool." Planning for the new franchise was soon underway.

Under the agreement, the Junior League would recruit and train the volunteers to answer phones for two hours each weekday, 10 a.m. until noon, Monday–Thursday. Volunteers were instructed to be courteous, take notes during each call, and follow-up with callers to make sure, if possible, their issues were resolved. KATV would be responsible for publicizing the endeavor and would handle public relations, giving the Junior League of Little Rock recognition on all printed materials. KATV also provided office space, phone lines, and office equipment—basically financing the operation.

7 On Your Side debuted in Arkansas on October 26, 1987. The agreement and effort would be reevaluated after a year. One big question remained: Who would be the first face of this new franchise? Pitcock decided on John Dewey, who had been working in KATV's Pine Bluff bureau for several years.

"Dewey had a journalism degree from the University of Missouri, was excited about the new challenge, and with his background was someone we could trust to cover the sensitive (client- related) topics," recalls Pitcock. At the time, Dewey co-anchored weekend newscasts with Kelly Minton.

"When station management told me that I would be the first 7 On Your Side reporter in 1987, it was described as a part-time role. I would report general assignment news when called to do so, while also identifying several consumer stories a week for 7 On Your Side," says Dewey. "Due to the promotable nature of the segments, news management generally wanted more pieces than I could generate in a week."

The popularity of 7 On Your Side with the public was almost instant. Lawyers cost money and nonprofit advocacy groups are often understaffed and overwhelmed. The segment offered Channel 7 viewers free and fast assistance. Dewey says he would routinely walk upstairs from the second-floor newsroom to the fourth floor (where the 7 On Your Side offices were located) and ask the first volunteer coordinator, Sandy Turner, to share any interesting calls or trends. "Amazing is all I can say about the work Sandy did," says Dewey. "Her files were very good. Her positive attitude and her volunteer commitment never changed."

The mix of stories reported by Dewey and subsequent 7 On Your Side reporters included successful advocacy, matters of consumer education and, on occasion, a healthy dose of confrontation.

"Sometimes, but not often, we became confrontational," remembers Dewey. "I did so only after getting news management's blessing, which generally was accomplished by detailing the extent to which Sandy and I tried to get the business to simply respond to a steady volume of complaints. By confrontational, I mean waiting next to the business owner's parked car and putting a camera and microphone in their face waiting for a response or knocking on the door of their house while a camera videotaped from the sidewalk."

The original intent of the 7 On Your Side franchise was not to confront bad actors but rather to refer wronged parties to other agencies and let them do the confronting. But a few problems emerged with that approach. First, the volunteers were trained to follow-up and make sure problems were taken care of following a referral. Oftentimes, they discovered that the problem still existed. Second, you don't get highly promotable TV moments by simply referring Arkansans to other agencies. Getting more involved became necessary not only to produce successful outcomes but also to grow a successful franchise.

Of course, getting more involved in disputes carries more risks, like the risk of litigation and advertiser alienation. Stargardter understood that. Downplaying station involvement in her initial pitch helped get wary news directors to sign on to the idea of a consumer reporting segment. As management's comfort level grew and the segment's popularity rose, increased reporter involvement (and risk) naturally followed. Little Rock was no exception.

"News management tended to give me a lot of leeway, and I rarely ever heard from General Manager Dale Nicholson," recalls Dewey. "This was commendable and showed a strong commitment to keeping news and sales separate. I know there must have been times when our stories created uneasiness with the sales group. For example, one time we aired a story about a customer's bad experience at a Dillard's department store and the customer's subsequent failures to get their complaint remedied. The not-so-favorable customer review prompted a phone call to me from William Dillard himself, promising to make the customer satisfied."

Although Dewey was the first 7 On Your Side reporter, his tenure would be the shortest. Dewey left KATV in 1989 and doubled his salary by taking a job with KMOV-TV in St. Louis. He followed up ten years in television news with a twenty-year career in public relations and is now retired and living in Las Vegas.

Dewey's departure created an opportunity for someone else.

"I started looking and I learned about Dewayne Graham, who was working in Baton Rouge," recalls Pitcock. "I brought him up, and he had a great audition tape."

Graham was quite a departure from Dewey; he was intense and combative as opposed to calm and collected. Unlike Dewey, Graham brought with him to the job experience as a television consumer reporter. He'd created a consumer affairs program at WAFB-TV in Baton Rouge where he started working in 1980. Later a cross-town rival, WBRZ-TV, hired him to do the same thing and he became the 2 On Your Side reporter.

The transition from Dewey to Graham was smooth in large part because of 7 On Your Side coordinator Sandy Turner. KATV hired Turner shortly after the launch of the franchise when it became apparent that the overwhelming response from the public necessitated putting someone officially in charge.

Turner brought life and work experience to the job, including a degree in mathematics from the University of Mississippi, seven years as a buyer for Memphis department stores, and a stint working in Washington, D.C. for Arkansas Congressman Beryl

Anthony. After marrying an attorney, Turner became active in social and charitable organizations in central Arkansas, including the Junior League of Little Rock. She was a natural choice to serve as the first volunteer coordinator for 7 On Your Side. Turner was the only paid person in the office (other than the reporter) and worked about twenty hours per week.

By the time Graham arrived on the scene, Turner had trained the volunteers, had a good working relationship with the newsroom, and managed a case file system that was invaluable to all who used it. Turner helped Graham get acclimated, and then off he went.

Graham served as the 7 On Your Side reporter for ten years, from 1989 to 1999. Viewers loved him. His bulldog-like tenacity and in-your-face reporting style made for some powerful and memorable television moments. Pitcock remembers his new hire this way: "At times he could get out on a limb, but it made for great TV, so I gave him a lot of latitude ... and we were never sued. Threatened MANY times."

Graham instituted a segment he called the "Rip Off of the Week," another example of generating content wildly popular with the public but apt to create heartburn in the souls of KATV lawyers and sales executives.

After Graham's arrival, 7 On Your Side was stable until the spring of 1994.

That's when Turner was in a horrific car accident that left her paralyzed. She would later revisit the 7 On Your Side office in her wheelchair, but she was never able to return to her coordinator duties. Turner died in 2009 at the age of sixty-one after a battle with breast cancer. Her obituary states that she enjoyed "book clubs, bridge groups, and Bible studies" until her death.

KATV named 7 On Your Side volunteer Donna Catrone (later Donna Nunn) as Turner's replacement. Just as it was when Dewey passed the baton to Graham, the transition from Turner to Nunn was seamless. Also in 1994, the newsroom experienced a leadership change as Bob Steel took over for Jim Pitcock as news director.

Throughout these changes, the volunteers remained the backbone of 7 On Your Side. Without a team of volunteers willing to answer the hundreds of weekly calls, letters, and emails from Arkansans in need of assistance, the program could not work. And getting volunteers—at least in the beginning—wasn't easy. Minutes from a Sept. 2, 1987, planning meeting reveal the challenges: "Terri reported on the groups she and Gladys had spoken to trying to recruit volunteers. They are discouraged and concerned because at this point not many have volunteered."

This was less than two months before the launch of 7 On Your Side. The Junior League of Little Rock's committee was going before civic groups every week touting the new service and asking for volunteers. They visited several AARP chapters, other Junior League chapters, retirement communities, the Southwestern Bell Pioneers, Welcome Wagon, the Business Volunteer Council, the Urban League of Arkansas, Stepping Stone, several sorority groups, and Parents Without Partners.

A man named Gene Goss was in the audience at the pitch made to Parents Without Partners. Goss, sixty-two, and the president of the support group, had joined in 1980, three years after his first wife died of cancer. He met his second wife, Alice, at the group in 1986, and they married two years later.

Since Gene and Alice were now parents *with* partners, they would have to leave the group. Goss began looking for another way to serve his community. He signed up with 7 On Your Side and answered the first call that came into the Helpline. A retired Navy captain, Goss's work history included ten years with Arkansas Power & Light, twenty-seven years with the Social Security Administration, and a stint as owner of an insurance business. His work experience benefited countless Arkansans during the twenty-two years he served as a 7 On Your Side volunteer. Goss visited all fifty states before his passing in 2017 at the age of ninety-three.

Over the years, countless overqualified men and women have served as 7 On Your Side volunteers. Most were retirees with a burning desire to help others and do some good in this world. They included former teachers, former politicians, former civil servants, and former business owners. All volunteers are trained to be compassionate and not rush to judgment. They're taught that no matter how thin you pour a pancake, there are always two sides.

Wading into and trying to clean up the messes made by others is no easy task. But most of the time, the volunteers are able to do just that—take a complaint, research it, and find a solution. The 7 On Your Side coordinator and reporter are involved in only the tough, sensitive, or urgent cases.

At one point, there was an allegation made to the Arkansas chapter of the NAACP that 7 On Your Side volunteers did not treat all complaints or callers equally. While the volunteer team has included minorities over the years, and while efforts are made to increase diversity, for the most part the retirees who volunteer are all Caucasian.

To investigate the complaint, the president of the Arkansas NAACP chapter at the time, Rizelle Aaron, went through volunteer training and for many months served as a 7 On Your Side volunteer. He worked cases and was able to listen to how other volunteers worked their cases. Aaron left his time as a volunteer without sharing his observations. The hope and belief is that during his service he found a team of volunteers focused on justice, service, and fairness—and nothing else.

In the mid-1990s, Dewayne Graham began to focus on something else: politics. While he wasn't ready to make a run for office, a 1997 profile in the *Arkansas Times* indicated that he was thinking about it. "[Graham] knows he would have to give up his television career should he run for the Senate, or any other political office. He wonders if he's better able to help people 'where I am, as opposed to in the political arena.' He has called friends, some of whom are legislators, to ask their opinion about making a race. 'I've had some positives when I call people.'"

Steel, who as news director inherited Graham, was asked by the *Arkansas Times* reporter in the same article about Graham's salary. "He's paid well," responded Steel, "I can just say it's enough to keep somebody of his ability in a market this size." Steel went on to say that KATV President and General Manager Dale Nicholson "...is a native Arkansan, and he has an abiding interest in those things that are going on in Arkansas. And he believes in what he calls civic journalism. This is part of that. If there is somebody in Arkansas who is ripping off fellow Arkansans, we need to expose them to the people. It makes for great television. From my standpoint, it's—yeah, it's a ratings driver. People are interested. You put on television the news, and you also put on television those things that people are interested in."

By the time Steel took over as news director, 7 On Your Side had become a prominent part of the station and its branding. Research showed that only Sports Anchor Paul Eells and Meteorologist Ned Perme were more popular with KATV viewers. Dewayne Graham enjoyed name recognition usually reserved for anchors—people with high profiles who spend more time on camera.

In 1999, Graham jumped into the race for Congress in Arkansas' 4th district. Also in the Democratic primary were State Senator Mike Ross, State Senator Judy Smith, and former congressional aide Bruce Harris. Graham narrowly edged out Smith (20,575 votes to 20,341 votes) for the right to take on Ross (41,668 votes) in a runoff. Ross easily defeated Graham in that runoff and later narrowly defeated Republican incumbent Jay Dickey to earn a seat in Congress.

In 2006, Graham would take another stab at politics, jumping into the race for Pulaski County Sheriff. This time, Graham ran as a Republican (Graham had previously run for Congress as a Republican in Louisiana in 1985). But six years out of the limelight and a lack of law enforcement experience equaled an easy victory for the Democrat in the race, Doc Holladay.

Little is known about how Graham spent the remainder of his days. He died after an extended illness in 2012 at the age of sixty-three. Donations made by the public he once served helped pay for all his funeral expenses.

Stability in the producer and volunteer coordinator position remained. Nunn served in the role from 1994 until 2013, an incredible run of nearly two decades. Nunn not only expertly managed the reporters and volunteers and all the varied personalities that existed, but she was also an accomplished public speaker who often addressed civic groups about 7 On Your Side's history and value to the community.

But, eventually, the pull of family and grandchildren proved too much and Nunn resigned at the end of 2013. She's now happily retired out east, still enjoying a glass of wine with good friends.

Once again KATV made a promotion from within by naming volunteer Wincie "Dan" Daniel the new volunteer coordinator. Daniel had retired in 2007 after a fifty-three-year career in the United States Air Force. He became a 7 On Your Side volunteer not long after that and served as coordinator from 2013 until his death in early 2020.

As for the "face of the franchise," Graham's departure as 7 On Your Side reporter in 1999 created a rare vacancy in that position. For valid reasons which I will explain in Chapter Four, I jumped at the chance.

CHAPTER TWO

THE RACETRACK
(ST. CROIX MEADOWS)

VALET PARKING

EMPLOYEE	MAT. 4-2-91	EVE. 4-3-91	MAT. 4-4-91	EVE. 4-4-91	EVE. 4-5-91
NATE ALBERTSON		16.00			46.00
RON BUNDY			11.00		
CINDY BUNNELL	15.00	15.00	29.00	3.00	
BRIAN CAMPBELL			19.00		
CHRIS CAMPBELL		23.00	15.00		
PAUL CAMPBELL			26.25		
NICK CERNOHOUS		27.00	6.00	11.00	16.00
KOBIE CONRATH	20.00		22.00		19.00
SCOTT CURTAIN	22.00		20.00	14.00	14.00
JAMEY DYE	16.00			27.50	21.00
MIKE EHLERS		24.00	13.00	15.00	
PETE FELLAND	11.00				25.00
BRAD HAUSER		26.00	2.00	20.00	33.00
MATT LARSON	3.00		16.00	20.00	
JOEL LEE		21.50			
PAT MOSSBARGER	1.00		16.00		33.00
SEAN O'BRIEN	10.00		14.00		
JASON PEDERSON	19.00	23.00	23.00		
JAMIE PIRIUS			19.00		
ROBBIE RISLER		20.00	9.00	9.00	18.00
LUCAS ROMAN			17.00	6.00	
JAMIE ROSENOW	16.00	17.68	33.75	29.00	34.00
DAN SORENSON	18.00	11.00	20.00		14.00
MATT SORENSON		27.00	19.00	27.00	
BRIAN STEFFEN			4.00	26.25	9.00
BRADD WALTON			35.75	3.00	26.00
TIM WILHELM	13.00	26.50			
SEAN ZEPPER		1.00	10.00		29.00
BRENT BJERSTEDT					29.00
TOTAL:	164.00	298.68	399.75	238.75	418.00
MIKE'S TOTAL:	142.00	256.00	367.00	217.00	373.00
DIFFERENCE:	$22.00	$42.68	$32.75	$21.75	$45.00
	13.4%	14.3%	9.2%	9.1%	10.8%

NOTE - OUR TOTALS ARE ON THE LIGHT SIDE AS MIKE HIMSELF IS TIPPED WHEN OPENING DOORS FOR AND GREETING CUSTOMERS AND WE HAVE NO WAY TO CHECK HIM.

ALSO - SOME OF THE VALETS HAVE WORKED 40+ HOURS IN A WEEK AND WOULD LIKE TO BE PAID TIME-AND-A-HALF FOR THEIR SERVICES BUT HAVE BEEN TOLD THAT THIS IS EITHER NOT POSSIBLE OR WON'T BE DONE.

Notes from my first "investigation" into
theft at a Wisconsin dog track.

ON JUNE 20, 1991, RD'S Flyinbullet won the first race on opening day at St. Croix Meadows dog track. The $40 million facility, built in Hudson, Wisconsin, and less than thirty minutes east of Minneapolis and St. Paul, brought live racing and gambling for the first time to western Wisconsin.

St. Croix Meadows was the fifth greyhound racetrack to open in Wisconsin in less than a year. Financial backers from the Badger State and beyond saw new gaming opportunities in Wisconsin as sure bets. So did the state's Native American tribes. By 1994, eleven Native American-owned casinos had opened across Wisconsin. Although they tried, the greyhound dog tracks could not compete or establish partnerships with the tribes. St. Croix Meadows would close a decade after it opened, and by 2009 all the greyhound tracks had gone under.

But when it opened, St. Croix Meadows was the talk of the region. And that region includes River Falls, where I was about to start my senior year of college as a journalism major at the University of Wisconsin-River Falls. Tens of thousands of people were expected to flock to the new dog track, and the recruiting and training of future employees started in the spring. My college roommate and I were hired as valets.

Parking vehicles for the hordes of gamblers was great fun and quite lucrative. Usually those who used the valet service drove nice vehicles and had plenty of money. This meant that we got to drive, if only for a short distance, BMWs and Chargers and Corvettes—and get tipped to do it. The coolest car to roll through that summer was a DeLorean. Think *Back to the Future*. And no, I wasn't the valet who got to park it. But I did park lots of Lincoln Town Cars, which were like driving on air compared to my '78 Dodge Diplomat.

A valet would average about $20 in tips per shift and most of us were college students. Our "adult" supervisor and boss was Mike. I think his last name was Stipes, but I might be confusing him with Michael Stipe, the lead singer for the band REM. In any case, I am sure his first name was Mike. I am also sure that Mike was a thief.

Mike had a system of distributing the valet tips: he'd collect all the money, take it home with him, and then "distribute" the tips the following day. To my young mind, it seemed like a system ripe for fraud.

When I shared my suspicion that our boss might be skimming tips, my fellow valets weren't bothered. In their estimation, we were all making good money, so no harm, no foul. Furthermore, they cautioned, people who rock the boat often find themselves tossed overboard.

I, however, continued to be bothered by the possibility that we were being ripped off by our boss, so I asked my dad for advice. Should I report the possible theft, or should I just go along to get along?

His response? "You can't shave with your back to the mirror."

Meaning, I needed to do whatever allowed me to be at peace with myself. Whatever allowed me to look in the mirror and like what I see, that's what I should do. Dad warned me that no higher-up was going to take my word over the word of my boss. If I was going to report him, I would need more than my suspicions.

So, my course was set. I was going to go after my boss, but how was I going to do it?

There were about thirty valets. On a weekday, around twelve were scheduled to work a matinee, about fifteen worked the evening session, and on weekends in those early days it was all hands-on deck. Twenty-five or more valets ran back and forth competing for vehicles and tips. Our boss, Mike, would park cars and get tips, too.

For five straight shifts, I polled all the valets afterward: How much tip money did you give Mike? I had no way of knowing how much Mike made in tips, but I could ask everybody else. They were curious and willing to share as long as I kept their name out of whatever I planned to do with the information.

The totals collected each day came to $164, $298, $399, $238, and $418.

The day after each shift, I polled each valet again to find out how much tip money Mike gave them back.

The totals returned the next day came to $142, $256, $367, $217, and $373.

Mike was skimming anywhere from 8 to 14 percent of our tip money after each shift, and that didn't factor in his tips. I created a chart with the names of each valet, the shifts worked, how much tip money was received on that shift, how much Mike collected, and how much Mike returned.

It was then time to share the information with St. Croix Meadow's general manager (GM). I remained wary of the risk involved and the warnings from my friends. I was making good money and didn't want that to change. I just wanted to change the way tips were distributed. I made the decision to put my findings in an envelope and leave them on the GM's desk anonymously. I don't know how I gained access to his office undetected so easily, but I did. I set my findings on his desk, left, and then waited.

And waited. And waited …

Days went by, then a week, and nothing changed. Mike continued to take all the tip money home and continued to distribute less than he should have the following day.

It seemed that without a face, my data would not be taken seriously. So, I walked back up to the GM's office. This time he was there. I introduced myself and informed him that I had left the envelope on his desk the previous week. He said he appreciated the information and that he would handle things. The next day, Mike announced a change: tips would now be pooled and distributed immediately at the conclusion of each shift. Hooray! Case closed; everybody wins … except Mike.

And me!

The next week when Mike released the new work schedule, my name was on it … but only once. Clearly, Mike knew who met with the GM, and I would now pay a price for it. My fellow valets had warned me, but the unfairness still made me angry.

I was also angry when I learned that Mike was still running and parking vehicles alongside the valets, but when it came time to pool tips, it always seemed that Mike had served all the worst tippers.

He was still skimming. And I was still scheming.

I recruited my mother to help me expose Mike's continued shadiness. I asked her and a friend to go to the track and be sure to use the valet service and tip Mike $20—a marked $20 bill that I provided her. At the end of that day's shift when everybody got together to pool tips, we would see how much Mike would throw in.

The answer? Nineteen $1 bills. Mike kept the $20 bill for himself.

Back to the GM's office I went to report this latest development. Again, he assured me he would handle things. And he did. He fired Mike the next day. I enjoyed the look Mike gave me as he left the facility carrying a box of his stuff. It felt like justice, and I liked that feeling. The day after that, the GM transferred me from the valet team to the parking lot team, citing "personality conflicts." That felt like injustice.

Members of the parking lot team received a higher hourly wage but no tips, which was definitely a demotion. But that didn't really matter. Within a couple of weeks, managers no longer scheduled me on either team. I was a casualty of my own principles. But, I could look at myself in the mirror, and that is what mattered most.

My college education offered me "Intro to Broadcast Journalism." But this real-world education offered "Intro to Cheats and Scammers." It cost me my job to learn that I am good at uncovering fraud. Both types of education would prove beneficial to my future as a consumer reporter.

> **LESSON LEARNED:**
> *Anonymous complaints aren't taken as seriously.*

This is especially true when an anonymous complaint lacks "official" supporting documents or a way to be independently verified. My complaint included information that I'd compiled and trusted, but the GM could not verify the information short of interviewing every valet involved.

This doesn't mean anonymous complaints are without merit. My complaint was totally true. Those who desire to remain anonymous often have valid reasons not to come forward.

I believe all complaints, including anonymous ones, are at least worth checking out. In my experience, you end up wasting time in some cases but winning awards in others.

> **LESSON LEARNED:**
> *Those who love you most tend to offer the best advice.*

Young people often make decisions with only immediate or short-term consequences in mind. Parents, grandparents, and others can offer perspectives with more life experience behind them.

On a side note, I gained another valuable nugget, unrelated to my future in journalism, from this valet experience: ***Casinos and dog tracks aren't built for winners.*** Many of the valets, including me, found it hard to avoid the temptation of the track. We would take our tip money and go straight inside and bet on the greyhounds. It only took the rush of one $300 trifecta payout to get hooked. I wasn't gambling with rent, grocery, or tuition money, as I worked several other jobs. But after a summer of working at the dog track—a summer of paychecks, tips, and gambling—I ended up with a net loss of $800.

That ended my gambling days!

CHAPTER THREE

THE INTERNSHIP
(WCCO)

I HAD NO IDEA THAT the lessons learned during the summer of 1991 as a parking valet would one day benefit me as a future journalist. However, the summer of 1992 was designed to do precisely that. I would be interning at WCCO-TV, the CBS affiliate in downtown Minneapolis. I would walk the same sidewalks that Mary Richards walked as she tossed her blue beret into the air during the opening credits of *The Mary Tyler Moore Show*. And I would be learning the same trade: journalism.

My journalism instructor, Ray Neikamp, offered me some advice: "Do as much as they will allow you to do, and take advantage of working with actual professional news photographers." Neikamp said a goal should be to put together at least two stories that could be used on a resume tape after graduation.

At WCCO, all the interns went through a brief orientation and building tour before being assigned to a reporter. I was paired with Silvia Gambardella. She worked as the station's consumer reporter (although that meant little to me at the time). A veteran reporter and graduate of City College of New York and New York's

Columbia School of Journalism, Gambardella didn't smile much, chat much, or care much for what college students hoped to get out of their internships.

The first thing she did after we exchanged greetings was introduce me to her "beat checks" list. There were about twenty local and national consumer-related organizations that I would be calling each day, asking if there was anything going on that would interest folks in Minnesota and western Wisconsin. For example, the Consumer Product Safety Commission might be issuing a recall on a product, or the Federal Trade Commission might have information about a new scam targeting senior citizens. Remember, this was 1992, and newsrooms were not equipped with the internet. Google searches were still six years away. If WCCO viewers were going to learn the latest consumer-related information, Gambardella had to find it and deliver it to them ... after I found it and gave it to her.

The "beat checks" list included a Washington, D.C. activist organization called Public Citizen. Many times, the group's founder would answer the phone and visit with me. I had no idea that I was casually chatting with a man who would one day be a U.S. presidential candidate and help develop and pass such landmark legislation as the National Traffic and Motor Vehicle Safety Act, the Freedom of Information Act, the Clean Water Act, the Consumer Product Safety Act, and the Whistleblower Protection Act. His name? Ralph Nader.

Truth be told, I had no interest in being a consumer reporter at the time. I just wanted to be a "regular reporter." I envied the interns who were assigned to a collection of younger and more fun general-assignment reporters. They visited crime scenes and took notes at press conferences while I worked the phones back at the station.

However, Gambardella's eventful summer resulted in her missing quite a few days of work and me getting to work with those "regular" reporters. Her sister got married in New York and her father had a heart attack the same weekend. She was representing the union in its contract talks with management (a strike was narrowly averted). There also were doubts as to whether Gambardella's own contract would be renewed. That's because two years earlier, Gambardella committed an unpardonable sin in journalism: she upset major advertisers.

Late in the summer of 1990, auto dealers complained about Gambardella's award-winning stories on defective seat belts and how car buyers can find bargains at rental agencies. The auto dealers wanted her fired … or else. Newsroom allies, including longtime WCCO anchor Don Shelby, supported Sylvia. Shelby let it be known that if Gambardella went, so would he. The Arkansas equivalent would be if legendary KATV sports anchor Paul Eells were to have done the same. That is how respected and liked Don Shelby was by both his colleagues and viewers.

St. Paul Pioneer Press media reporter Brian Lambert summarized the showdown in an article written six years later: "Eventually, WCCO management, in the person of then-General Manager Bob McGann, a former salesman, was convinced the station risked a worse blow if it appeared to cave in to advertisers than if it actually lost hundreds of thousands of advertising dollars."

Like Philadelphia consumer reporter Herb Deneberg once said: "Everyone loves it if you're chopping up the city of Philadelphia. But if you're chopping up car dealers or department stores, [most media] don't want to touch it."

Gambardella kept her job. In fact, management extended her contract, with conditions. Lambert wrote about that also: "The hollowness of the 'contract extension' is evident in that, from that point on, Gambardella was effectively muzzled, and her contract was not renewed two years later. Translation: She was neutered and fired."

Gambardella is also quoted in the article: "Was I muzzled? Yes. It was thinly veiled, but I was muzzled. I remember my assignment for the May [sweeps period] the next spring. It was a 20-part series on how to decorate your home. There was nothing investigative about any of the pieces I did after that. And whenever I'd kick up my heels about it, I'd be accused of insubordination."

All to say, there were many reasons for Gambardella's summer of discontent in 1992. By visiting with her, I learned things college professors never mentioned, like the relationship between the news department and the sales department, the power of advertisers, and how good journalism can create enemies.

Midway through my internship, I decided on a couple of stories that I wanted to use for my resume tape. One was a Gambardella report on the dangers of rear seatbelts (back then they only crossed a passenger's lap, not the shoulder and torso). A husband and wife were involved in a rollover accident. The husband, who was driving and protected by a shoulder-harness seat belt, survived with minor injuries. The wife, who was buckled up in the back seat with only a lap belt, suffered major head injuries and died. What you are about to hear is a pure Midwestern accent before it was softened by southern charm.

The other story I decided on was reported by weekend anchor Amy Marsalis. It concerned two children sitting on a blanket at a drive-in movie theater who were hit by a vehicle. I went out on both stories, took my own notes, and gathered the raw footage to choose my own soundbites and write my own stories. I purposefully chose not to watch how Silvia or Amy put their reports together. I wanted to do my own versions and see how they compared to the professionals.

Eventually, I presented a script of my "Backseat seat belts" story to Gambardella for her review. The following excerpt is from a report on my internship experience that I turned in to my professor. It summarizes how things went:

> "Judgment Day" I jokingly call it now, although it wasn't very funny at the time. Obviously, I had plenty of time to write the script for my seat belt package, and when I presented it to Silvia, I was confident—even proud—of it. She looked it over for about five minutes and then told me what she thought: it editorialized, it was too long, and it wasn't written conversationally. It was probably slanderous, or at least incorrect, at some points.

> I was an English minor and have always considered myself a good writer. So, it stung when she said that, judging by the script, I couldn't write (or I could write, but poorly). But the worst part was that she backed up every one of her criticisms. Every one of her criticisms made sense to me. She was right. It sucked.

> This was the first time I had ever wondered to myself "What am I doing? What am I getting myself into?" I wondered if I had missed something in my journalism education here at River Falls and if so, was it my fault or the fault of my professors or curriculum?

It turned into a long weekend of soul searching, and I decided that I was hardly going to give up on my future and
ambitions because of one failure. If there is that much
more I must learn, then I'll have to learn that much more.
The main problem with my story was that it was too flashy.
Too much "A Current Affair" and not enough basic "CNN."

Gambardella did not hold back, but her blunt, dare I say harsh, critiques helped me improve. Still, I believe there's a way to critique
someone's work without demoralizing them. My second draft of
the story received a lot of her red ink as well, and even the third
didn't satisfy her completely. By that time, I'd learned that nothing
probably would, and the third version is what I would put to tape
and later send to news directors around the country to try to get
my first job.

The WCCO photographers were very kind and willing to shoot
video of the interns to add to our resume tapes. We were even
allowed to sit at the anchor desk and deliver a few news stories,
although I had no interest in being an anchor. I wanted to be a
reporter. Anchors make more money, but the hours they work,
generally 1:30 to 10:30 p.m., are not family-friendly. Plus, while anchors leave the office on occasion, reporters leave the office every
day. That is the job I wanted, and I hoped that the tape I'd put together during my internship would be enough to persuade some
news director somewhere to give me a shot.

After graduating in December 1992, I spent the first few months
of the new year mailing resumes and VHS tapes to small market
news directors all over the country. Bangor, Maine. Eugene, Ore-
gon. Bakersfield, California. Augusta, Georgia. Duluth, Minnesota.
Eau Claire, Wisconsin. I mailed over three dozen tapes before I got
a job offer.

It came from Jerry Mayer, the news director at KTVE in Monroe,
Louisiana. Jerry needed a reporter to work in KTVE's bureau in El

Dorado, Arkansas. The job paid $12,500 per year with the opportunity to make more by working overtime. I would be expected to cover news, politics, weather events, and sports across eight south Arkansas counties. I would be a one-man band, meaning in addition to finding and writing my reports, I would shoot and edit them as well.

I took the job, packed up my 1985 Pontiac Parisienne (an upgrade from my '78 Dodge) and hit the road for south Arkansas.

> **LESSON LEARNED:**
> *A first draft is far from a final draft.*

At some point you must be satisfied with whatever you've written, especially in the news business where you are often under serious time constraints and deadline pressure. But you can *always* write it better *if* time allows.

> **LESSON LEARNED:**
> *Allow criticism to improve you, not define you.*

Criticism should light your fire, not extinguish it.

> **LESSON LEARNED:**
> *Speak truth with love or risk being ignored.*

After that first knockdown, the criticisms offered by Gambardella lost their sting. I spent more time avoiding her than listening to her. By the time she called me a terrible speller because I added an extra "z" to hazard, her critiques were almost welcomed as it gave me more stories to share with incredulous friends. Follow the Golden Rule or you risk losing your influence.

> **LESSON LEARNED:**
> *Reputation trumps revenue.*

The only thing that scares a TV station more than a decrease in revenue is an increase in bad publicity. But this lesson only applies in the short term. Companies play the long game. So, if you take on management and win, brush up your resume. Of course, I didn't need TV news to teach me this one. I learned it at the dog track.

CHAPTER FOUR

THE START
(FROM KTVE TO KATV)

JASON PEDERSON
Reporter

CHANNEL NEWS 7

My first publicity photos at both KTVE and KATV.

I STARTED WORK AT KTVE in April 1993. The thirty months I would spend in El Dorado would be life-altering. I met and married my best friend and El Dorado native, Mary Carol Spencer. I had the opportunity to learn from the mistakes of a young journalist in a small market—errors that, if made in a large market, would likely cost a person his job. And I made connections that would help get me to Little Rock.

The annual Associated Press awards banquet was an ideal place to network. The banquet was held in Hot Springs, and since most KTVE employees lived and worked in Louisiana, I would attend and accept my awards and any other awards for the station. During one such year, Mary Carol accompanied me, and we were seated at the KATV table along with News Director Bob Steel and his wife Sherry. While Bob and I visited about the TV business, Mary Carol and Sherry visited about all sorts of things. They hit it off, and Bob would later tell me that Sherry would ask him from time to time, "When are you going to hire that young reporter down in El Dorado?"

In 1995, breaking news gave me a pair of golden opportunities to remind Bob of my El Dorado existence. KATV had recently purchased NewsStar 7, a satellite truck that allowed reporters to go live from anywhere in Arkansas and beyond. While the truck was always fueled up and ready to go, there wasn't always a reporter ready to go along with it.

When an elderly Avon saleswoman named Trudy Scott from Hamburg was kidnapped and thrown into the trunk of her vehicle, her quick thinking likely saved her life and made for a great story. As her abductors were driving her to an unknown fate, Ms. Scott broke out the taillight and extended her hand through it. A trailing motorist saw her hand sticking out of the back of the car and alerted police, who rescued Ms. Scott. I interviewed her, got video of the suspects, and headed back to El Dorado.

I soon learned that Channel 7 wanted the story and that NewsStar 7 was heading my way without a reporter on board. This was terribly exciting—and nerve-racking. In my two years of reporting, I had little experience reporting live. Almost all my reports were recorded to tape and edited by me. If I screwed up, I could just record it again until I got it right. Channel 7 wanted me to report live! Thankfully, I overcame my nerves, and my reporting and live shots went well.

That summer, the same scenario played out again when a lightning bolt hit a giant Lion Oil refinery tank. The strike resulted in a massive fire that would take well over a day to burn itself out—a towering, raging visual that both KTVE and KATV wanted to see live. Both would include my live reporting in their 6:00 p.m. newscasts.

After sending my packaged report to both stations, I stood and waited a safe distance away from the blazing inferno behind me.

Five minutes before the news started, I had a producer from Monroe talking to me in one ear and a producer from Little Rock talking to me in the other. I had a KTVE microphone in one hand and a KATV microphone in the other. The Channel 7 producer, Jeff Whatley, wanted to know when he could put me in his newscast. I couldn't give him a definitive answer because it depended on when Channel 10 was finished with me. After all, Gray Communications (the owner of KTVE) was paying my salary, not Allbritton Communications (the owner of KATV).

Despite juggling the needs of two stations at the same time, things went smoothly, and Bob Steel got to see my work again without leaving his office. Steel wrote me a note dated July 26th in which he stated, "We were all impressed and really appreciate you doing the live shot for us." He then added, "I don't have any reporter positions open at the present time, but I will tell you that I know who you are, and I have been impressed with your work. Please stay in touch with this newsroom and monitor our job situation here from time to time."

Three days later, Mary Carol and I married and left for a weeklong honeymoon on Margarita Island, off the coast of Venezuela, a generous gift from our parents. When we returned, my job hunt ramped up. Over two years in a small market is enough to prepare most reporters for a larger market, plus Mary Carol had just graduated with an MBA and would find more job opportunities in a larger city. I sent tapes and resumes to TV stations in Austin, Tulsa, Springfield (MO), Lexington, Louisville, Memphis, Oklahoma City, Kansas City, Shreveport, and Little Rock. In October, both Little Rock (KATV) and Lexington (WKYT) offered me jobs.

Both were the top-rated stations in their market. Both were in state capital cities and would offer the opportunity for political reporting, which I enjoyed. The money offered at each station was around $20,000 per year. I wasn't sure what to do.

I once again sought the sage advice of my dad. He and Mom had slowly accepted that I would not be returning to the Minneapolis market as I had originally intended when I moved south to Arkansas. Mary Carol is a "Southern belle," and she made it clear long before my proposal that the snow and cold of the upper Midwest were not for her. Dad's advice: if I wasn't going to live near my family, I should try to live near Mary Carol's family. It made little sense to take a job in Kentucky where we would be far from everyone.

KATV had a new reporter.

Over the years, the wisdom in that advice has been constantly evident as we have been able to love, help, and enjoy many wonderful memories with Mary Carol's side of the family. Plus, we get up to Wisconsin at least once, usually twice, and sometimes even three times each year.

I later received a card from Trudy Scott, the Avon saleswoman who had been kidnapped in Hamburg. She said each of her abductors (both female) got thirty years. "I'm sure glad you got the job with Channel 7," Scott wrote. "That is my favorite. Something good did come from that kidnapping. Miracles do happen. I've had a big time since then. Heard from so many people who saw me on TV and couldn't believe what happened. If you come back to Hamburg, come by to see me." Unfortunately, I never got the chance. Ms. Scott died in March 2000 at the age of eighty-seven.

Even though I accepted a job in Little Rock, I had committed to putting together a special report for KTVE that was scheduled to air in early November called "Zoned Out." The series focused on El Dorado's notorious "Thunder Zone," an area east of downtown and across the railroad tracks, located in the city's impoverished

3rd Ward. Nightclubs and drug activity pervaded the small area. The imaginary boundaries of the "Thunder Zone" had spread over time in the minds of wary El Dorado citizens, negatively impacting property values and making it hard for those who lived in the "Thunder Zone" to get out. My reports would explain where the name came from, if it was deserved or exaggerated, and the impact such a label has on an area. In order to get the job done and keep my word, I traveled back to Union County on weekends until the story was finished—unpaid work ultimately rewarded with an Arkansas Associated Press award in the documentary series category.

I started at Channel 7 on October 23, 1995. Just like at Channel 10, I began as a general assignment reporter, but I would not have to shoot and edit my own stories. KATV had an incredible team of photographers, reporters, and editors. Many of them would become like family to me.

Usually, the first day at a new job is full of meeting people, touring the building, and filling out paperwork. Things changed when a call came into our newsroom about a house fire. Assignment Editor James Thompson suggested I ride along with photojournalist Carey Kelly to the scene.

Kelly, a former Arkansas Razorback basketball player, was the tall, quiet type. We arrived in the southern Pulaski County community of Sweet Home and easily found the blaze: a fully involved inferno. I asked a few questions and quickly learned that three people had been inside the white, one-story structure at 9408 Young Road. They were forty-four-year-old Larry Young, forty-four-year-old Betty Young, and twenty-two-year-old Chris Young. All three died, and when I called Thompson and shared this, he told me I would now be the evening's top story at 5:00 and 6:00 p.m.

The job of a general assignment reporter often creates a whirlpool of emotions; the solemn sadness and empathy for the suffering and loss of life, but also the adrenaline rush that accompanies the duty and responsibility of sharing the top story of the day. Especially on your *first* day.

Sweet Home is unincorporated. There were no fire hydrants, and the pumper trucks sent to the scene had long since exhausted their supplies of water. In fact, one fireman had taken a knee and was leaning against a tree, still holding a fire hose with only a trickle of water coming out of it. All he could do was watch the home burn. The rural location was part of the story, and the visual of this helpless firefighter helped convey that. I suggested to Kelly that he get the shot so when I wrote about it, people could see what I saw.

Kelly had yet to really speak to me, but at this point he looked down from his 6' 7" vantage point and said, "Listen Sparky, I don't miss a thing."

Gulp. Message sent, and message received! I no longer had the total control that I'd enjoyed as a one-man band. I needed to trust the professional photographers and editors to do their jobs while I focused on mine. Of course, over time working relationships formed and the news gathering process and presentation would become much more collaborative. But, as the newest of new employees, I had overstepped on day one.

My first week at KATV went well. So well that I came back to the newsroom one day to find a note written in black Sharpie on my desk from General Manager Dale Nicholson. "Good first week. Keep it up. Also, this article is required reading for new employees. Dale." Attached to the note was a newspaper clipping titled "Vacuum Therapy for Impotence."

What a sense of humor! I had been meaning to go up to the third floor and introduce myself to Dale, seeing as how we'd both gotten our start at KTVE in El Dorado. I saw his outreach as a good reason to do just that.

I went upstairs and we enjoyed a nice chat, at the end of which I said, "My wife and I are newlyweds and don't plan on having kids anytime soon, but I'll keep that article handy in case we have any problems." Then I laughed but Nicholson did not.

"What article?" he asked.

Uh-oh! I pulled the note and article from my pocket and showed it to Nicholson. He looked it over and then looked back up at me.

"I didn't write this. But I'm damn sure going to find out who did!" He pounded his fist on the table, as if his words needed more emphasis. They did not. I went directly to my news director's office and told Bob Steel what had transpired. He laughed and said he had a pretty good idea who the prankster was, and he was right.

Anchorman Chris May.

Apparently, reporter Tom Ryan had previously left the same article with a "note from Dale" on May's desk, only Chris was smart enough to recognize it as a joke. He did not march up to the GM's office expecting to share a laugh over it. Chris never dreamed that I would do such a thing, and while he wasn't in any serious trouble, he certainly wasn't too happy or impressed with "the new guy."

Veteran photojournalist Jim Casey offered a theory as to why Nicholson may have objected so strenuously to someone signing his name. According to Casey, back in the day when Robert Doubleday served as KATV's GM, Dale got lectured following a similar offense.

The KATV sales floor had a break room and, as the story goes, every morning about the same time the phone would ring and whoever picked it up would hear "This is Doubleday. Is the coffee ready?" When the answer was yes, it was usually Dale Nicholson, not Robert Doubleday, who would be the first to show up.

The way Casey tells it, one day Doubleday himself was in the break room and answered the phone. When Nicholson showed up a minute later to get his cup of coffee, he got a lot more than that. And so, according to Casey, Nicholson learned the gravity of such misrepresentation, however harmless.

Over the next four years, the reporting opportunities presented to me at KATV would make any general assignment reporter in the nation envious. Months after the note fiasco, Chris May and I reported together from downtown Fort Smith after it had been hit hard by a tornado. In early 1997, we were in Washington, D.C., covering President Clinton's second inauguration. Of course, before that there was election night in 1996 in Little Rock.

I stood on the risers across from the Old State House, from which the Clintons would emerge once it was clear Bill had won. An exciting evening of national significance to be sure. But there was also plenty of state politics: Whitewater, prosecutor Dan Harmon's trial and conviction, and the indictments and convictions of several state lawmakers come to mind.

Natural disasters during this time included the April 15, 1996, tornado that hit north of Mountain View along Sylamore Creek. Among those killed were NFL Hall of Fame quarterback Kurt Warner's in-laws. Even more powerful storms hit Arkansas the following spring. On March 1, 1997, twisters cut a destructive path from Arkadelphia to Little Rock and beyond, resulting in a full week of coverage and a visit from President Clinton. More tornadoes pounded the state in January 1999, including a direct hit to the city of Beebe.

The notable crimes, criminals, and trials covered during those four years included the "Star City Swindler" Murray Armstrong, the robbery and murder of the Mueller family (a crime later linked to the Oklahoma City bombing), the Blue Light Rapist (Robert Todd Burmingham), Boy Scout leader Jack Walls, Rohypnol (a.k.a. date-rape drug) rapist Steven Sera, and court hearings involving the West Memphis Three.

Stories that I reported on during this period that attracted national interest included the 1996 conviction and resignation of Governor Jim Guy Tucker,

the fortieth anniversary of the desegregation of Little Rock Central High School in 1997, the 1998 shooting at Westside Middle School near Jonesboro (and the subsequent trial of Mitchell Johnson and Andrew Golden), and the 1999 plane crash of United Airlines Flight 1420.

In addition, there were assignments that took me to New York, California, Haiti, and the previously mentioned Washington, D.C. It was a whirlwind four years for a young reporter in Arkansas that would be difficult for any reporter in any other U.S. market to match.

As exciting and rewarding as reporting can be, two aspects of the job weighed on me, and I'm sure on many journalists. First, the job sometimes involves approaching people on what may be the worst day of their lives. And second, reporting doesn't pay much. As a young married couple, Mary Carol and I had our sights set on starting a family, and a general assignment reporter's salary can make that difficult.

I addressed the salary almost immediately after our move to Little Rock. Mary Carol had yet to find a job and my $20,000 a year salary was cutting things too close, so I took a job in the mornings at the Books-A-Million near our apartment and then worked at KATV 1:30–10:30 p.m. Soon, customers started recognizing me. That made me uncomfortable, and I didn't think it reflected well on KATV to have me working a second job. Also, Mary Carol found a good job. So after about a year, I quit.

Here is what KATV News Director Bob Steel wrote in my 1997 annual review: "Jason has his priorities set. He wants to be the best reporter he can be, and he is among our best. He is the best at story development. His live shots are excellent, very comfortable to watch. Crisp, clear writing. Good on background. He understands difficult stories and makes them understandable to the viewer."

Here is what I wrote in the same review: "This is not a complaint—I am happy working here—but eventually (two years from now) I will expect to make enough to support a family. I don't expect to get rich, but the only reason at this time I can imagine looking for a job elsewhere is money."

I told Steel that I wanted to be making $40,000 per year by the year 2000. He said he appreciated me giving him a couple of years to try and make it happen, but it was a big jump. He made no promises or guarantees.

Six months later I received a nice raise, inching me a little closer to my goal. And then again in November of 1998, I received another raise after my annual review. Between those two raises, I wrote a note to Steel informing him that once again I would be working a second job. The letter is dated 8-18-98 and reads in part: "I realize that you want to pay me more, and that it would be considered somewhat embarrassing for the station to have an on-air personality seen out in public working a second job. That is why I have gone out of my way to choose a second job that is extremely low profile. Beginning this week, I will be throwing the morning paper for the Arkansas Democrat-Gazette in a west Little Rock neighborhood. This extra income will help allow Mary Carol to quit work once our family is started and which will, if the salary amounts we have discussed by the end of next year come to be, allow me to stay with Channel 7."

I threw a paper route for several years, every morning between the hours of 2:00 and 5:00 a.m. Only on a very few occasions did I have to call in because overnight news required me to report to my primary job, and my route manager David Rogers knew that might happen when he hired me.

One such example was the crash of American Airlines Flight 1420. The pilot of the plane attempted to land during a severe thunderstorm at Little Rock National Airport a few minutes before midnight on June 1, 1999. The plane overran the runway, hit a structure built to support approach lights, and broke into several pieces just short of the Arkansas River.

The phone rang right after midnight, a few hours before my alarm for my paper route. I spent all night in the rain and chaos at a staging area set up for survivors, gathering as much information as possible. Most were amazingly articulate considering what they had just survived hours earlier. Our crew did live reports all morning for KATV's morning show Daybreak followed by live shots on CNN and Good Morning America. I did a Q & A with Diane Sawyer. While it aired live on the East Coast, it was tape-delayed... meaning the same segment was broadcast as if it were live...an hour later in most of the Midwest, including Wisconsin, where my parents lived. I was able to call and give them a heads up, and they watched me reporting on a national news program. It was a big moment for them and for me.

I shared about the weather conditions, how the crash occurred, and the fatalities. But the official number of victims would not be determined until sixteen days after the crash with the passing of fourteen-year-old Rachel Fuller. Her death brought that total to eleven—Captain Richard Buschmann and ten passengers. In addition, forty-five other passengers and crew suffered serious injuries.

Later that morning, I handed the baton to other Channel 7 reporters and left the airport to meet Mary Carol for a scheduled appointment at a clinic where we'd learn the gender of our first child. I nearly fell asleep waiting for the sonogram review. We were told we would be having a boy! By then, I was excited and fully awake!

Those first twelve hours of June 2, 1999, were an incredible mix of emotions that I'll likely never experience again. It all came only hours after completion of what was scheduled to be my first official day as the new 7 On Your Side reporter.

After Dewayne Graham's departure, I applied to replace him as the third reporter to serve in that position for KATV. Getting the job had the potential to solve both of my reporter dilemmas. The new job title came with a substantial raise. And it would eliminate, or at least greatly reduce, the necessity of approaching people dealing with the loss of loved ones or other personal tragedy.

I worked hard to properly and empathetically memorialize Arkansans killed by a tornado, accident, or act of violence. Many of the families I approached were truly grateful for the opportunity to talk, making their loved one more than just a name in the minds of KATV viewers. But there were other times when the knock on the door or the phone call was not well received.

I learned this lesson in south Arkansas while at KTVE. In Ouachita County, a state trooper once protected me from a raging son whose father had just been killed in a logging truck accident. I had not approached him. I was just getting video of the wreck. But my mere presence gave him a direction in which to channel his overwhelming grief. The trooper assured the man I was leaving, and then he told me I had one minute to get what I needed and to get out of there.

In a small TV market, the instances of tragedy are fewer and farther between. In a large market, with other competing stations, the stakes and opportunities increase. You didn't want to be the reporter who failed to get a photograph of the victim or an interview with a grieving relative. However, on more than one occasion this aspect of the job troubled me.

A letter dated April 11, 1997, captures the conflict within. I wrote and mailed it the day after the search for a missing Saline County boy. The boy was discovered to have drowned.

To the parents, family, and friends of Carmie Cash,

My name is Jason Pederson, and I am a reporter with Channel 7 News. Let me first express my deepest sympathy regarding the loss of your son, grandson, and family member and/or friend.

When I arrived on the scene yesterday, Carmie was a missing child. My plan for a news story at 3:00 p.m. was to put Carmie's picture on the news with hopes that someone would see it, see Carmie, and bring him home.

But the story changed. My story of hope turned into a story of tragedy. It was still my job to tell that story. The pain of your family and community was shared with the rest of the state. I wish it could have been your joy and relief instead.

I did the best job I could, although one family friend has already expressed to me that he was unhappy with my story...that he thought it was insensitive to the family. I tried to be sensitive. If I failed, I am sorry. The news gathering process at times can be very intrusive. It is part of the job that I don't enjoy. Like all of you, I didn't sleep very well or very much last night.

My wife and I prayed for you all last night and asked God to both comfort and give you strength, especially Carmie's mother and father. I am not a father. It is hard for me to imagine your pain.

Again, with deepest sympathy, Jason Pederson

Ten days later, I received a card in the mail. It was from Ronnie, Karen, and Courtney Cash.

Jason, I received your letter about the tragic story of my son Carmie. You know I watched the news. I couldn't believe my eyes, my hurt of losing my baby was the big news of the day. I would love to tell you my side of the story of what I think of the graphic pictures that were at the top of the news.

Judging by the handwriting, I believe the note was written by Carmie's mother. There was no phone number included, and I have no record of any follow-up notes or memory of any further correspondence or conversations.

I believed that my promotion to the 7 On Your Side reporter would take me, for the most part, out of the general assignment duties that sometimes necessitated such uncomfortable encounters. I much preferred knocking on doors and having uncomfortable encounters with individuals who ripped people off. In addition, a promotion would give my news director an opportunity and reason to meet the salary demand I'd laid out two years earlier.

Thankfully, I was blessed enough to get the job with its new duties and the requested raise. And true to my word, it kept me at KATV not only for the immediate future, but for the next twenty years.

> **LESSON LEARNED:**
> *For success, ability usually precedes opportunity.*

Sometimes this is out of your control. But I knew when I got to El Dorado that I needed to be there for a while and learn my craft. Had Ms. Scott's kidnapping or the Lion Oil lightning strike happened earlier in my career, I doubt Bob Steel would have wanted to hire me. Improvement is a process.

> **LESSON LEARNED:**
> *When your goal is dependent on others, be reasonable and communicate your expectations.*

Had I waited until 1999 to tell my boss I wanted to make $40,000 by the year 2000, it's doubtful it would've happened.

> **LESSON LEARNED:**
> *If at all possible, live near your loved ones.*

It's much easier to see family members on holidays, birthdays, moving days, graduation days, and difficult days when you live nearby, especially when you have a demanding job with limited time off. It is especially a blessing when you're able to help those you love.

> **LESSON LEARNED:**
> *The seemingly meaningless can have great meaning.*

Sometimes what table you sit at can later determine where you work. You never know.

CHAPTER FIVE

THE SCOUNDRELS
(THE DISHONEST EIGHT)

"Take no part in the unfruitful works of
darkness, but instead expose them."
—Ephesians 5:11

IN RECOUNTING TWO DECADES AS the 7 On Your Side reporter, it seems logical to start with the scoundrels. Without the cheats, thieves, and scam artists, the job would be a lot less fun. We would still be able to educate and instruct. We would still remind you that your property taxes are coming due or that a child safety seat has been recalled. However, it's the exposure of the scoundrels that viewers crave most. Such revelations not only serve to protect the consuming public at large, but public exposure is a powerful deterrent to others who might be considering illegal or ill-advised activities.

The men (and one woman) profiled on the following pages are the "repeat cheats." Each generated multiple complaints from

Arkansans, from people outside our state, or both. I did multiple stories on all of them. Some of the scoundrels were prosecuted, some were sued, some are no longer a threat, others remain open for business, and one has graduated to even bigger problems.

I shared the same message many, many times with their many, many victims... resist feeling ashamed. These con artists are good at what they do. Just as honest folks pay their bills and support their families by working, the dishonest pay their bills and support their families by scamming. You can be the best cornerback in the NFL and Tom Brady may still beat you. All the victims got beaten out of some money. But they learned from it and used their experiences to help educate others.

These scoundrels are not listed here in any particular order. They're all opportunists and equally devious. I'll start with one of the first and most memorable confrontations I experienced as the 7 On Your Side reporter. It happened one weekday afternoon when I paid a visit to a North Little Rock office building to interrogate a man who represented himself as a man of God while preying on primarily young women and their dreams of home ownership.

JOSEPH CARTHRON

"I KNOW you're not here for my benefit! I KNOW the DEVIL sent you here!"

Those are the words that Joseph Carthron yelled across his desk at photojournalist Sandy King and me after we entered his second-floor office along JFK Boulevard to ask him some questions. Many of Carthron's clients were claiming they had paid him $1,500, $3,500, and in some cases $5,000 in exchange for cleaning up their credit scores and helping them become homeowners.

The first complaint against JC Affordable Homes came in May 2003. Sandra Price wrote to 7 On Your Side the following: "Me and several coworkers here at Arkansas Children's Hospital have signed contracts to get a new home built and also have paid more than $3,500 each so the company can start building and nothing has happened."

In June we heard from Kwanna Brown. She also was out $3,500 and told us that Carthron was now calling his company Carthron Development. He also operated JC Mortgage Funding.

In August, Joyce Adams filed a formal complaint with the Pulaski County Sheriff's Office, and Carthron refunded $900 of the $1,125 she had paid him. She said a neighbor of hers had done the same and had also received a partial refund.

Price, Brown, Adams, and others had met Carthron over the previous year and trusted him to make their dreams of home ownership come true. Carthron promoted his business on Christian radio station KITA AM 1440. Carthron wore a clerical collar and represented himself as a pastor or apostle. When we pressed him about his church and congregation, Carthron told us he was part of "Spiritual Delivery Street Ministry" and that he goes to different neighborhoods. He claimed his business clients could not get traditional financing because of the discriminatory practices of mainstream lenders. Carthron promoted himself as their best, last hope for homeownership.

He told clients, usually single mothers, they could get land. They couldn't. He promised to improve their credit scores. He didn't. Carthron took thousands of dollars for restoring credit and for appraisals, down payments on land, and construction. The money didn't go to any of those things.

The same people who complained to 7 On Your Side also filed complaints with the Arkansas attorney general's (AG) office, alleging Carthron violated the Arkansas Deceptive Trade Practices Act, which states it is "Unlawful to make a false representation or to knowingly take advantage of a consumer who is reasonably unable to protect his/her interests because of an inability to understand the language of an agreement."

We interviewed several of Carthron's victims on August 29 for a report to be broadcast on September 3. The story included an impromptu interview with Carthron at his office. We confronted him with a stack of complaints and questions from his clients about their deposits and the lack of progress toward becoming homeowners. Carthron accused the attorney general's office of poisoning the minds of his clients and pointed to a lawsuit he had filed against the AG seeking $25 *billion* in damages!

When pressed about the whereabouts of his clients' deposit money, Carthron became animated. "Whether it's $3,500 or $5,000,000, any contractor can charge, or any developer can ask for a deposit—whatever is relevant. That's my freedom to do that. You've lied to me . . . your staff has lied to me since they picked the phone up. And it's not unusual, it's not uncommon, for the devil to lie!"

When asked for the name of his attorney, Carthron replied "Jesus Christ." When asked about the AG's investigation into his business dealings, Carthron replied, "These crackers in Arkansas are trying to run me out." And what would he do if a court asked him to account for all the deposit money he'd received from clients? "I am going to leave that question a mystery. No comment."

We contacted radio station KITA and were told that Carthron had paid for airtime and broadcast a thirty-minute show once a week called "Deep South," but he had stopped coming in. KITA had tapes of all the shows and shared copies with me. During those shows, Carthron promised listeners that he could get them in a house. "I can do it—100 percent guarantee to get financing." In reality, Carthron now owed the station $1,500 and the debt had been turned over to a collection agency. When asked about this, Carthron said, "I quit. They were shorting me spots."

Immediately after we aired stories on September 3 and 4, a slew of new complaints against Carthron flooded into the 7 On Your Side office. The attorney general's office filed suit against Carthron less than two weeks later. The lawsuit stated in part that "... Carthron has neither the intent, nor the ability, to assist Arkansas consumers in obtaining a home in the time or manner in which he promises the consumer." It added, "Carthron cannot legitimately engage in credit repair and cannot actually repair credit."

The walls continued to close in on Carthron as more complaints surfaced and court dates grew near. In March 2004, he filed for bankruptcy protection. At the hearing, Carthron admitted that he had no money, had no intention of paying back any money, and that any paperwork or computers linked to his business had been destroyed. Carthron told the court he had not filed a tax return since 1996.

Eventually, the Pulaski County prosecutor filed criminal theft-of-property charges against Carthron and on January 20, 2006, he entered into a plea agreement. On April 21, a judge sentenced him to twelve years in prison, with six of those years suspended if Carthron agreed to pay restitution to his victims. The judge's order also required Carthron to begin repaying two dozen victims upon his release from prison. The total owed? $55,650.

Carthron did not stay behind bars long. He was released on October 30, 2006. The Arkansas Department of Community Correction set his monthly restitution payment at $927.50 per month by dividing the amount owed ($55,650) by 60 months (five years). Under threat of returning to prison, Carthron made seven payments before filing a federal lawsuit claiming the monthly amount was too steep.

The court agreed, ordering Carthron to pay whatever monthly amount he wanted so long as the total amount owed was paid in full within not five years but ten years (2018). Carthron moved out of state and other cases soon captured the attention of the court, prosecutors, and parole officers. In the end, he did not pay his restitution in full and there've been no consequences for Carthron.

This from Kwanna Brown in 2021: "I only received two to three payments totaling less than $600 of the $3,500 dollars that I paid [to Carthron]. I tried to follow-up and track progress and never received feedback from the Department of Community Correction."

In 2016, Carthron started Joseph Carthron Outreach in Houston, Texas. A description of the business found online is shared here verbatim: "After being falsely accused Dr. Joseph E. Carthron wanted to make sure no one else would suffer the injustices, of racism in the American judicial system. Fighting to make sure poor students receive the same quality education of those whom parents are wealthy and privileged. We have helped hundreds of families from across America and will continue with God's grace."

Also...

> My name is Dr. Joseph E. Carthron I'm an education advocate and spiritual counselor to those hurting needing an answer and guidance to living a life of freedom from drugs and alcohol, and suicide prevention. At the age of thirteen, I became heavily involved with drugs and alcohol over a ten year span. I have been clean and sober for 23 years as of 2017. I now fight to free those that have been taken advantage of in the criminal justice system. I fight for those that attend Title 1 schools for a more quality and equal education to help make their lives better for great opportunities.

It is a pleasure and honor to serve as the founder of Legal Professionals for Equality in America.

Carthron's LinkedIn profile also lists him as senior vice president of operations at Baker & Williams Industries for the past ten years and as president and legal investigator of Citizens for Better Criminal Defense, Inc., founded in Houston in 2016.

MARSHALL HANCOCK

Many times scoundrels threatened to sue 7 On Your Side, KATV, and me. Marshall Hancock of Hot Springs was one of the few who actually did.

In January 2007, Hancock's attorney, Justin Hurst, argued that an interview with a state employee about Hancock's business practices contained false information that hurt Hancock's business, which was renting inflatable entertainment (bounce houses) and rock climbing walls to the public.

In a 7 On Your Side report that aired June 26, 2006, Mike Watson with the Arkansas Department of Labor made the comment that, "Mr. Hancock has not notified our office of his intent to operate in this year or since May of last year." Watson also stated that, "We haven't inspected him at all in over a year." The suit claimed this was a false statement and had tarnished Hancock's reputation and cost him business. It also alleged that KATV had failed to verify Watson's statements prior to broadcast. None of which was true.

Months later Hancock would admit to ninety violations of the provisions of the Arkansas Amusement Ride and Amusement Attraction Safety Insurance Act; forty-five admissions of failing to notify the state of his intent to operate his attractions at an event; and another forty-five admissions of operating without liability insurance. Hancock entered into a settlement agreement with the Arkansas Department of Labor.

The agreement prohibited Hancock from operating, buying, selling, leasing, or acting as an agent for the operation of any amusement rides and attractions in the state of Arkansas. Watson, the Labor Department employee, was also dropped as a codefendant in Hancock's lawsuit against KATV, and the entire lawsuit was dismissed shortly thereafter.

Hancock had been a thorn in the sides of consumers for years, and that wasn't about to change —despite the agreement and a $10,000 penalty looming if he tried any shenanigans in Arkansas again.

But let's go back in time to May 2005, when 7 On Your Side received the first complaint against this Spa City shyster. Lake Hamilton High School had contracted with Hancock and Bounce Around Party Rentals to supply bounce houses for an after-graduation party. Hancock had cancelled the day of the event citing insurance issues and promised to refund the school $2,000.

Then Hot Springs High School contacted 7 On Your Side with a similar story. Hancock threatened bankruptcy if the schools didn't give him six months to repay them. I looked into Hancock's bankruptcy history and discovered that he had filed for bankruptcy seven times since 2001. He never followed through with any of them, so they were all dismissed.

New stories generated new complaints. Hancock never ducked requests for interviews. And at least in the beginning, he was willing to answer my questions and usually complained later about what he considered unfair coverage. Over the summer, 7 On Your Side received complaints from religious groups like the Arkansas District of Assemblies of God churches and McArthur Assembly of God. We also heard from the Chambers of Commerce in Nashville, Murfreesboro, Yellville, and Mountain Home. All alleged that Hancock took deposits and later offered dubious reasons why he could not show up on the day of a scheduled event. City leaders in Nashville sued Hancock and won. A judge ruled his cancellation, based on a national and inaccurate weather forecast, was unjustified.

In October of 2006, more complaints came in from the towns of Gentry and Lake Village. In November, it was Ash Flat and Melbourne.

Hancock used many excuses to pull out of contracted events: a chance of rain, a brother's heart attack, heart surgery or stroke, a sibling's death, or vehicle trouble. The names of Hancock's businesses were almost as numerous as the complaints against him and the excuses he used: Bounce Around Party Rentals, Moonwalks for Fun of Arkansas, Marshall's Fun Jump, Roger's Amusements, Fun Inc., Fun Time Rentals, Fun Time Inflatables, and MBH Concessions were some of them. Hancock also used the aliases Roger Fulton and Marshall Wallace.

After the settlement agreement with the Department of Labor in 2007 put Hancock out of business in Arkansas, he expanded his schemes to other states. Hancock listed amusement rides and equipment for sale on websites like www.usedrides.com and www.amusementtrader.com (which is no longer in operation). Not just inflatables or rock walls but also cotton candy and popcorn machines and motorized trains that kids can ride.

By March 2010, 7 On Your Side reported that people in twenty states were claiming that Marshall Hancock had ripped them off. They all claimed they'd sent Hancock money for merchandise and received nothing in return. Jameson Jumpers out of Louisiana paid Hancock $10,000 for six inflatables. A Michigan pastor paid $3,300 for a batting cage and other games. A Connecticut man paid $2,000 for a set of eight teacup rides. All they and many others received from Hancock were excuses.

Hancock filed bankruptcy again in 2010, listing seventy-five people or businesses that he owed money to. If you're wondering why so many people could be owed so much money without any criminal charges filed, well, all those victims wondered the same thing. Many had tried to get Garland County prosecutors interested, but they were consistently told these were contract disputes or civil matters, and not criminal.

One detective from Hot Springs Village disagreed. In February 2010, Detective Thomas Hickox reached out to me via email. "I am investigating Roger and Marshall Hancock for fraud, theft, etc. I was told that you did a 7 On Your Side piece about them once. I was wondering if I could get a copy of what you did on them. Thanks." Roger Hancock was Marshall's brother.

My response: "I have done about a dozen stories over the years on Marshall Hancock. I have a file on him two inches thick. I will be happy to provide you with whatever you want but you might want to be more specific. The Garland County prosecutor considers Mr. Hancock's fraudulent activities, despite the large number of victims in many different states, to be civil matters because a contract is usually involved. The FBI is not interested because it generally doesn't get involved unless the dollar amount tops $250,000. The AG's office has worked with the U.S. Postal Service to do a couple of things but, for the most part, Hancock has been allowed to operate in your county without fear of penalty."

I'm not sure how Detective Hickox did it, but prosecutors finally charged Hancock with five counts of felony theft. Ultimately, the con man made a deal with prosecutors and pleaded guilty to one count of felony theft of property over $500 on April 4, 2011.

Hancock didn't get prison time, but he did get four years' probation and a judge ordered him to pay $2,441.02 in restitution to

Stewart Sparks of Calgary, Canada. Sparks had paid Hancock for a mini donut machine advertised online. "He's a smooth operator," Sparks told us in a phone interview following Hancock's arrest. "He certainly knows how to scam people. I tell you he got me good. I'm a smart businessman and I didn't think anybody would ever get me but boy … he got me (laughs)."

Hancock, who was morbidly obese, left the courtroom in a motorized wheelchair. I peppered him with questions as he entered the courthouse elevator. He said nothing. Photojournalist Richard Newman and I were waiting for him on the first floor with more questions when the elevator doors opened. His brother walked alongside Hancock as they left the Garland County courthouse and made their way to a pickup truck waiting in the parking lot.

Marshall, still uncharacteristically silent, got in the front seat while his brother leaned two boards up against the tailgate and prepared to guide Marshall's wheelchair up into the bed of the truck. It was a struggle, and Marshall's brother decided he no longer liked the presence of a camera capturing his every move. "Get that camera off me man!" He moved toward Newman, and Newman issued a warning that I later mass produced as a T-shirt with his picture on it: "I'm not the one," he warned Roger Hancock. It worked. The brother backed off, loaded the wheelchair, slammed the tailgate, and drove off in a huff.

Hancock paid half of his restitution the day he entered his plea, with the rest to be paid within ninety days. At the deadline, he still owed $641.02, and the presiding judge issued a warrant for his arrest. I emailed him about the warrant, and he quickly paid the balance … and then replied to me. Here is the last exchange we shared, offered verbatim, from August 16, 2011:

> Well you need to check there is no warrant and the money was paid so stay out of my business and life and try leaving other people alone and you need to pray for all the lives

that you have destroyed and hope nobody ever does you the way you do others god bless you with your poor pitiful life.

To which I replied:

Marshall,

If you feel there have been any inaccuracies in our reporting, you are certainly entitled to file suit against us (again).

As risky as it is, I will take your word for it that the terms of your guilty plea agreement have been satisfied. Better late than never. It is a shame that it takes the threat of incarceration for some people to do the right thing.

As always, I wish you much success in finding an honest way to make a living. I will be pleasantly surprised if I don't get any more complaints against you in the future.

Jason Pederson
KATV Channel 7

I never did receive another complaint against Marshall Hancock. He died at a Hot Springs hospital in June of 2021 at the age of 54.

I appreciate the work of Detective Tom Hickox and all the men and women in law enforcement who realize that property crime and financial theft steal much more from individuals than money.

CHESTER SANDERS

There is a search engine called "Court Connect" that allows you to enter the name of a business or individual and look up the number of court existing cases involving that person or company.

When you enter the name "Chester Bernard Sanders," you'll see twelve pages of entries, 227 in all the last time I checked, dating back to 1979 when Sanders was twenty-six years old. An outfit called Corporation Service Financing had filed a lawsuit against

Sanders and collection efforts continued for six years. In 1981, Tommy Griffin sued Sanders for damages of some kind (records do not specify) and Griffin won a default judgment of $2,278. Sanders finally paid in 1989 but not without a lot of court intervention. Coleman Auto (1982), Union Pacific (1984), and Missouri Pacific (1987) were all ordered to garnish Sanders' wages and send a cut to the courts to pay Griffin.

There's no doubt that Sanders hated having his paychecks garnished, and it may explain why he eventually went into business for himself as an auto mechanic. Complaints to 7 On Your Side against Sanders and Mabelvale Automotive preceded my tenure, and they continued throughout my twenty years.

In 1981, prosecutors in Pulaski County charged Sanders and he pleaded guilty to assault and fleeing, the first of many criminal charges over the years. Sanders has also been taken to court by customers. He has been sued by ex-wives and by women trying to establish paternity. He has been sued by insurance companies. He has been sued by banks. He has been sued by the City of Little Rock. He has been sued by the state, both the Department of Revenue and the Department of Finance and Administration.

In 2020, attorney Sylvester Smith filed a lawsuit on behalf of Mabelvale Automotive customer Anna Phifer. The lawsuit accused Sanders of a bait-and-switch, agreeing to tow, inspect, and store Phifer's 2010 GMC Terrain for $300 and then demanding $3,500 in storage fees before he would release her vehicle, more than ten times the original estimate.

From the lawsuit: "This person (Sanders) brought her in there under the guise of inspecting her vehicle, towing it, and storing it. And instead tried to leverage her with the exorbitant and unreasonable fees. They're frankly unconscionable!"

Smith's allegations were not the only case of unconscionable charges. We had previously interviewed Maybelline Miller, who agreed to pay Sanders $1,800 to put a new engine in her 2003 BMW only to later be presented with a bill for $5,500. Silvek Pupkowski experienced similar price hikes in 2017 but was able to pull the money together to get his two vehicles back from Sanders. He then sued and won a judgment for $7,805. Gail Lindsey paid Sanders $1,300 for repairs that weren't done properly. When she demanded the warranty on the work be honored, she said Sanders cussed her out and told her not to come back. The list of such instances goes on and on.

Nearly two decades earlier, in 2001, I presented Sanders with two dozen police reports filed within the previous fifteen months, reports in which his customers called police to help with a dispute. The reports alleged that Sanders used profanity, physical force, and dishonesty against his customers. Sanders' response to the charges? "People get angry. You can't control peoples' feelings. I don't try. I try to work on cars and solve the problems."

"Almost twenty-five incidents where the police have been called. They're all lying?" I asked.

"They're all lying," Sanders insisted.

A year later, another of our conversations became a showdown. At some point, Sanders decided it was no longer in his best interest to do interviews with us about complaints. When he saw us coming, he'd lock the office door or retreat into his garage where he couldn't be seen. He made it clear that Channel 7 was not welcome on his property.

So, when a new complaint came in, we interviewed the unhappy customer on the lot next to Mabelvale Automotive. Latreece Freeman paid Sanders $1,200 for a new engine, a bit more than was owed, and Sanders refused to give her any change. To make matters worse, her 1989 Lincoln Town car still wasn't running right. Freeman returned and threatened to call 7 On Your Side after which she said Sanders cursed her out and said, "F%@ & 7 On Your Side ... they can't do anything to me!"

After the interview with Freeman, photojournalist Ray Hamilton and I set up across the street from Sanders' garage to get some video of his shop. Sanders watched us through the window for a while, then suddenly marched outside and toward an RV on his property. Apparently, he knew he couldn't order us off property he didn't own, so instead he decided to position the RV to block our view of his business.

So began a comical dance between Sanders and Hamilton. Hamilton would set up his tripod and aim it at Mabelvale Automotive and Sanders would drive the RV into the shot. Hamilton would pick up the camera and tripod and move one direction or the other, and Sanders would put the RV into drive or reverse depending on which way Hamilton went. This went on for several minutes and while amusing to me, Sanders became more agitated with every move.

Finally, Sanders gave up, hopped out of the RV, and walked directly up to me. Hamilton, as I always wanted each photographer to do when things got heated, continued to capture video of the ensuing confrontation.

After the confrontation aired on the evening news, a slew of new complaints against Sanders were shared with the 7 On Your Side office.

But back to the lawsuit filed by Sylvester Smith on behalf of Anna Phifer in December of 2020, which stated "... that Chester Sanders and Mabelvale Automotive continue to refuse to release the vehicle to Anna and now have raised the storage fee charges to $3,500 due to the fact that Anna got the police involved in the matter. Separate, Defendant Sanders yelled at and threatened Anna before hanging up. After the call ended Mr. Sanders failed to properly hang up, and Anna heard him tell his female employee that Anna would 'eventually forget about the car just like the rest of them do, then we can sell the car and make some money off of it.'"

Sanders failed to reply to the lawsuit in the thirty days required, so a Motion for Default Judgment was filed. The entire case was slowed due to the COVID-19 pandemic and Sanders' changing attorneys. If Phifer prevails, she will be awarded a judgment that will be next to impossible to collect. Just like all the rest of them.

In December 2022, the now sixty-eight-year-old Sanders was arrested and charged by the Pulaski County prosecutor with several felonies including rape, battery, aggravated robbery, and terroristic threatening. At the time this book went to press, Sanders was awaiting trial and his shop on Mabelvale Pike was boarded up.

ERIC HOLMES

Just like Joseph Carthron, Eric Holmes presented himself as someone who could make dreams of homeownership come true. And just like with Carthron, most of the complaints 7 On Your Side received against Holmes were from single women.

Just like Marshall Hancock, Holmes didn't mind being interviewed. The best con artists always believe they're the smartest person in any room and that no one, not even an investigative reporter, can see through their ruse. And just like Chester Sanders, the complaints involving Holmes spanned the entirety of my time as the 7 On Your Side reporter, from my first report on Holmes in 1999 to the last one in 2019.

The first centered on the complaints from two women, Priscilla Jones and Rose Taylor. Jones and Taylor contacted 7 On Your Side in August of 1999. Both claimed to have given Holmes substantial down payments (Jones/$1,300 and Taylor/$7,000) toward buying two different homes, only to be later told that financing fell through. Holmes was operating as Circle H Industries. Prosecutors reviewed the evidence brought to them by police and charged Holmes with felony theft by deception.

While investigating Holmes, I learned that the Arkansas Real Estate Commission had revoked Holmes's license in 1997 after it found he had stolen money from an elderly woman and had lied on his application. In its decision, the commission stated that "... Holmes's acts involve fraud, dishonesty, untruthfulness and untrustworthiness" and that "...he is unworthy or incompetent to act as a real estate salesperson."

In February of 2001, a judge found Holmes guilty of theft of property in connection with the Jones and Taylor complaints and sentenced him to ten years in prison (or five years if Holmes paid $8,300 in restitution). Prosecutor Stewart Cearley stated right after the verdict that Holmes's own testimony did him in.

Two months later, there was a surprising twist to the case. Judge Marion Humphrey, the same judge who found Holmes guilty and sentenced him to prison, reversed his ruling and set aside the guilty verdict after the request was made by Holmes's attorney, Jack Kearney. Judge Humphrey then sealed the court record and expunged Holmes's criminal record.

Prosecutor Larry Jegley felt blindsided. "There wasn't any new evidence or anything else," said Jegley. "It was a rehash of the same arguments that were made at the trial and the conclusion of the state's case and just represented a 180-degree reversal. Eric Holmes has a long, lengthy, and sordid history of ripping people off and of threatening individuals. He's been convicted of felonies on more than four separate occasions."

Holmes eagerly shared the news of his exoneration. "Frankly, I just couldn't see how the judge found me guilty from the beginning. Judge Humphrey . . . I have high respect for him and his decisions and opinions. He's a friend of mine, and I respect him highly. And I don't really question what he does."

Humphrey still required Holmes to pay back all the money Jones and Taylor lost to him on the bogus real estate deals. Holmes told us he was just fine with that, but Jegley was not. Prosecutors appealed Judge Humphrey's reversal to the Arkansas Supreme Court. In February of 2002, the court sent the case back to Humphrey with orders to impose his original sentence. In May, Humphrey ordered Holmes to prison.

Sidenote: Holmes had appeared in Judge Marion Humphrey's courtroom before. In 1996, Holmes entered a guilty plea to the charge of felony possession of a firearm. Humphrey imposed a sentence of three months' probation and a $460.50 fine. Humphrey later decided that paying the fine would cause "a severe and undue hardship upon the defendant" and he reduced the amount to $250 plus community service.

As a sitting judge, Humphrey would not comment on Holmes's claims of friendship or the rationale for the decision to release him from jail. But Humphrey has been retired for over a decade, so I asked him again. "I was more concerned about his paying her money back than I was in him going to prison," Judge Humphrey explained in an email. "My recollection is that the lady wanted some money more than a jail sentence for Eric. I got that for her. I think that was justice for her. Moreover, Eric exaggerated his being a 'friend.' I knew him, but I would not describe him as a friend. I, also, knew the victim."

At Judge Humphrey's suggestion, I also reached out to Priscilla Jones. She noted that the original order required her to be repaid regardless and she would have preferred Holmes stay in jail as long as possible. "We were never consulted about his early release," says Jones. "I was very surprised and upset. We both got our money back, but Eric should have stayed in jail! My father was U.S. Magistrate Judge Henry Jones. Judge Humphrey called my father to apologize to him. But he never offered me an apology. Eric is still up to his old games. Some lady contacted me on Facebook in 2020. He ripped her off for $5,000!"

As we learned with Joseph Carthron, a prison sentence of five or six years is in reality less than twelve months (about one-sixth of the time ordered). It wouldn't be long before Holmes was released and 7 On Your Side again started hearing from more people unhappy with him.

In February of 2004, Holmes operated Above and Beyond Real Estate Development Co. and according to Rochelle Gamble, Holmes was representing himself as a real estate agent. Gamble said Holmes accepted from her a partial down payment ($1,320 of $2,500), but she was later told by Code Enforcement that the home she thought she was buying was not for sale. Holmes claimed it was his wife's company, not his, and his promises to refund Gamble's money were broken.

In late 2007, Holmes resurfaced doing contracting work under a license in the name of Anita Holmes. Code Enforcement found Holmes had done electrical work and put in a new HVAC unit without the required permits. Also, the work done was deemed substandard. I called Holmes to ask him about it.

"I just want you to know that that ditch you're trying to dig for me ... you're going to fall in that ditch yourself," Holmes warned.

"So just keep on digging. And remember—I'm gonna always be standing."

Next, we learned Holmes was trying out his hand at remodeling homes. Dennis Carroll needed to add on to his home after his sister died and he took in her children. Carroll made the mistake of hiring Holmes, operating as BH Construction.

"He came and gave me a good spiel about how he is sent from God and he's the perfect man for this job," Carroll told us at the time. "He really sold himself quite well. We've given him $13,500, which is enough for labor to at least do the addition. But he wants more money."

"Phase One" of the project, the room addition, was to cost $15,000. But it became obvious to Carroll that Holmes had no idea what he was doing. Other contractors who came to look at the work done by Holmes were appalled. Water was coming into the home, and the ceiling was falling in.

"He's actually taken our money and put us in a worse condition than we were to begin with," Carroll lamented. "So, it's just been bad all around."

In September 2009, Judge Willard Proctor issued a ruling in Carroll's favor and ordered Holmes to repay the $13,500 he was paid, plus the amount of money needed to repair the damage done to the Carroll family's home and personal belongings. The total award: $57,000. Less than two years later, Dennis Carroll died at the age of forty-three. It's unknown if the debt was paid prior to his death.

Over the next decade, while Holmes made regular appearances in Pulaski County courtrooms, he made only a few appearances on Channel 7.

I broadcast my first story on Eric Holmes a few months into my two-decade run as KATV's 7 On Your Side reporter. And my final story on Eric Holmes would be shared in July of 2019, a few months before my tenure would end.

Holmes accepted $5,000 from Rotonda Williams to help remodel her Little Rock home. When Holmes asked for an additional $2,500 and Williams refused (because of substandard work), Holmes refused to come back, saying he had already done $12,000 worth of work. In a phone conversation, Holmes admitted he was not licensed to do the work but claimed he was working with licensed contractors, although when asked for the names of those individuals, he refused to provide them.

The Arkansas Contractors Licensing Board filed suit against Holmes, accusing him of working without the necessary license. It's basically the same offense that Holmes was committing when he lacked a real estate license in 1999. Some things never change.

According to LinkedIn, Holmes is now going by Erick Holmes and is listed as a Real Estate Investor at The ACMB Group in Little Rock.

JERRY COLLINS

Only one of the scoundrels I chased can rival Marshall Hancock when it comes to the number of out-of-state complaints. While Hancock was forced to find victims in other states after our reports poisoned the well for him in Arkansas, the complaints against Jerry Collins came from other states right from the start.

Our first report on Collins aired on October 2, 2013. The Arkansas Better Business Bureau had issued an alert on Collins based on a growing number of complaints and his lack of responsiveness. We went to Morrilton, where Collins was operating at the time, and found him at his shop. At that time, thirty-one people had filed complaints with the attorney general's office against Collins and his company, RV Ice Box, in 2013. Aaron Sadler, spokesperson for then Attorney General Dustin McDaniel, told us that eighty complaints had been received since 2009.

I asked Collins about all the complaints.

"Sometimes our efforts aren't good enough and that is where some of the complaints are going to come," said Collins. "But I can tell you this—we're in here to make sure that every customer is satisfied, happy, and we've got lots and lots of customers that way. But we do have a few more that are not."

Before leaving, Collins promised he would do better to limit new complaints and address old complaints.

We checked back eight months later when someone emailed a new complaint against Collins to the 7 On Your Side office. The AG's office had received forty-two complaints against Collins in the twelve months prior to our first report. There were only thirteen filed in the first six months after our report aired, so it seemed we had helped make some progress.

Unfortunately, it was a mirage. Collins began doing business as Tate's Welding. Over the years, he would change the name of his business many more times as online anger grew, and shippers/suppliers would cut him off for nonpayment or complaints. RV Ice Box, RV Fridge House, NuCold Refrigeration, Tate's Welding—whatever name Collins chose to use, he paid Google to make sure that his companies came up first when someone searched for "RV refrigerator repair."

From 2014–2016, the Arkansas attorney general received 125 complaints against Collins from thirty-seven states totaling $87,417. The average age of each victim was sixty-two years old.

The average amount lost was $699. And who knows how many people lost money to Collins and never bothered to file a formal complaint.

All the complaints followed a similar pattern. The high cost of replacing an RV refrigerator shocks an RV owner and prompts an online search for repair services. That would turn up one of Collins's companies, which required money up front. Long delays were blamed on back orders, delivery mistakes, or illness. Refunds were promised but never came. Warranties were offered but not honored. Complaints fell on deaf ears and eventually contact was lost or became unpleasant.

After sending Collins the core from his RV refrigerator along with $870 for its repair and receiving nothing in return, Lee Adams from Idaho wrote: "After looking into the history of this company, we find that we are just one of hundreds of people who have been sucked into dealing with this company which has very unscrupulous business methods. Why is this company still doing business in the state of Arkansas?"

When David Craft of California lost $820 to Collins, he called the attorney general to complain. "What the AG told me (in 2015) was that because it was sold out of the state of Arkansas it was basically out of their jurisdiction. There was nothing they could do for me."

I asked Craft if he believed Collins was aware of this. "Oh yeah, I do. I mean, it's been years he's been able to carry on like this."

And this is what Hank Kinsley told us after he lost $499 to Collins: "If it is to the desire of your attorney general's office to allow this business to continue to operate within your state, that is your business. I am highly disappointed that there have been so many complaints and this business is still allowed to operate."

We interviewed an in-state competitor of Collins, Wick Weck-werth of RV Cool in Greenbrier, about his frustration with what Collins was doing to the reputation of Arkansas and his industry.

"Not everybody can afford to buy a new refrigerator when an RV refrigerator fails," Weckwerth told us. "They're expensive, you know, anywhere from $1,700 to $3,000–$4,000 for a new refrigerator. And we can rebuild or repair the customer's refrigerator for a fraction of that."

Negative online comments about RV fridge repairman Collins (who lived nearby in Plumerville) were hurting Weckwerth's business. In May of 2014, his wife Stacey wrote to Attorney General Dustin McDaniel and begged him to "Please do something" about Jerry Collins.

Nothing happened.

On October 13, 2016, 7 On Your Side made a request to interview Arkansas Attorney General Leslie Rutledge about Collins. I even took the unusual step of sharing some of the questions I planned to ask. Here is the request sent to Rutledge's spokesperson Judd Deere:

> Judd,
>
> I would like to schedule an interview with Attorney General Rutledge focusing on the consumer protection duties of the attorney general's office.
>
> I am going to specifically zero in on Nucold/RV Fridge House complaints.
>
> By my tally (and assuming there have been no new complaints over the past two months) there have been 79 complaints from 29 states against Jerry Collins since Ms. Rutledge took over as our state's attorney general.
>
> However, none of those complaints were made by an Arkansas citizen.

This raises several questions in my mind—questions I would like the opportunity to pose to Ms. Rutledge. For example:

Is it the duty of the Arkansas AG to primarily serve and protect Arkansas citizens, or is there also a duty to protect citizens from other states when they are dealing with a bad actor based in Arkansas?

What specific power does the attorney general have to address out-of-state allegations made against an Arkansas business?

Since 2001, at least 200 complaints have been filed with the Arkansas Attorney General's office against this business. Is there any record of any action being taken by any attorney general against Jerry Collins during those 15 years? If so, what was it? If not, why not?

Is 200 complaints filed with the Arkansas Attorney General's office against an Arkansas-based business (that is not a national corporation) common or unusual?

I may have other questions based on the answers that are given but this should give you an idea of the direction of the interview.

I am available today, tomorrow, or any day next week. We have set October 27 as an airdate for this report. Thanks in advance.

Jason Pederson

The day of our planned broadcast came, and we still had not been able to interview Attorney General Rutledge. At the time, I was doing one hour of morning radio once a week on sports/talk station 103.7 The Buzz. Attorney General Rutledge did a morning segment on the same station once a month and took calls from listeners. It just so happened that her appearance that month fell on October

27, so I took the opportunity to call in and ask her about Collins and her seeming reluctance to do an interview about his company for a story that was to be broadcast that evening.

It was an uncomfortable conversation, bordering on confrontational, as I didn't appreciate her lack of availability and action, and she no doubt didn't appreciate me pointing the finger at her office on air. In truth, complaints against Collins had been coming in for years. Attorneys General Mark Pryor, Mike Beebe, and Dustin McDaniel had all received complaints against Collins.

Our report on Collins that aired October 27, 2016, included this comment from Attorney General Rutledge, taken from our phone conversation broadcast on 103.7 The Buzz that morning: "You and I are on the same team. We are going after the bad guys. And Arkansans need to know that the folks at the AG's office work hard every single day and that we go after the bad guys on their behalf."

Less than two months later, on December 21, AG Rutledge filed a lawsuit against NuCold Refrigeration. A statement issued by Deere quoted Rutledge as saying, "After receiving over 200 complaints from citizens across the country and conducting a multi-year investigation, I am taking action to shut down this bad business."

Things did not improve after the attorney general filed suit. Less than a year later, in August of 2017, we reported that fifty new complaints from twenty-four states had been filed with the Arkansas attorney general's office with incident dates *after* the December 2016 lawsuit. The total amount allegedly lost was nearly $30,000 and much of it was lost to veterans. How did we know that? The attorney general's complaint form contains a box to check if you're a veteran.

In December 2018, nearly two years after filing suit, Attorney General Rutledge obtained a default judgment against Collins in the amount of $1.63 million dollars. Others had received much smaller judgments against Collins previously, including Regions Bank ($250,000), UPS ($25,000), and First Security Bank ($4,000).

The judgment included $81,454 in restitution to be paid to Collins's past customers. Most of the fine constituted a $10,000 civil penalty for each offense. But the real purpose of the lawsuit was to put Collins out of business, as the judgment prohibits Collins from working in recreational vehicle refrigerator repair in the future.

So far, that seems to have been accomplished.

DARA BOOTH

During my two decades of reporting, there is only one *woman* who rises to the level necessary to be included in this rogues' gallery: Dara Booth. The primary reason for Booth's inclusion is her penchant for targeting one of society's most vulnerable, our elderly. Plus, she has a manner so slick she could fool a federal judge.

The first complaints that 7 On Your Side received concerning Dara Booth came in 2009 from employees of Arkansas Home Care for Seniors. They called to claim they worked but weren't paid.

It didn't take long to determine that wherever Booth went, trouble and drama followed. We were soon hearing about all kinds of plots and storylines worthy of daytime television.

In May 2009, Sandra Tindall's aging and ailing mother needed round-the-clock care, so she hired Arkansas Home Care for Seniors. Tindall prepaid for services each month. Her mother died at the beginning of a pre-paid month, so Tindall was owed a refund of more than $4,000. She called 7 On Your Side when Booth refused to pay. We did not name Booth or her company because producer Donna Nunn secured Tindall's refund prior to broadcast.

Despite not naming Booth or her company, we started receiving other complaints against her. She managed to satisfy each complaint and keep her name and face out of our broadcasts. But often when this is the case, a scoundrel is robbing Peter to pay Paul, and it's only a matter of time before the Peters run out.

While we were helping customers get refunds and employees get paychecks, Booth was being sued by TV station KTHV ($13,000) and the *Arkansas Democrat Gazette* ($2,000) for advertising debts. Baptist Health sued Booth for $14,797 for unpaid medical services. But her real trouble was with the IRS, who claimed she owed nearly $300,000 in unpaid taxes based on her company's earnings from 2005 to 2008.

In August 2011, Booth appeared before a federal judge to plead guilty to two counts of misdemeanor failure to pay taxes (the judge reduced the charges due to Booth's cooperation with federal prosecutors in another case). When asked by Judge D.P. Marshall where the money went, Booth replied that she gave most of it to a man named Cary Gaines with whom she had been involved. Gaines was a former North Little Rock alderman who was sentenced to federal prison after pleading guilty to wire fraud in connection to a city contracts and kickbacks scheme (this was the other case). Booth claimed she gave Gaines nearly $400,000, telling Judge Marshall that Gaines had taken advantage of her.

Booth avoided prison time by convincing Judge Marshall that she'd learned her lesson and would stay out of trouble.

"I've learned that being true to myself and God is what is most important," Booth said in court. "I've learned it the hard way, but I have learned that. I know beyond a shadow of a doubt that I will never find myself in a situation that I'm not proud of. I've hurt my family and friends and I've let a lot of people down. I cannot change the past; however, I can do something about the rest of my life, and I have purposed in my heart to be the best I can be from this point forward."

What I've learned in dealing with scammers and scoundrels over the years is that they're not bashful about wrapping themselves in religion if they think it will help get them into your pocketbook or help get themselves out of trouble.

Booth was sentenced in November 2011 to five years of probation and agreed to pay $278,000 in restitution to the IRS.

Three years later, she faced a new felony charge after being accused of stealing $16,000 worth of rings off the fingers of an elderly Little Rock neighbor. Federal prosecutors immediately requested a probation revocation hearing.

This situation would only worsen. The very next day, Maumelle police arrested and charged Booth with stealing $50,000 worth of jewelry from another elderly woman's home. In both cases, Booth had been stopping in for visits and bringing pies. Without admitting she took anything, Booth returned a $27,000 diamond ring to police after being charged.

At her probation revocation hearing, the judge learned that Booth hadn't made a restitution payment in over two years. She'd missed mandatory probation check ins. She'd been associating with convicted felons. And she'd failed to report within the required seventy-two hours of her new felony charges. All were violations of her probation. Yet federal prosecutors decided to wait and see what happened with the state charges she faced before deciding what to do.

Booth pleaded not guilty and seemed content to attempt to drag out her prosecution for as long as possible—potentially well beyond the end of her five years of federal probation. If that were to occur, then the federal government would no longer have a probation to revoke. She needed to get to November 30, 2016, and more than a year after being charged with stealing jewelry her case had progressed very little. That is until Booth's own mouth derailed her plan. I asked her in the hallway outside one of her court appearances about rumors that she planned to plead guilty.

"Why plead guilty if you're not guilty?" I asked her. "I wouldn't plead guilty to something I didn't do."

"I'm not pleading guilty," Booth answered.

"You're not pleading guilty? You're not entering a deal with prosecutors? Because the trial was supposed to be for today, so you must have some kind of deal going with prosecutors."

"No," Booth replied flatly.

Well, when we shared Booth's comments with prosecutors, it was news to them. Realizing that Booth was not dealing with them in good faith, they immediately called her back before Judge Leon Johnson, who said that in June he would either entertain a guilty plea or set the case for trial—and no more delays would be allowed.

But Booth did manage another delay in June by changing attorneys. Her trial date was set for December, but federal prosecutors filed a motion to extend her probationary period so she could not run out the clock prior to her state charges being resolved.

Booth was convicted on both counts of felony theft in December, but her punishment was limited to 120 days in the county jail and seven years of probation. Booth never spent a night in jail. She reported for work (picking up trash, mowing grass, washing vehicles) on Saturdays and Sundays (6:00 a.m. to 2:00 p.m.) and received two-for-one credit, meaning one day of work counted as two days toward her 120-day sentence.

In May of 2017, Booth appeared before Judge Marshall and once again professed that she'd learned her lesson. Booth told the judge she suffered from a mental illness and believed with help she could get better. She confessed to being untruthful at all her previous court hearings. She admitted to all her probation violations.

"I'm a hot mess," she explained. "I'm just a hot mess. And I just need to get better."

Judge Marshall sentenced her to four months in federal prison in Mason City, Tennessee, which was on the more lenient end of the sentencing guidelines. We asked veteran federal prosecutor Pat Harris after the hearing if he believed Booth was being sincere this time.

"You know, I don't know. I've heard a lot of stuff over the years. Sometimes people come in and they are sincere. And you know the way we will tell is time. If she gets out, if she changes, that will be great."

I spent my final thirty months as the 7 On Your Side reporter without hearing Booth's name again.

GENE HICKMAN

Unlike all the scoundrels so far, Gene Hickman didn't have one particular way to get into his victims' wallets or purses. He found multiple paths of entry, which would land him in prison.

When we first called Hickman about a customer complaint in October 2011, he asked for and we gave him two weeks to rectify the matter. Our goal is always to first work to make a victim whole (assuming their complaint is legitimate), not put people on TV. In fact, putting a dispute on TV is usually a last resort. It becomes more difficult to resolve conflicts in favor of the victim after that step has been taken.

Hickman sold storage sheds near the Highway 67/167 overpass at the Highway 5 exit in Cabot. He would also sell pole barn kits (large metal buildings supported by laminated wood posts anchored into the ground that lack interior load-bearing walls) and offer to visit a customer's property to assemble the structures. And that is what Ruth Horton of Vilonia purchased from Hickman. Horton had paid Hickman $6,200 and had little to show for it.

"I guess it is a $6,200 stupid tax," lamented Horton. "There is nothing else I can do. I'll just have to hire someone else to do the work he was paid to do."

In investigating Hickman, we learned that the Lonoke County Sheriff's Office had fielded over a dozen complaints against Hickman that were about to be sent to prosecutor Chuck Graham. We suggested Horton add her name to the list.

In mid-November, Hickman filed for bankruptcy protection, listing fifty-four creditors—including Ruth Horton.

A month later, three days before Christmas, Hickman was arrested and jailed (at least until he complained of chest pains and was transferred to a hospital). Prosecutors alleged the number of victims had risen to over thirty and the amount of money involved was approaching $140,000. While often considered civil matters, prosecutor Chuck Graham said that the number of victims and the fact that it appeared Hickman had no intention of fulfilling contracts after taking money convinced him that Hickman's conduct was criminal.

As was the case with Dara Booth, Hickman entered into what Graham thought was a good-faith negotiation to resolve the criminal charges with a negotiated guilty plea; Hickman could avoid jail time by agreeing to pay restitution to his many victims.

On January 24, 2014, Hickman appeared in Lonoke County District Court, over three years after he was arrested and charged with ripping off a group of people that had grown to thirty-three in number. In lieu of a trial, Hickman was given one last chance to avoid jail time.

"He has thirty days to come up with a significant amount of money, which if he does it will allow us to help those victims," explained Prosecutor Graham. "If not, he'll face a judge and be sentenced for all those charges."

"How much money?" I asked Graham. "What is 'significant?'"

"It's $175,000. That's what he needs to come up with within thirty days," answered Graham.

Well, just like when 7 On Your Side gave Hickman two weeks to make things right the first time we dealt with him, Lonoke County didn't have any better luck. On March 17, 2014, Judge Sandy Huckabee sentenced the serial scammer to sixteen-and-a-half years in prison. The losses of his victims ranged from $3,900 to $35,000. The judge ordered Hickman to pay them all back but after prison. Graham told the many victims at court that day not to get their hopes up.

"They always order it, but I always tell victims—when we're sending them to jail it's not about the money," said Graham. "They're probably never going to see it."

Hickman did report to Cummins Prison, but within months he was transferred to a work release program in Benton. As a nonviolent offender, Hickman was eligible for the transfer and for an earlier release. Hickman was paroled in March 2016, part of an effort to ease prison overcrowding. Hickman was to make his first $1,500 restitution payment within ninety days of his release. He did not. He moved to Springfield, Missouri, and just like with Joseph Carthron, moving to a different state made collecting restitution payments more of a challenge.

But unlike Carthron, Hickman couldn't stay away. He moved back to Arkansas and quickly got into more trouble. While operating a roofing company, HGH Development, he took money from customers to repair roofs but failed to return and do any work.

We featured Hickman in another 7 On Your Side report in April 2018 when the Arkansas Residential Contractors Committee cited him for working as a residential contractor without a contractor's license. Hickman had taken $6,500 from a homeowner for a roofing project but never performed the work. He refunded $2,500 after the police got involved.

In August 2018, the committee cited Hickman again for the same thing. This time he was operating as JZ Roofing and had taken $9,885.95 from a homeowner to replace a roof damaged by a hailstorm. Hickman did not perform any work on the project, nor did he return any of the money. In this instance, the Garland County prosecutor charged Hickman with felony theft. In November 2019, Hickman pleaded guilty before Judge John Homer Wright and avoided jail time. He was given six years' probation and ordered to pay $6,000 in restitution ($300 per month starting on December 15, 2019).

In August 2019, 7 On Your Side heard from three more Hickman customers/victims. Joseph Taylor ($4,436), John Bukowczyk ($2,000), and Robert Robertson ($13,580), all of Jacksonville, AR, had given Hickman money toward new roofs, only to never see him again. And in October 2019, another Jacksonville man, John Buck, called to share a similar story. Buck had given Hickman $2,000.

In October 2020, a judge threatened to dismiss the case against Hickman filed by the Arkansas Residential Contractors Committee due to lack of activity, but the committee responded with the following: "That good cause exists for this case to remain active. It is Plaintiff's reasonable belief that the Defendant continues working in the state without a license from the Contractors Licensing Board." In May 2022, Judge Alice Gray issued an order permanently prohibiting Hickman from working as a residential contractor without a contractor's license.

GLEN DANIELS

The actions of the scoundrels profiled thus far have been devious and deceitful, but not dangerous. Only one of the con artists I reported on was violent: he shot a customer in the face. And the man who did it continues to serve the central Arkansas public at his place of business.

The first complaints against auto mechanic Glen Daniels started in the early 2000s and were usually resolved with the return of a vehicle or a refund issued to the complaining party. KATV would feature such individuals in "success stories," where we would allow the viewer to explain how 7 On Your Side helped without naming the offending business or individual.

Glen Daniels Transmission is located off Mabelvale Pike in southwest Little Rock, just down the street from where Chester Sanders operated Mabelvale Automotive. The complaints against Glen Daniels Transmission seemed to go from a trickle to a flood in the summer of 2011. For instance, one man hired Daniels to put a new transmission into his 1994 pickup truck. When he stopped by after a week to see how things were going, his truck was nowhere to be found. He was informed that his truck had been stolen and five other vehicles had been broken into. He learned that the security cameras on the property were not operating; they were dummy cameras to give the appearance of surveillance. No arrests had been made, and no one had bothered to call him to let him know what had happened.

Daniels refused to do an interview with us about the situation, but a year later he did do an on-camera interview with us about a complaint made by another customer, Sandra Bell. Bell had her car towed to Glen Daniels Transmission and paid $400 toward the repair of her 1992 Toyota Camry to a man (Lamont Foster) in a Glen Daniels Transmission uniform. Bell was later told that no money had been paid but she had a receipt.

My interview with Daniels about the situation was frustrating. I started with a simple question:

Me: "Lamont Foster. Who is he in relation to Glen Daniels Transmission?"

Daniels: "No ... no relation."

Me: "He's never worked for you?"

Daniels: "Yes."

Me: "So ... that is a relation."

Daniels: "That's not a relation."

Me: "It is an employer/employee relation."

Daniels: "So? So what?"

Me: "She paid a man in a Glen Daniels Transmission uniform $400 towards getting a transmission."

Daniels: "So? I could put on a Channel 7 shirt ... what that mean? You know, you about a pain in the chest."

I then presented Daniels with a copy of Bell's receipt.

Daniels: "That is not my receipt."

Me: "That's not what your receipts look like?"

Daniels: "No. I get a lawyer to sue you too."

Me: "To sue *me*?"

Daniels: "Yeah."

Me: "For what?"

Daniels: "Well ... you'll see."

Although Daniels originally agreed to show us his receipt book, he later changed his mind.

He also never sued KATV, but a year later he found himself in court facing a criminal charge after shooting a customer in the face with a .22 caliber pistol.

In May 2013, Daniels was charged with a felony of first-degree battery after an altercation at his shop with customer Quinton Moore. The six-foot-eight-inch, 395-pound Moore went to pick up his truck and told police that Daniels became agitated and, despite Moore's size, started pushing him. When Moore pushed back, the much smaller Daniels fell. Moore told police that Daniels pulled out a gun and started fiddling with the gun's safety. Moore told police that he said, "Really? You're going to shoot me over my transmission not being fixed? You did this . . . and you're going to shoot me? Really?" And then Daniels shot him. The bullet hit him in the chin, traveled along his jawline, and exited out the back of his head.

Prosecutors later upped the charges against Daniels due to his habitual offender status, adding a felony possession of a firearm charge, and arguing that "Defendant Glen Daniels has been previously convicted of four or more felonies, and consequently his sentence should be increased as provided for in Arkansas code."

In March 2014, Daniels avoided a jury trial and a possible prison sentence by accepting a plea deal. The deal added two more felonies to his criminal record, and the agreement required him to spend 120 days at the Pulaski County jail (on weekends only if he chose). The deal also required six years of probation, one-hundred hours of community service, a $1,500 fine, anger management counseling, and random drug testing. Daniels left court without commenting; Moore was happy with how the case was resolved and, thankfully, complaints against Glen Daniels Transmission decreased in the years that followed. When this book went to press, Glen Daniels was open for business and appeared to be busy.

> **LESSON LEARNED:**
> *Business name changes are a major red flag.*

Each of these scammers (except Sanders and Daniels) changed the name of their business multiple times. These phony fresh starts allow dishonest individuals to evade their damaged reputations. Searching court databases as well as the internet can help protect consumers. So can consulting the Better Business Bureau, licensing boards, the attorney general's office, and other organizations and agencies that keep tabs on both good and bad individuals and businesses.

> **LESSON LEARNED:**
> *Just because someone looks like you doesn't mean they can be trusted.*

It's sad, but many of us are inclined to trust somebody who looks like we do. That's a mistake, because in almost every case I reported on the scammer and the victim shared the same skin color. The only color that matters to a con artist is green.

> **LESSON LEARNED:**
> *Restitution is a racket.*

It sounds good, especially after losing your money to a scoundrel. But time and again, promises of restitution are often used to convince victims to agree to a plea deal that helps swindlers avoid jail time. And when that money is not repaid to victims, nobody gets sent to jail for violating the terms of the plea deal. That's just the way it goes. I've seen it often. If I'm ever in that position and given the choice, I will tell the prosecutor to forget about my money: lock the thief up.

MORE SCOUNDRELS
(SCAM LETTER)

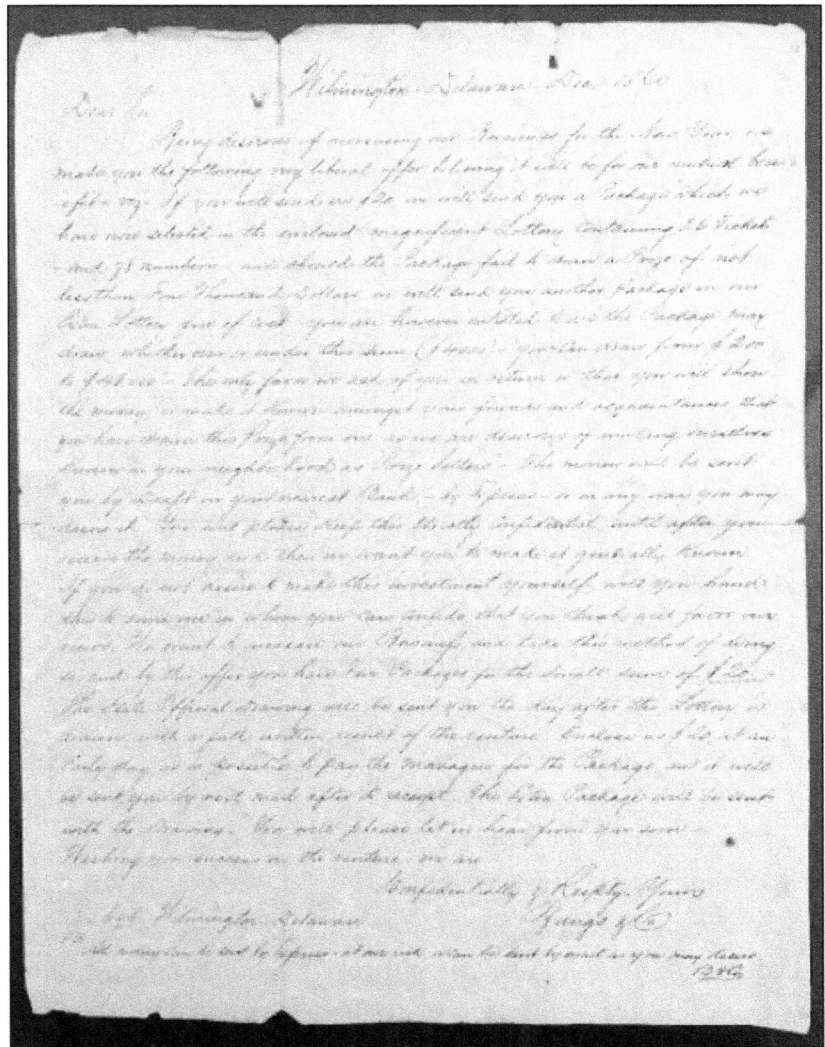

Scams and scam artists are nothing new. Human nature creates in all of us an instinct to get as much as we can for as little as possible. This instinct, when not controlled by a conscience, can cause people to lie, cheat, and steal to get what they want. While vacationing in Wisconsin, I discovered the above letter for sale in a binder of old documents at a flea market. I paid $20.00 for it. It's an example of a lottery ticket scam from 1860. It's hard to read, so I have retyped its content here.

Wilmington, Delaware—Dec.1860

Dear Sir,

Being desirous of increasing our Business for the New Year, we make you the following very liberal offer believing it will be for our mutual benefit - viz - If you will send us $20, we will send you a Package which we have now selected in the enclosed magnificent Lottery containing 26 tickets - and 78 numbers - and should the Package fail to draw a Prize of not less than Four Thousand Dollars we will send you another Package in our Extra Lottery free of cost - you are however entitled to all the Package may draw, whether over or under this sum ($4,000) - "you can draw from $200 to $48,000" - The only favor we ask of you in return is that you will show the money, or make it known amongst your friends and acquaintances, that you have drawn this Prize from us as we are desirous of making ourselves known in your neighborhood as "Prize Sellers." The money will be sent to you by Draft on your nearest Bank, - by Express - or in any way you may desire it. You will please find this strictly confidential, until after you receive the money and then we want you to make it generally known. If you do not desire to make this investment yourself, will you hand this to someone in whom you can confide that you think will favor our views. We want to increase our Business, and take this method of doing so, and by this offer you have Two packages for the small sum of $20. - The State Official Drawing will be sent you the day after the Lottery is drawn with a full written result of the venture. Enclose us $20, at and Early day as is possible, to pay the Managers for the Package and it will be sent you by next mail after this receipt. The Extra Package *will be sent with the Drawing - You will please let us hear from you soon - Wishing you success in the venture - we are -*

> *Confidentially and Respectfully Yours,*
> *Bangs and Co.*
> *Box 696 Wilmington - Delaware*

PS

All money can be sent by Express - at our risk or can be sent by mail as you may desire.

B @ Co.

CHAPTER SIX

THE MONEY
(DREW CO. BURIAL ASSOCIATION)

STORY IDEAS CAN COME FROM almost anywhere—an observation, a tip, a hunch, a neighbor, or even a national story that might have a local angle. But before an idea becomes a story, there needs to be trust, verification, and due diligence.

In 2014 or early 2015, a former colleague gave me a story idea. During my time in El Dorado with KTVE, the station also employed a reporter named Vince Sims who worked in Monroe, the northern Louisiana city where KTVE was based. Although we worked for the same station, we didn't work in the same city, so we rarely saw each other. Vince, who was born and raised on a cattle farm near Monticello in southeast Arkansas, was working as a reporter in Atlanta when he reached out to me. He called with a tip about the Drew County Burial Association (DCBA). Black residents of southeast Arkansas, including Vince's parents and about 250 others, belonged to the DCBA. It was one of about 135 burial associations in the state at that time, and one of only a few that was super funded. There was well over a million dollars in the bank and the members wanted to dissolve the DCBA and divide up the money. So, they did. Checks were cut, sent, and a few were cashed. However, a state board called the Arkansas Burial Association quickly voted 4–2 along racial lines to freeze all funds and suspend DCBA officials. Sims believed that in doing so, the board had exceeded its authority. He wanted to bring attention to what he considered an injustice.

I knew and trusted the source of the tip, so I was naturally interested, but I had more to learn and confirm. For example, what is a burial association, and why do they exist? What records exist for the DCBA and other such associations? Who serves on the Arkansas Burial Association board, and what reasoning or conflicts of interest might be driving their decision? What if any precedence or guidance exists for such situations?

According to a 1979 Arkansas Supreme Court decision (Drummond Citizens Ins. v. Sergeant), *Burial associations arose out of the depression years in our country for the mutual benefit of those who desired assurance at a modest price that they would be given a decent and proper burial.* The Arkansas Burial Association Board was created in 1953 and a cap on benefits paid to any association members was set at $500, which at the time was enough to guarantee a complete and respectable funeral and burial.

White burial associations may have formed due to the Great Depression, but minority burial associations were often formed due to discrimination. Black Americans in Arkansas and many other states could not buy burial insurance in the early 1900s. To prepare for the death of a loved one, members paid into a fund regularly, a little at a time, so they could pay collectively for the funeral and burial of the next member to die.

After decades of regular deposits and with a maximum payout limited to $500, well-managed burial associations grew exponentially in the U.S. When I learned of DCBA's existence, the members had $1.2 million in the bank. In 2012, the members voted to dissolve the association and sought permission from the Arkansas Burial Association's board to do so. Permission was denied. The

DCBA sued, but the case moved slowly. Eventually, DCBA decided to cut checks to its members. In December 2014, the Arkansas Burial Association's board took action to halt the process, which was when Sims contacted me.

I did a few stories on this dispute in January and April of 2015, when the Arkansas Burial Association Board held meetings and the matter was on the agenda. But it was a complex issue and needed more time than the usual two minutes that each reporter is allowed during a newscast. Fortunately, there are several months during the year when a reporter is allowed to go over this two-minute time limit. Stories during "sweeps" months, also known as ratings periods, can be more in-depth (Chapter 14 will examine ratings periods in greater detail). In May of 2015, I shared the following report:

State Senator Jason Rapert and State Representative Mark Lowrey sponsored legislation on burial associations that passed in 2015. However, it only applies to a small number of overfunded burial associations. It doesn't address the dissolution of an association, but it does allow money in excess of a stated policy amount (whether that be $500, $1,000 or $2,500) to be paid to members as long as such action doesn't jeopardize the financial integrity of the burial association.

Two months after my story aired, the Arkansas attorney general's office weighed in on the dispute. It found that not only did DCBA have the legal right to dissolve and distribute its money to its members, but the Arkansas Burial Association Board lacked the authority to prevent such an action.

Five days later, on July 22, 2015, the Arkansas Burial Association board reconvened and reversed its previous decisions to freeze DCBA's account and to suspend its president and secretary. Board member Scott Berna of Fayetteville changed his vote, allowing for the reversal. We were with DCBA members in Drew County as they listened via teleconference to the board's vote. Joseph Cavaness then spoke on behalf of the group.

"Prayer to our Heavenly Father means a whole lot. And we have been praying . . . we have been hoping for justice to be done. And I think today it has been done. I'll be relieved when the checks start clearing the bank. Simply because I don't know . . . I . . . but I'm hopeful and I'm praying that this is over."

There were no more surprises. The checks cleared the bank.

Arkansas Burial Association board member Chuck Dearman, owner of Stephenson-Dearmon Funeral Home in Monticello, recused himself from the vote. His opinion can be found in the notes from previous board meetings: He warned that allowing this dissolution ". . . will be the beginning of the end of burial associations." He called allowing dissolutions " . . . the first step in destroying burial associations as we know them. Even though there may not be many super funded associations, there will definitely be more dissolutions to follow. There has never been a burial association dissolution and there is a reason for it."

Time has proven Dearman wrong. There have been no mass dissolutions of burial associations in Arkansas. Bob Brooke, auditor for the Arkansas Burial Association board, explained that the DCBA was a unique case, being the only association in the state not linked to a specific funeral home. Had it been linked to a funeral home (as Dearman desired via a merger), that funeral home would undoubtedly have objected to any dissolution plan. Why? Because former DCBA members can spend the money they receive on anything they want. They might set it aside for a future funeral, or they might buy a new living room set. It's their choice. Prior to dissolution, the money had to be used to help pay for funeral and burial expenses.

Members of most burial associations in Arkansas would not elect to dissolve because they're grossly underfunded. For example, if members of the Stephenson Burial Association, managed by Chuck Dearmon, had voted to dissolve at the same time as the DCBA, each member would've received a paltry $1.64.

How can that be? Some members have paid into the funds for decades. So where did all the money go? Brooke says that burial associations or their managers, who are often funeral home directors, can use up to 25 percent of the dues collected for burial policies for overhead or operating expenses. But 75 percent is supposed to remain in the association's fund and be set aside for members. Dozens and dozens of burial associations do not adhere to this policy. The semi-annual reports issued at the end of June and December of each year by the Arkansas Burial Association are proof. They detail the number of members and the amount of cash on hand for every burial association.

Most burial association members have no idea that the fund they've paid into for years is grossly underfunded. As stated in the report I aired in 2015, there's no public outcry because the policies aren't paid to members. Instead, they're paid to the funeral home. If a member holds a certificate for $2,500 and the funeral home reduces a $10,000 bill to $7,500 . . . everyone is happy. The funeral home still makes money, and a family saves some money, even if their deceased loved one may have paid in far more than $2,500 over the years.

There are audits of burial associations but little oversight. A 2009 article in *The Village Voice* quoted Hayden Burrus, a Florida-based expert on the financial management of cemeteries, who said, "Burial societies have added risk for abuse because people tend to trust more, the laws are generally lax, and you usually have non-financial experts running it. When you can pull money out with no oversight, that's going to create a temptation."

LESSON LEARNED:
Even more so than black and white, green is the color that concerns many the most.

If you want to figure out why a particular decision was made or why a person voted a particular way, look for financial interests. While racism certainly exists, many decisions detrimental to racial minorities in this country were motivated more by love of money than hatred of skin color.

MORE MONEY
(SEWCO)

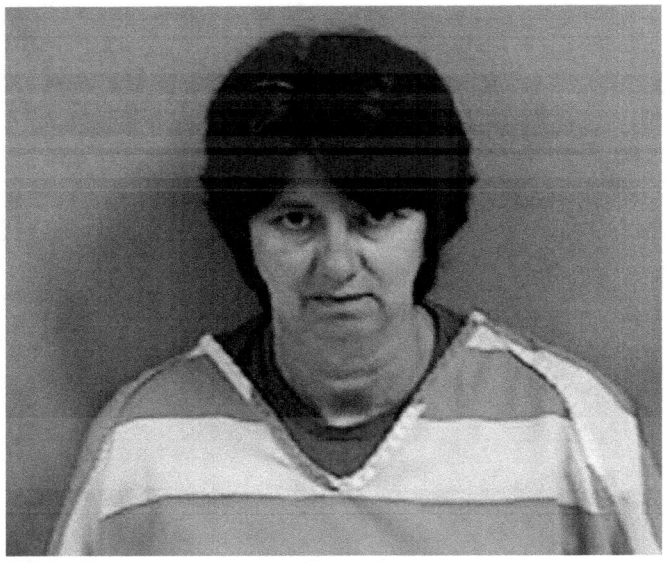

Mugshot of Diana Woodle following her 2017 arrest.

Another story idea that I received involving a lot of money origi-nated from an anonymous source. You may recall that one of the "lessons learned" from Chapter Two was that anonymous sources aren't taken seriously. This is true unless there's a way to verify the tip or information provided. I spent a lot of hours unsuccess-fully trying to verify anonymous tips over my career. This is one case where the information checked out, and our story resulted in criminal charges.

Based on research conducted in 2017, there are 704 rural water systems in Arkansas. Some serve as few as thirty-eight customers, such as Crabapple Point Water Association in Union County. Hav-ing safe, clean water is essential, so these rural water associations are a lifeline to the people they serve. They collect money from their customers in exchange for maintaining the system, monitoring quality, and providing water.

In spring 2016, I received a tip via email that the manager of the Southeast White County Water Association (SEWCO) had resigned. SEWCO is headquartered in the White County town of Higginson, population 752. I easily confirmed the tip by checking the minutes of SEWCO's board meetings, which are posted online. Those minutes also reflected that the water association's board of directors immediately voted to "remove Mrs. Woodle from all SEWCO PWA bank accounts, CDs, and lock boxes." Interesting.

The tipster said that Diana Woodle had been caught stealing, and SEWCO had quietly allowed her to resign, most likely because her husband is a deputy with the White County Sheriff's Office. Later, the tipster would encourage me to examine SEWCO credit card statements for irregular purchases.

On April 22, I emailed the tipster what I'd uncovered up to that point. I share this email in its entirety because it gives you a good look into the process a reporter goes through to dig into a story:

> OK...here is how this has played out chronologically. All the following took place prior to your credit card tip.
>
> I used our research tools to find possible addresses and phone numbers for all of the board members, but I wasn't able to reach any of them.
>
> I called the water company and Cynthia told me if I had any questions I would need to visit with Steve Merritt. She gave me a number, but it was not a correct number.
>
> I called back and Bobbi answered. She looked it up and gave me the correct number for Mr. Merritt. I also figured out that the "manager" you were referring to was Diana Woodle, since she was the only member of the business personnel I had yet to speak with.

I called Mr. Merritt and he was at lunch. I left a message.

I called the Arkansas Rural Water Association and was informed that Mr. Merritt had recently contacted the organization with a hiring question. Merritt stated that he needed to replace a manager but did not indicate why. The ARWA also informed me that all such rural associations must submit annual audits to the Bureau of Legislative Research.

I called the Bureau of Legislative Research and learned that the last audit submitted on behalf of SEWCO was for calendar year 2013. I printed it out and called the accountant in Fort Smith.

The accountant said that the 2014 audit was completed a year ago and he just forgot to file it. The 2015 audit was recently completed and will be filed very soon with the state. I asked if there were any red flags in the audit, and he said yes. He was nervous, as private accountants are rarely, if ever, quizzed by a reporter. He didn't want to tell me anything that might get him in trouble. I told him I understood and asked if there was a law enforcement agency I could contact. He said no...there was no investigation like that. I gathered that a problem had been discovered and that a private agreement had been worked out between the parties. In fact, he said he had received two emails just after 1:00 pm (from Merritt, I assume) about such an agreement. He said he would check with his partner before discussing anything further but that his audit findings would be public once submitted to the state.

I called the White County sheriff's department to ask if they were looking into anything involving the water company. I did the same with the Arkansas State Police.

Eventually both told me that no ... they were not investigating anything.

Mr. Merritt called me back. He told me that the general manager had resigned to pursue other interests. I asked him if her resignation had anything to do with the recent audit. He said no. I told him I had visited with the auditor and that there were some problems found and asked him if he was sure there were no financial improprieties involving the former manager. He said no. I told him the audit should be available in a couple of weeks. He said the SEWCO board went into executive session and discussed a personnel matter at the last board meeting but that none of that discussion can be shared. I asked him for a copy of the resignation letter and any other emails, texts or documents related to the resignation. He eventually emailed me back and told me to contact Heartsill Ragon III with any requests/questions. I assume this is an attorney.

I called the female sergeant back with the WCSO and I asked if there are any deputies with the department with the last name of Woodle. She stuttered a bit before sharing that yes, there is a Deputy Dee Woodle. Why did I do this? To further confirm the accuracy of the information you have provided me.

What I suspect is going on here is there was a misuse of a credit card, and Ms. Woodle (because she is liked and because her husband is a deputy) is being given the opportunity to resign and pay any money back without any notification of law enforcement or public exposure.

I will now have to wait for the audit report to be made public. And I will ask SEWCO's attorney for copies of not only the resignation letter but all the water company credit card statements for the past two years.

When such requests are made, they're often rejected because the desired documents are part of an ongoing investigation. Well, in this case, there was no investigation. So, under the Arkansas Freedom of Information Act, Mr. Ragon had no choice but to share the information I requested from this public entity.

On May 3, I had enough information nailed down to broadcast the first of what would eventually be over three years' worth of stories on the financial scandal that would envelop the Southeast White County Water Association. Here's a look at four of those reports:

At the time of my first report, attorney Ragon told me Woodle had paid back all the unauthorized charges, but he couldn't say how much she had repaid or how much of her past credit card charges had been reviewed.

So, I submitted another Freedom of Information Act request for that information. It revealed that two weeks after she resigned on April 21, Diana Woodle delivered to SEWCO a cashier's check in the amount of $25,944.06. Without a tip and further questioning by me, that would've likely been the end of it.

Just prior to Woodle's resignation on April 7, auditors notified the board of approximately $25,000 in questionable credit card spending attributable to Woodle and another $23,000 attributable to service technician Brandon Johnson. Eventually, my review of fifteen credit card statements (January 2015–March 2016) revealed nearly $60,000 of unusual activity, including charges to Dish Network ($1,956.48), Sirius XM ($108.16), Lucky Dog Racing ($1,038.86), Schwan's home delivery ($1,305.29), Starbucks ($594.10), and Amazon ($598.94) among others.

But things would get worse for Diana Woodle. On May 17, the SEWCO board voted unanimously to pursue criminal charges against Woodle. In June, the legislative audit for 2015 was released and the prosecuting attorney asked the Arkansas State Police to get involved. A forensic audit of SEWCO's books would look at every bank statement since January 1, 2011, and every check written during that time.

It revealed that the losses were much greater than expected. The total amount Woodle was alleged to have stolen between Jan. 1, 2011, and April 7, 2016, exceeded $360,000 ($255,346 in salary overpayments, $92,000 in credit card charges, and $36,980 in medical reimbursements). She was charged with felony theft of property in July 2017.

Not everyone was surprised. A member of the community sent this email in May after our third report aired:

> I have been keeping up with this report since I live in the area that the water company serves, and I went to school with Diane. I drive by their house every day going to and from work. I always wondered how they were living the lifestyle that they were living, knowing what she did for a living and what her husband does for a living. That's what I want you to know, what her husband does for a living. He is an investigator for the White County Sheriff's Dept. For some odd reason, the water company isn't pressing charges on her. You can't sit there and tell me that her husband didn't know what she was doing. He was enjoying the extra money too. And he is still employed by the Sheriff's Dept? Maybe you can check on this.

Under a best-case scenario, Detective Dee Woodle failed to detect that his wife was using her company-issued credit card to pay for private school tuition, supplies for their backyard pool, and trips to Starbucks. He failed to question who was paying for over a hundred home- shopping-network deliveries made to his home. He also failed to notice that his wife's original salary had more than doubled over the years.

Under a worst-case scenario, Detective Woodle knew what was going on and allowed it. Either way, it could've disqualified him from service as a law enforcement officer. If there were any professional consequences for him, they were not made public.

As for Diana Woodle, rather than risk a trial and the possibility of a twenty-year sentence, the fifty-two-year-old pleaded guilty in January 2018 and was sentenced to seven years in prison. The state released her in November 2018 after serving only ten months. It is not uncommon for first-time, nonviolent offenders who participate in a reentry program to be released early.

Unlike many defendants, Woodle was not saddled with crushing restitution payments upon her release from prison. In her plea agreement, her attorney, Paul Petty, negotiated repayment to Arkansas Legislative Audit in the amount of $26,880, to be paid in $600/month installments following Woodle's release from prison. No other restitution was ordered.

Woodle did face a civil suit filed by SEWCO. In March 2019, she filed for bankruptcy protection and in April, SEWCO's civil suit was closed. Bankruptcy protection would not get Woodle out of her court-ordered restitution. She tried unsuccessfully to get the $600 a month payment reduced. At the time of the bankruptcy filing, Woodle said she worked as a hostess at a Searcy restaurant and was making about $1,000 per month.

> **LESSON LEARNED:**
> *Sometimes your job is to just to get the ball rolling.*

My interest, research, and reporting took months, first getting the attention of the public, then the prosecutor, and ultimately the state police. Auditors, investigators, and attorneys have access and abilities that most reporters lack. In many cases, you have to trust others to continue and finish what you start.

> **LESSON LEARNED:**
> *Public entities hate negative publicity more than financial losses.*

The plan was to allow Diana Woodle to resign and accept $26,000 in reimbursement without looking much deeper into her possible malfeasance. One concerned citizen helped prevent that from happening, but who knows how often fraud goes undetected or is swept under the rug.

CHAPTER SEVEN

THE MADDENING

(TENANT RIGHTS)

IN THE CIRCUIT COURT OF PULASK_____ DIVIS

STATE OF ARKANSAS, *ex rel.*
LESLIE RUTLEDGE, ATTORNEY GENERA

v.

CASE NO. _____

ENTROPY SYSTEMS, INC and
IMRAN BOHRA

IN OCTOBER 2013, A CLIP from a 7 On Your Side report "went Hollywood" when Jimmy Kimmel of *Jimmy Kimmel Live!* included it in his late-night monologue.

A renter in rural Pulaski County outside of Jacksonville had contacted us because her toilet had been backing up into her bathtub, bathroom sink, and even the kitchen sink. Diane Alford told us she'd been going to the bathroom outside in a five-gallon bucket. "Suppose somebody comes through there driving down the highway and sees my butt," declared Alford. "That wouldn't look good. They'll be calling the sheriff on me for indecent *disposal*," she told us when we visited her rent house for an interview.

Photojournalist Chato Wilson and I kept our composure, but as soon as we got into our news vehicle, we agreed the sound bite provided by Alford was pure gold! Of course, what Alford meant was indecent exposure, but indecent disposal worked even better. Alford's misspeak and earnest delivery made her comment an instant classic. It went viral, and thanks to our involvement, her landlord fixed her plumbing.

Kimmel's audience laughed at Alford's comment, but "do-little landlords" are no laughing matter for the families who live in their properties. Poor plumbing, erratic electricity, unreliable heat, and leaky roofs can be unhealthy and unsafe.

One thing I've consistently done during my time in central Arkansas is volunteer to mentor young men. It started with a group of young men at our church and evolved into mentoring under-resourced youth through VIPS (Volunteers in Public Schools), CityChurch Network, and STEP Ministries.

Most at risk youth that I mentor live with single mothers and multiple siblings in questionable rental properties. The worst one stood on a corner near the intersection of Roosevelt and Martin Luther King, Jr. Drive in Little Rock. The toilet in the mostly brick home did not work, and if you moved any object on the kitchen counter or table, cockroaches scurried in all directions.

I asked my mentee's mother for the name of her landlord. "Imran Bohra," she replied.

Five months later, after the sun had set on Christmas Eve, Bohra visited the property and tacked an eviction notice to the front door. The mother had finally run out of patience and had withheld December rent in hopes of getting Bohra to fix some basics at his property. It's a risky play, and not surprisingly it resulted in the family being given ten days to move out.

I'll get back to Bohra, but first let me say there is no doubt her landlord held all the power in this situation. Over the years, Arkansas lawmakers have decided that you must have a license to hunt alligators and elk, that the state is properly pronounced "ARkan-saw," and that Arkansas renters have few rights.

Arkansas is the only state where you can be criminally charged and put in jail for not paying rent, and the only state that doesn't require landlords to maintain minimum health and safety standards for their rental properties. Some cities have minimum standards and code enforcement officers, but there's no statewide warranty of habitability to help ensure that all rental properties are structurally sound and have working plumbing, locks, heat, and electricity.

Are many Arkansans jailed for not paying rent? No. But the statute allows landlords to use police and prosecutors to help get a tenant out rather than having to rely on the courts. This is a savings in both cost and time.

Are there landlords with horror stories about bad tenants who tore up their properties, refused to pay rent, or refused to vacate a rented house? Sure. But these are isolated incidents. One bad landlord can own dozens of neglected properties and negatively impact many families at the same time.

The Uniform Residential Landlord Tenant Act (URLTA) was created in 1972. Since then, *every* state has adopted all or some of the protections it affords renters—except Arkansas.

"Arkansas landlord-tenant law is not balanced and it's out of step with the 20th century," said Bill Rahn, who at the time he made this comment was a lawyer with Arkansas Legal Service Support Center. "It's probably out of step with the 13th century."

"If a tenant doesn't pay rent when due, all rights to further occupation cease," explained Rahn. "If after given a ten-day notice to move the tenant remains, he becomes guilty of a crime and a penalty of twenty-five dollars a day every day he holds over. Arkansas is the only state in the country with a law like this. Another deficiency in Arkansas law, but practiced in forty other states, is a warranty of habitation. That is an implied condition in lease agreements that promises the rental property will meet minimum health and safety requirements."

Those comments from Bill Rahn could have been stated in 2022. But he made them in 1990 as fair housing advocates geared up for the 1991 legislative session and another attempt to level the playing field between landlords and tenants in Arkansas.

Months later, the April 15, 1991, headline in the Arkansas section of the *Arkansas Democrat* newspaper would read "Rejected landlord-tenant bill patterned on law in 20 states."

Here is the information reporter John Haman included in that article:

> Phillip Carroll of Little Rock, an attorney with the Rose Law Firm and a member of the conference that drafted the (Uniform Residential Landlord Tenant) act, said another bill based on the act was considered by the 1979 Arkansas Legislature, but it never emerged from committee. The 1991 bill met a similar fate under fierce opposition from real estate interests.
>
> "Generally, the major landlord interests said we don't care how you amend the bill; we're going to be against it anyway," Carroll said.
>
> Bob Balhorn, executive vice president of the Arkansas Realtors Association, thinks the law is fine the way it is. "The main reason we opposed the bill is that it was too much, too fast," Balhorn said.

Now, more than thirty years later and despite numerous efforts at the Capitol, nothing has changed. Changing too much or too fast is hardly the issue.

Actually, 2001 brought change—change in favor of landlords. And in 2007, lawmakers passed the Arkansas Residential Landlord-Tenant Act (sponsored by Rep. Robbie Willis, D-Conway), which tipped the scales in favor of property owners even further. State lawmakers voted to adopt the landlord protections included in the 1972 URLTA, but not the tenant protections; Arkansas is the only state to do so.

The main reason that little progress has been made on behalf of Arkansas renters since 1979 (the first time legislative efforts to strengthen renters' rights were defeated) is because the Arkansas Realtors Association's resistance has remained consistent and strong over the decades.

Who gave the most money to Arkansas legislative campaigns in 2020? The Arkansas Realtors' political action committees. The Arkansas Realtors Association has 9,000+ members. Spokesman Cameron Kuhn told a reporter with the *Arkansas Democrat-Gazette* that his group supports state candidates "whose values closely align with the values of realtors."

Those donations, along with power lobbyist couple Ted and Julie Mullinex, beat back any legislative attempts to improve the lives of Arkansas renters via a warranty of habitability during the 2021 legislative session. There's no organized, well-financed Political Action Committee (PAC) lobbying lawmakers on behalf of Arkansas renters (even though renters make up approximately 40 percent of Arkansas's population).

Over the years, Sen. Bill Lewellen (D-Marianna), Rep. Bill Townsend (D-Little Rock), Sen. Sue Madison (D-Fayetteville), Sen. Jon Woods (D-Springdale), Rep. Greg Leding (D-Fayetteville), Rep. Warwick Sabin (D-Little Rock), and Rep. Jimmy Gazaway (R-Paragould) are some of the legislators who have tried without success to level the playing field in Arkansas between tenants and landlords. In 1991, then-governor Bill Clinton and then-senator and future governor Mike Beebe both encouraged a compromise. Unfortunately, there would be none.

Representative Sabin's bill in 2017, like others before and since, sought to require all landlords to provide living spaces free of roof leaks and with functioning door locks, working heating and plumbing, plus safe electrical connections and access to running water.

"We really do not guarantee those basic provisions in our law, and I think it's quite shocking and surprising when people find out about that," said Sabin after his bill died in committee.

Julie Mullenix, the lobbyist who represents the Arkansas Realtors Association, argued maintaining the status quo is necessary to preserve the low rates that Arkansas renters enjoy. "We believe the laws of the State of Arkansas provide a unique balance of rights that have proven optimal evidenced by healthy investment in rental properties and some of the most affordable housing for tenants in the nation," reads a statement issued by Mullenix at the time.

A change in the law would have little or no impact on how most landlords currently do business, as most of their properties already meet minimum housing standards. The decades-long effort by a handful of lawmakers not in the grip of the Arkansas Realtors Association is aimed at getting a small, dangerous minority of property owners to do the same.

Property owners like Imran Bohra.

A week before my first story on Bohra aired on 7 On Your Side in July 2011, a judge warned Bohra to improve the conditions of his properties or risk jail time. He owned 200 in all, making him a landlord to hundreds. I spent over a month looking into a handful of tenant complaints as well as Bohra's track record with courts and the code enforcement divisions in both Little Rock and North Little Rock (NLR).

Being in court was nothing new to Bohra. I found that over the previous fifteen years, the landlord had received hundreds of citations and been fined tens of thousands of dollars. But code enforcement officers told me they'd seen little change in his behavior or his properties.

"He is the premier," NLR code officer John Roberts told me. "We have several [landlords] that are not really trying that hard. But he is the worst. He pressures tenants into signing a contract. And then once the contract is signed, if there is a problem, well, you fix it. Or he won't even talk to them."

The first court action I found involving Bohra dated back to early 1985. More than a decade later, in February 1998, the *Arkansas Democrat-Gazette* ran an article with the headline "Tired of being had, NLR to swing at condemned buildings." In the article, Bohra is quoted as saying, "It takes a long time and a lot of money to fix [condemned buildings] up. Sometimes the city just doesn't give us enough time, and so the landlords don't have any choice." Municipal Judge Steve Morley had found Bohra guilty the year before for maintaining six condemned structures—buildings not safe or fit to live in—and renting a condemned structure.

In all my years of dealing with Bohra, he would always run away after court rather than answer any of my questions. Once I chased him across Markham Street after he left a Little Rock courtroom, noting in my story that he was running from me but several of his tenants did not have running water.

In January 2019, the *Arkansas Democrat-Gazette* did an exposé on Bohra. Then in August, the Arkansas attorney general filed a lawsuit against Bohra and his company, Entropy Systems, Inc., citing the newspaper article. The lawsuit alleged that Bohra rented properties after they failed inspections and were found unfit to live in. Seven of his 150 or so properties were specifically listed in the lawsuit. A jury trial was scheduled for May 3, 2022, in the court of Judge Herb Wright.

Ultimately there would be no trial. Nearly four years after Attorney General Rutledge's press conference, and with Rutledge about to take over as the state's newly elected lieutenant governor, a new lawyer was assigned to the case (Senior Assistant Attorney General David A.F. McCoy), and he brokered a deal with Bohra's attorney. Under the consent judgment, Imran Bohra admitted to no wrongdoing or liability. He agreed he would not engage in any activity that violates the Arkansas Deceptive Trade Practices Act, including renting any properties with one or more known life/safety violations. And Bohra paid a $5,000 fine to the AG's Consumer Education and Enforcement Fund.

Bohra has remained an active landlord, especially in court. In 2020, during the pandemic, he filed lawsuits against fifty-nine tenants, attempting to evict them under Arkansas' Unlawful Detainer statute. In 2021, Bohra sued thirty-three tenants. And in 2022, the seventy-six-year-old Bohra took forty-four tenants to court. Tenant responses filed with the court almost always cited Bohra's refusal to fix problems and miserable living conditions. Many allege their evictions are retaliatory actions taken by Bohra after they called Code Enforcement.

Bohra uses the lack of renter protections to his benefit as he seeks to evict tenants and collect unpaid rent. For example, Bohra's longtime attorney, Edward Adcock, makes this argument in a filing related to Bohra's efforts to evict tenant Mona Hinojosa: "Instead of denying the facts set forth in the Complaint and Plaintiff's Affidavit, Defendant complains about the condition of the premises. However, even assuming arguendo that they were true, her complaints are legally irrelevant. Under Arkansas law there is no implied warranty of habitability on rental properties and the contractual obligation to make regular monthly rental payments is not mitigated by the condition of the property."

Here is some of what Hinojosa told Judge Herbert Wright: "May 2019 started renting. Was promised he would have his guy come fix and make livable. Never did. Bathrooms only had water in bathtubs. Kitchen only had hot water. The bathrooms had no plumbing to sinks. Washing machine had no plumbing. Back bedroom has no electricity. Electric receptacles ... most do not work and are hanging out. Every month took my $500 and said he would send someone. Never did. He came to America and got a piece of the pie and makes women and children live in unsafe conditions. Please help us!"

There is nothing in the court record to indicate how this case was resolved.

Over the years, I've done many stories about landlord/tenant disputes and the failed efforts to improve the imbalance in Arkansas between the two.

Mason-Dixon polling in 2019 found that 73 percent of Arkansans strongly favored a law that would require all landlords to provide a minimum level of habitability to renters (again, something all other states have). This was a popular idea across all regions, political parties, ages, races, and genders.

A study presented to lawmakers in 2017 linked the high rates of cancer, asthma, depression, and fire-related deaths in Arkansas to substandard housing. Dr. Alesia Ferguson with the University of Arkansas for Medical Sciences' (UAMS) Institute on Public Health told legislators that inadequate heat, structural issues, leaks/mold, pests/rodents, electrical/plumbing deficiencies, and improper ventilation can all jeopardize health.

"We have a significant number of older homes in Arkansas," said Dr. Ferguson. "Older homes means that we're going to have more structures that are not maintained. They're dilapidated. They're falling apart. It means that appliances in the homes are likely to be old and not maintained, which means carbon monoxide threats, right? HVAC issues ... leading to poor homes."

A study requested by the legislature in 2011 and completed two years later recommended reforming state laws.

Yet, neither public opinion, studies, testimonies by medical professionals, nor anything else has been enough to persuade legislators to support changes. After an effort went down in flames in 2015, I summed up the situation in my six o'clock report this way: "The easy answer is ... the people who collect rent or finance rental properties have lobbyists, and the people who pay rent do not." This remains true.

Efforts to repeal Arkansas' regressive grocery tax took several decades. We'll see if the same can be said one day for the efforts to strengthen the rights of renters in Arkansas. There was a bit of progress made in the 2021 legislative session. Act 1052 of 2021 allows renters to move out without penalty and have their security deposits returned if landlords don't provide a sanitary sewage system, hot and cold running water, electricity, a roof that doesn't leak, and functioning heating and air conditioning (provided it worked when the tenant signed the lease). In order for a tenant to exercise this option, they must be current on their rent and give the landlord thirty days to address issues. But the legislation doesn't protect tenants from possible landlord retaliation.

I asked Rahn, the Little Rock attorney who has been fighting for change for over thirty years, for his perspective on the issue now. "I am glad to see heightened interest and more resources devoted to creating balance with our residential landlord and tenant laws," he said. "Maybe the efforts of 7 On Your Side back in the 1990s and during your tenure can claim some credit for this growing awareness. The way things are trending in our legislature, I am not optimistic change will occur but always remain hopeful."

> **LESSON LEARNED:**
> *Blame people, not parties.*

From 1972 (when the Uniform Residential Landlord Tenant was passed) until about 2012, Democrats were in power in Arkansas. They had forty years to improve the rights of renters, and they didn't. Since then, Republicans have been in charge. And so far, tenant advocates say their efforts have fallen short. Lobbyists, in general, don't support parties; they support causes. They're effective and relentless advocates for those causes because the people and organizations who pay them demand it. The people get the electorate they deserve. If renters want better policies, they need to elect better politicians.

MORE MADDENING
(RESTITUTION, REPUTATION, REHABILITATION)

RESTITUTION

At the heart of most 7 On Your Side stories is money: lost money, stolen money, needed money, love of money. And when justice is served, it's often served with a healthy side of restitution.

Restitution is a popular concept. Any person or organization that has lost money to a scam or a scoundrel no doubt wants to get that money back. Prosecutors use the promise of restitution when negotiating plea deals. Here is what might be said to a victim: "He will agree to pay you back if you agree to allow the judge to sentence him to probation rather than jail time." The problem is, at least from my experience, far too often the promise to pay restitution is broken without consequences.

In theory, if a criminal defendant on probation fails or refuses to make restitution payments to their victims, they'd be locked up. But in reality, this rarely happens. Prosecutors, judges, and the system at large move on to other more immediate and pressing matters. There's little time or inclination to look back and make sure the promises made in plea agreements are adhered to. Instead of getting repaid, victims are often left feeling betrayed.

In all honesty, is it reasonable to ask and expect the scoundrels profiled in Chapter Five to pay tens of thousands of dollars in restitution after incarceration?

In Joseph Carthron's case: $55,650.

Or, in the case of Jerry Collins: $81,454.

Gene Hickman: $175,000.

Dara Booth: $278,000.

After their guilty pleas, these people are now convicted felons. This information comes up on a background check, which makes getting a job that pays decent money more difficult.

Marshall Hancock did pay his restitution, but it was only $2,441.02. Even then, he only did so under the threat of having his probation revoked.

I stated in an earlier chapter that restitution is a racket, which is an overstatement. Some felons do pay, and some victims do get repaid. Using it as a negotiating tool does prevent many trials, eases courtroom backlogs, and saves taxpayer money. But former state and federal prosecutor Cody Hiland agrees that changes are needed. "Arkansas has a restitution problem," Hiland told me. "In 2013, the legislature changed it, so court fees and fines were prioritized over victims. And there is no space in the jails, which takes away the ability to enforce restitution orders."

Some counties (for example, Washington County) have a victim restitution coordinator within the prosecutor's office. Some have a victim assistance office or victim services office. But most do not.

The collection of court ordered restitution varies by county. In many counties, it's the sheriff's office that collects and distributes restitution payments. It can also be the prosecutor's office, the

circuit clerk, the court/judge, or Arkansas Community Correction. There's no central agency across the state that tracks restitution across jurisdictions.

In 2012, a report was issued at the request of the legislature that
focused on the Arkansas victim restitution system. The fifty-one
page document, produced by The JFA Institute, included information on other states, as well as input from probation and parole
officers, prosecutors, public defenders, judges, community correction officials, and those responsible for collecting and disbursing
restitution payments. Here are a few excerpts from that report:

> Efforts to improve collection of victim restitution across
> the country and provide some measure of support for vic-
> tims with monetary losses have had limited success. The
> reality is that victim restitution competes with several
> other financial obligations that are placed on offenders.
> Despite the political benefits of placing the costs on the
> perpetrators, offenders are often in the worst position to
> assume such financial responsibility. While their criminal
> conduct may warrant such a burden, the fact is offenders
> have very few means when they leave the criminal justice
> system to pay these obligations and their prospects of im-
> mediate and lawful employment to satisfy their debt is
> equally limited. (p. 7)

> Most officers reported that judges will not revoke a proba-
> tioner for not paying victim restitution. This makes the
> possibility of revocation an empty threat. At the same
> time, officers are sympathetic to judges who see a revo-
> cation as unhelpful. As one officer put it, "Why throw a
> guy in jail for not paying restitution when you know it's
> even less likely to result in payment? The victim wants
> payment, and jail is not going to do it." Judges must also
> abide by the law that a probationer cannot be revoked for

failing to comply with an order of restitution unless there is a finding that the probationer has not made a good faith effort to comply with the order. (p. 24)

People on probation have few resources and struggle just to maintain stability. Pressure to pay financial obligations can often create a sense of futility in a probationer that may dissuade the person from searching for a job, staying clean of substances, and avoiding antisocial associates. (p. 25)

The report offered five conclusions about Arkansas:

1. There is no systemic mechanism for ordering or tracking restitution;
2. Other financial obligations are a higher priority than victim restitution;
3. The state has no idea how much in victim restitution is ordered or is collected;
4. Offenders are encumbered with many financial obligations that are unrealistic;
5. Most victims probably do not receive the restitution that they are owed.

The report also offered several recommendations, including:

- expanding the role of community corrections (which at the time handled restitution collection/disbursement in only five counties);
- increasing support for victim/witness coordinators;
- creating uniform data collection and information sharing criteria for all victim restitution ordered and collected;
- using the data collected to submit a report annually to the Governor and others reflecting the state of restitution collection in Arkansas; and

- monitoring and evaluating the job being done in each county.

If any of these recommended reforms were implemented, they didn't solve the problems with restitution in Arkansas. In fact, three years later a headline in the *Arkansas Democrat-Gazette* dated November 15, 2015, read "Restitution system broken, official says. Prison board told of need for statewide agency to collect money for victims." From the article: "The state's collection system for restitution - a monetary amount a judge can order an offender to pay to a crime victim - is so disjointed that state officials said they cannot determine the total outstanding amount for the state. 'Something has to change because people are not getting their restitution,' said Arkansas Board of Corrections member Mary Parker-Reed.

Gee ... if only the state would commission a study and issue a report with recommendations that could be implemented.

> **LESSON LEARNED:**
> *Studies and surveys are worthless as agents of change without commitment and implementation.*

Anyone can describe a problem and propose a solution. It takes leadership to implement the changes necessary to improve a situation.

> **LESSON LEARNED:**
> *If you're the victim of a scam or a crime and lose money, that money is more than likely gone.*

Learn from what happened, but don't obsess over it. Move on in life with greater knowledge and awareness.

REPUTATION

Chapter Three showed how scoundrels often change the name of their businesses to help avoid bad word of mouth and negative online reviews. Not all company name changes are made for this reason. Some companies with good reputations will change their name ever so slightly for another reason: to escape obligations.

A lifetime warranty is good for the entire time you own a product OR the entire time the company that sold you the product remains in business.

During the 2013 Arkansas legislative session, 7 On Your Side asked our viewers what proposals they would like to see lawmakers consider. One of the ideas shared concerned the issue of "lifetime warranties" offered by, in the case of this complaint, window and siding companies. The problem, according to the complaint, was that the warranties weren't being honored.

Louise Spivey hired Hanke Brothers Siding and Windows, Inc. to put siding on her Benton home. Twenty years later, she had a problem. But she also had a lifetime warranty.

"Yes, in writing," explained Spivey. "Signed by Kim Hanke. Saying for the lifetime of the structure—any problems or repairs—they would take care of it." But when Spivey called the number on her contract, she was told the company that sold her the siding no longer exists. The company was now Hanke Brothers and Sons, Inc.

I tried without success to get an interview with Kim Hanke to explain the change. Instead, I received a letter from the Davidson Law Firm explaining that Kim Hanke is "... Vice President of the new company, which is owned by his son. Gregory K[im] Hanke, the father, is in charge of sales and marketing for the new company and is a paid employee on a commission basis. Gregory K. Hanke, the father, does not own any interest in Hanke Brothers and Sons, Inc."

Attorney Charles "Skip" Davidson explained that Gregory Kim Hanke, II (Kim Hanke's son) was the sole stockholder, director, and president of the new company. Davidson also made sure we realized that the new company "... is a legitimate corporation that was established pursuant to Arkansas law and is being operated in a legal and proper manner. Any insinuation otherwise and KATV ...could be subjected to claims for defamation including libel and slander..."

The new company had incorporated the same year the old company went out of business. Kim Hanke filed both personal and business Chapter 7 bankruptcies in 2011 and received a discharge of debts the following year.

We asked Greg Crow, executive director of the Arkansas Contractors Licensing Board, about the arrangement. "I would remind people that any warranty you ever get—whether it is from General Motors or whoever it is from—is only as good as the company that stands behind it," said Crow. "When that company is gone, then your warranty is gone."

But Kim Hanke was not gone.

"They told me that Mr. Hanke is still involved, but his son was the main owner now," Spivey told me. "But they're still at the same address. I called the same phone number I'd called twenty years ago, I think. There's something wrong when they can do that."

Spivey suggested that there should be a law that prevents a company from being able to get out of past debts and obligations but still retain name recognition by reopening under a slightly different name. Although she wasn't against someone getting a fresh start, she thinks it should be under a distinctly different name.

Crow said there was no evidence that the name change and re-incorporation were done solely to escape past obligations. If the Contractors Licensing Board suspects that to be the case, Crow said, the agency will and has in other cases refused to issue or re-new a contractor's license.

Hanke Brothers isn't alone in this practice.

Gary Goldman of Jacksonville purchased $18,000 worth of windows from Royal Windows and Siding in 1999. The seventeen windows came with a lifetime warranty. When the rubber in between the windows started to bubble, he called Royal and asked that someone come out and take a look. Nothing happened.

Unbeknownst to Goldman, in March 2006 Royal Windows and Siding was sold to Jim Draper in a deal known as an asset purchase. Draper bought the assets (the client list, building, phone number, etc.) but NOT the liabilities such as lifetime warranties.

Royal Windows and Siding became a new company: Royal Windows and Siding, Inc.

Same building, same address, same phone number, but legally it was a new entity and therefore not bound to old sales agreements and old "lifetime" warranties.

In 2009 I contacted both company owner and President Jim Draper and General Manager Tiger Jordan and asked them about the change. They told me that every Friday, complaints about old jobs are forwarded to the "old ownership group." Jordan told me he had no idea what, if anything, happened after that. Draper told me they were trying to work out a service agreement with the "old ownership group" that would benefit past customers.

It seems clear these companies are having it both ways: using legal methods to ditch obligations while maintaining the benefit of name awareness built on years of advertising.

Tim Lemons, a state representative at the time, agreed. He was already sponsoring a bill to extend the warranties on roofs to subsequent owners of homes and agreed to sponsor another bill to make the changes that Spivey suggested. Ultimately, a problem with the bill developed—it conflicted with an existing bulk sales law—and there wasn't enough time in the session to make an amendment and get the issue resolved. To my knowledge, it has never been proposed again.

Some good news: Wilson's Home Improvement volunteered to step in and help Louise Spivey. Owner Paul Wilson says he operates under the same name he started with and therefore remains obligated to honor all past warranty work. It puts his company at a disadvantage as running all over the state taking care of warranty issues is not a money-making endeavor. But, Wilson says, to do otherwise would be dishonest and unethical.

> **LESSON LEARNED:**
> *Do some research and point-blank ask.*

Before you enter into a contract with any company, find out if they've ever changed their name and, if so, why? If they did it before, they may do it again, and you may be the one left with a worthless warranty.

REHABILITATION

The stated mission of Arkansas Rehabilitation Services (ARS) is to prepare Arkansans with disabilities to work and lead productive and independent lives. ARS offers assistance to some and training and career preparation programs to others through nineteen field offices that serve citizens in all seventy-five counties.

One segment of the Arkansas population that greatly benefits from these services is the deaf and hard of hearing community. ARS can help with communication barriers by providing interpreter services and technologies that improve communication. In addition to maintaining a list of qualified interpreters, ARS coordinates a statewide Quality Assurance Screening Test to evaluate the skill level of interpreters.

I learned all about this agency and the test when an interpreter named John West contacted me in 2012, at first anonymously, about a matter of great concern to him. According to West, ARS had recently hired a sign language interpreter who was unqualified for the job. West and several other qualified candidates had been passed over for the position. While that bothered West, what concerned him more was the possibility that clients who are deaf or hard of hearing might suffer a consequence due to a misinterpretation or miscommunication made by an unqualified interpreter.

It sounded like a good story, but it could also just be sour grapes from a guy who applied for a job and didn't get it. I needed proof to move forward. What were the qualifications of the candidates who applied for the interpreter position? What was the hiring criteria? Who ultimately made the hiring decision? Thankfully, West had already used the Arkansas Freedom of Information Act to research the matter, and he provided all this research to me.

My reporting never named the woman hired for the position. She saw an opportunity to improve her life by applying for a good-paying job with great state benefits, so she took it. Seven other candidates tested better, and six of them had sign language certifications, but she was hired instead.

Bill Walker, an appointee of Governor Mike Beebe to lead the Department of Career Education, told me in late June that he had nothing to do with the hire. Walker told me he trusts his managers, in this case Robert Trevino and Carl Daughtery, to evaluate all job candidates and to make the right decisions.

In mid-July, Walker told a legislative committee that despite lacking certification, the candidate hired had a family member who was deaf, had signed for members of her church (which was also Walker's church) for the past ten years, and had been a state employee for over twenty years. The committee tasked the Office of Personnel Management to take a closer look at the hire.

Meanwhile, the new interpreter was generating complaints from the deaf community she was attempting to serve. Interpreter Coordinator Cheryl Sugg shared some examples in an early August email: "Her communication (signing) was choppy, thus making it difficult to follow. She could not voice (read the signs produced by the deaf consumers) for anyone and refused to try to voice for anyone. The speaker gave specific facts in their statement and Ms. _____ omitted important details of those statements because of her inability to keep up. She was missing too much of the information and the consumer asked me, as the Interpreter Coordinator, to request that she please stop interpreting."

Tommy Walker, President of the Arkansas Association for the Deaf, wrote to Director Walker on July 31: "The lady hired for the interpreter position is totally unqualified for the role and needs to immediately vacate the job or transfer to a different non-interpreter job. WE do not believe another face-to-face meeting with you would be beneficial since you have stated that you will not remove the unqualified interpreter, period."

The deaf community was left wondering why Walker was doubling-down and continuing to defend a hire that seemed so blatantly bad.

The Office of Personnel Management's interview with Human Resources Manager Pam Harris on August 24 seemed to shed some light on that mystery. "Following the hiring of the interpreter, Ms. Harris said she called Mr. Walker and asked what he was attempting to do by this hire. Ms. Harris said that Mr. Walker explained that the interpreter field was a closed group, that no black applicants were being hired, and that he was going to change that practice." Director Walker, through a spokesperson, denied making those comments.

Black applicants did apply for the job, and they met the job qualifications, so it seems there was more in play than a possible quest for greater diversity, equity, and inclusion.

Carl Daughtery decided who to hire. He told those reviewing the hire that he did not think the woman who got the job was the best qualified candidate prior to speaking with Director Walker. Daughtery said that Walker gave her a very good reference and recommendation and that with such a good recommendation from the boss, Daughtery made the decision to hire the candidate.

But another manager, David McDonald, voiced concerns about the candidate's work history as a certified funeral director. Why? Because she'd worked closely with Premier Funeral Home for many years, and Premier Funeral Home is owned by Bill Walker.

Director Walker stood firm, insisting that the hire was "a good fit, a good choice." But things started to turn. Black community members, including Dr. Glenn Anderson, voiced objections. Dr. Anderson, who is also deaf and a professor at the University of Arkansas-Little Rock (UALR), wrote in a letter, "The deaf community is not very happy. It is an insult to both the deaf community and the professional interpreting community. We expected the agency to follow high standards in their hires of interpreters."

On Aug. 27, 2012, a national organization called the National Black Deaf Advocates, Inc., wrote a letter to Governor Beebe, who up until that point had refused to interject himself into the controversy. The letter reads in part, "The hired individual did not hold any of the interpreter degrees nor any interpreter credential, scored second lowest among nine applicants, and failed to translate a simple video in either of two types of sign language." Because of the hire, the letter warned, "...your state could potentially face a violation of the civil rights of deaf clients of ARS as well as a violation of the Americans with Disabilities Act.

Three days later Walker met with his boss, Governor Mike Beebe, who told him that the woman hired for the interpreter position was not the right choice. A spokesperson said Governor Beebe told Walker that he didn't make "the appropriate choice" based on input from the deaf community and that Beebe asked Walker to reflect on his decision. The next day, and after two months of defending the hire, Director Walker issued a statement saying, "I believe that I made a mistake in hiring her for the interpreter position." She was transferred to another job within ARS that paid the same salary.

> **LESSON LEARNED:**
> *Reality trumps good intentions.*

Becoming certified as a sign language interpreter is a lengthy and expensive process. Such costs can be a daunting barrier to low-income communities, making it more difficult to climb social ladders. If it was Director Walker's intention to diversify what he reportedly considered a field closed to minority candidates, he could not do so at the expense of reality. Some occupations require unique skills. Interpreting for the deaf is one of them. There were qualified candidates who applied and who could have been selected if diversity, equity, and inclusion were the ultimate goals.

> **LESSON LEARNED:**
> *If a command doesn't violate your faith or a deeply held conviction, swallow your pride, obey, and move on.*

It can be difficult for people in positions of power, who are usually left to operate without much oversight, to be reminded that they have a boss. Governor Beebe had to gently remind Director Walker who was in charge. And when Asa Hutchinson became governor, Walker was out.

I saw this lesson play out at Channel 7 too. Allbritton Communications pretty much left KATV General Manager Dale Nicholson alone because the station was a dominant #1 and made its owners a lot of money. Nicholson was rudely reminded that he had a boss when Allbritton made him do an on-air endorsement of President George H.W. Bush in advance of the contentious 2000 election. Arkansas was not yet a red state and journalism was traditionally neutral. Nicholson hated to do it, but he did as he was told. Afterward, he continued a successful career that pride could have easily ended prematurely.

CHAPTER EIGHT

THE UNSOLVED
(EAST END BOMBING)

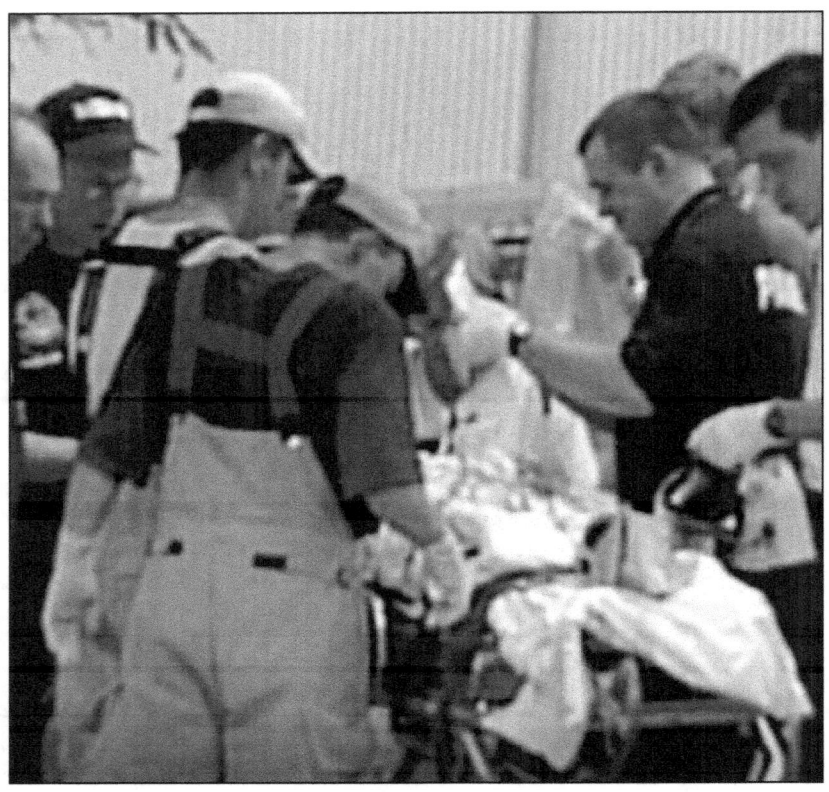

Paramedics prepare to airlift Johnny Rauch to Little Rock following a package bomb explosion in his home.

911 operator: "9-1-1. What is your emergency?"

Linda Rauch: "Help!"

911 operator: "What's the problem?"

Rauch: "9-1-1 ... there's a bomb! We just opened it and it exploded! I think my husband is dead!"

THAT'S THE CALL LINDA RAUCH made only minutes after finding a package addressed to her husband left on her carport steps. I arrived on the scene less than an hour after a package bomb blew up in Rauch's eastern Saline County home in 1998. I watched as paramedics wheeled Rauch on a stretcher that moments later lifted off for Little Rock. I secured the audio of Linda Rauch's panicked 911 call.

The bomb blew a two-by-three foot hole in the floor. It destroyed furniture, blew out windows, and seriously injured Johnny Rauch's head, hands, and legs. He was airlifted to Baptist Hospital, where part of his leg was amputated. Sixteen days after the blast, Rauch was pronounced dead.

I wrote many stories on Rauch's death after that day. To this day ... no arrest has been made.

THE SUSPECTS

Some investigations are frustrating because they produce no suspects. Some are frustrating because an obvious suspect is developed, but there's not enough evidence to bring a charge. Others are frustrating because there are so many people with possible motives that it's hard to know where to start. That was the situation following Rauch's death.

"I do know there were suspects that were looked at," said Grover Crossland in 2011 when he was the resident agent-in-charge of the Bureau of Alcohol, Tobacco, Firearms, and Explosives in the Little Rock field office. "Obviously, there was not enough factual information to do anything with that. It doesn't mean that they did or didn't do it. It's just that—you have to have enough facts to present to the U.S. Attorney's office and prove a case. And as of right now, those facts have not been developed."

There was an obvious suspect—a businessman who carried a $500,000 life insurance policy on Rauch. He filed to collect on the policy before Rauch's body was buried.

Another possibility? The businessman's partner/uncle, a man with a track record of collecting insurance money under suspicious circumstances.

A third suspect—Rauch's former business partner, no doubt upset about being jointly sued after more than one project had gone awry. Others suspects included the boss who threatened to kill not only Rauch but also his wife and son prior to Rauch's death, or the father-in-law who watched his daughter dragged through bankruptcy due to Rauch's well-intentioned but rarely successful business ventures, not to mention the two employees Rauch fired shortly before the bombing, and a host of other contractors and customers who claimed Rauch walked away from unfinished jobs, owing them money. Some filed lawsuits but most did not.

Whoever left the bomb packaged in a wooden container on the doorstep of John and Linda Rauch's East End home on June 10, 1998, is still out there. A $20,000 reward is waiting to be collected. Hundreds of interviews, scores of tips, and strong hunches have failed to produce an arrest.

THE BLAST

At the time of the attack, Johnny Rauch was working as a sales representative for All Seasons Roofing. He previously ran Linco Construction. Both positions might be relative to his murder.

The label on the package had been typed. Neither Johnny nor Linda had ordered anything, and neither was expecting a delivery. But the package looked official. It looked OK. Johnny commented to Linda that it was a joke. The package rested on the kitchen table as he opened it, with Linda nearby when it detonated.

Investigators immediately began asking neighbors if they'd seen any UPS or FedEx trucks in the neighborhood. No one reported seeing any delivery vehicles or suspicious vehicles. Investigators checked with parcel delivery companies and confirmed that none had visited the Rauch home.

Several days before the blast, Rauch served as best man in his son Justin's wedding. Justin described his father as his best friend, as did Johnny's wife, Linda. Rauch's two favorite things were riding horses and playing with his grandchildren.

Neighbors immediately offered comments regarding Rauch's character and expressed disbelief that someone would intentionally target him. Family members echoed those sentiments. But soon, investigators were tracking leads and discovering that Johnny Rauch's personal life was far simpler than his professional one.

THE MELBOURNE PROJECT

Johnny Rauch incorporated Linco Construction Company in 1993 with business partner Jerry Arnold. Two years later, Linco entered into an agreement with Cooper Management Corporation to build Pioneer Nursing and Rehab Center in Melbourne, Arkansas.

The $2 million project quickly fell behind schedule and was ensnared in problems. Linco had not posted a performance bond, architectural plans weren't being followed, subs weren't being paid, payroll went unpaid, and materials were missing. Linco left the project, and another contractor finished the job.

Pioneer Nursing and Rehab Center held an open house in September of 1996. In attendance at the ribbon cutting were owners Jim Cooper, his father Ben Cooper, and his uncle Carl Cooper, as well as Bobby and Brenda Hargis. The construction project may have been done, but Cooper Management still had business with Linco Construction. It chased Rauch and Arnold back to Little Rock with a lawsuit, hoping to collect more than $200,000.

A judge postponed the first two trial dates. Rauch had been unavailable for depositions due to his exceedingly poor health, which included severe depression, cardiac arrhythmia, and hormone deficiency. Rauch told the court he was seeing a cardiologist, urologist, and psychiatrist. The judge reset the trial for December 7, 1998.

Rauch didn't live to see it.

Rauch had already been through bankruptcy once and now he was piloting a failing company. Even if Cooper Management had won the civil suit, the chances of recouping much money by way of a judgment were slim.

But Cooper Management had a Plan B. During construction, a $500,000 life insurance policy was taken out on the life of Johnny Rauch. Commonly called a "key-man" policy, it helps ensure that a project is not set back or harmed if the man in charge suffers death or illness and cannot complete the job.

Unbeknownst to Rauch, Cooper Management continued to pay the premiums on that policy long after Pioneer Nursing and Rehab was completed, and long after Rauch had left Cooper's employ.

THE BUSINESSMAN

Jim Cooper served as administrator of Pioneer Nursing and Rehab Center, and he is a past president of the Arkansas Health Care Association. The organization serves as a lobbying arm for the nursing home industry. Four days after Johnny Rauch was pronounced dead and before his widow had buried him, Cooper submitted paperwork to Mutual of Omaha to collect on the half-a-million dollar key man life insurance policy.

Why had the life insurance premiums been paid long after the project was completed? Cooper explained in his deposition: "Well, that would be because we felt like - Pioneer felt that Linco Construction and John Rauch owed our company in excess of $200,000 and that we would obtain a judgment against he and his company for that. And as before, when we filed - when we obtained the insurance policy, really the only way the company would have been at risk was for him - if he would have died, we could have never recovered that money. So we, Pioneer, decided to continue to pay the premiums."

The only problem Jim Cooper encountered: Mutual of Omaha refused to pay.

Mutual of Omaha called Pioneer's effort to insure Rauch's life "a sham transaction." The insurer noted that "Federal investigators have not ruled out the Plaintiff, its agents and employees as suspects in the death of Mr. Rauch." It also argued that Pioneer "...never had an insurable interest in the life of John Rauch."

But in March 2001, Federal Judge Henry Woods ruled against Mutual of Omaha, ordering the insurance company to pay up. The Coopers and other owners collected more than double the amount they'd hoped to collect with their civil suit. My attempts to interview Jim Cooper about the insurance policy he maintained on Johnny Rauch's life were rebuffed.

Cooper said in his deposition that ATF investigators visited Melbourne and interviewed him within sixty days of the bombing. Cooper said he thought his younger brother, Robert, was also interviewed, even though Robert was an employee of Cooper Management, not Pioneer. Jim Cooper did not think any other Coopers were interviewed by investigators.

THE UNCLE

The Cooper family is one of Izard County's most powerful and most respected. A notice in the local paper for a Cooper family reunion put it this way: "The Cooper family is a pioneer family in Izard County and is also one of the county's largest families."

But while some Coopers excelled at sports, business, or politics, Jim Cooper's Uncle Carl Cooper seemed to corner the market on misfortune—and insurance claims.

In December 1981, Carl Cooper's home on Knob Creek Road—a stretch populated by Coopers for generations—was destroyed by fire. A front-page photo in the local paper with a caption stated, "The home of Mr. and Mrs. Carl Cooper was totally destroyed by fire last Friday morning, December 11th, about 8:15 a.m. No one was home at the time the flames started, apparently in the furnace room. The home was a total loss, but several guns were saved."

In a phone conversation on February 4, 2011, Carl Cooper told me that the photo caption was not true and that not only did he lose his guns in the blaze but his knife collection as well.

Three years later, a historic cabin inherited by Carl Cooper's wife burned to the ground. This time, the caption with the front-page photo read: "The historic former Jeffrey home in Mt. Olive burned to the ground Sunday, December 9th. The possibility of arson is being investigated by the Izard County Sheriff's Dept. The house and grounds have been under lease to a private hunting group from Jonesboro, but the house was unoccupied at the time of the fire. In the event that arson is proved, Carol Cooper has stated that a reward of $500 will be offered for information leading to the arrest of the person or persons responsible for the fire, with an additional $500 upon conviction." The State Fire Marshal's office also assisted in the investigation.

No reward was ever paid, no cause ever determined, and Cooper claimed the cabin had been uninsured.

Carl Cooper opened the Tally Ho restaurant in Melbourne, Arkansas, in 1991. He soon followed it up with the Tally Ho II in nearby Mountain View. But Cooper could not get a private club license that would allow him to sell liquor at his Stone County location.

A newspaper article in December 1995 details the third defeat in twenty-two months before the Alcohol Beverage Control board. Cooper's restaurant manager is quoted in the article as saying, "Carl wants out of the restaurant business."

In July 1996, Carl Cooper would get his wish when fire destroyed the Tally Ho II. The fire broke out shortly after 4:00 a.m. The fire chief suspected arson but could not prove it. Cooper is quoted in a newspaper article as saying that he had "…made no decision regarding plans to rebuild and that he would wait for the insurance company and investigators to complete their work." In the meantime, he said, he had been advised not to comment on the incident.

ATF investigators interviewed Carl Cooper following Johnny Rauch's murder. "They asked me a bunch of oddball questions for about fifteen minutes," Cooper told me. "I had only met John Rauch two or three times. Never really had a conversation with him. I didn't even know the guy."

THE PARTNER

When Johnny Rauch paid Jerry Arnold $10,000 in March 1996 for fifty-one shares of Linco Construction Company's stock, Arnold felt he was cashing out and resigned as secretary/treasurer of Linco. However, the companies hurt by Linco didn't see it that way. More than one, including Pioneer Nursing and Rehab, named Arnold as a codefendant when civil suits were filed in hopes of collecting money. When Rauch died, so did those legal efforts targeting Linco and Jerry Arnold.

Jerry Arnold died in April 2009. I spoke to his widow, Joanie, by telephone a few years after Jerry's death. She told me that ATF or FBI agents had interviewed Jerry twice in Benton following Rauch's murder. She said she is not surprised that her late husband was included in a long list of possible suspects. "Johnny screwed a lot of people over," she said. However, Joanie Arnold is confident her husband had nothing to do with the package bomb. When asked if Jerry ever shared his thoughts on who most likely killed her husband's former business partner, Joanie recalled his response: "Johnny was working with some mountain people, some hillbillies up north, that he should not have screwed over."

THE BOSS

When Johnny Rauch realized that he could not run his own company, he just wanted—and needed—a job. Walter Koon gave him what he was looking for.

Koon owned Four Seasons Roofing and hired Rauch as a salesman. Investigators also interviewed Koon following Rauch's murder. He figured it was because he was Rauch's employer. But actually, a story Rauch's son, Justin, told investigators is more likely what triggered the interview.

Justin Rauch worked both for and with his father, and Walter Koon agreed to let Justin rent a mobile home from him. At that time in his life, Justin admits he prioritized partying over paying rent. This resulted in a heated telephone argument one day between Koon and Justin Rauch, an argument that both agree happened. However, they disagree on one key element: Justin claims a drunken Koon threatened to kill not only him, but also Johnny and Linda Rauch if Koon didn't pay his rent. Justin told investigators that he immediately hung up and drove to his father's house to warn them. All parties agree that while Justin was there, Koon showed up. Johnny Rauch went outside to calm him down. Ultimately, Koon got paid and cooler heads prevailed.

Koon says he had nothing to do with Johnny Rauch's murder, and he hopes that one day whoever killed Rauch is caught. In fact, Koon shared an interesting story of his own with investigators that pointed them in yet another direction.

THE FATHER-IN-LAW

Koon told investigators that three days before he died, Johnny Rauch came to him and shared this comment: "If I ever get killed, send the police straight to my father-in-law."

And that is just what Koon did.

ATF investigator Glen Cook questioned Charles Bennett. While it's likely that Bennett admitted to Cook that he didn't care much for Johnny Rauch, Linda says she does not believe her father had anything to do with his son-in-law's murder.

"We were estranged at the time of Johnny's death," says Linda of her father. "Daddy liked Johnny at first. He even gave us land to build a home on, two doors down from him and his wife Freda. But my dad thought real workers had 9:00 a.m. to 5:00 p.m. jobs. Johnny preferred to work for himself. That resulted over the years in a bankruptcy for us, several lawsuits, and later the loss of our home. Over time, Daddy soured on Johnny. He would run him down to anyone and everyone. I told him that when he was running Johnny down, he was running me down—that Johnny was my husband and I had chosen him."

Linda says she felt she had no choice but to cut herself off from her overly-critical father. Of course, that didn't sit well with Charles Bennett, an Arkla gas-air-conditioning service man who'd retired early at age fifty-five and had entered into a period of his life where he really didn't have much to do. According to Linda's stepson, Justin, the estrangement started at least two years prior to his father's murder.

Bennett may have been bored and bitter at his son-in-law, but Linda says her dad would never put a bomb on his daughter's front porch—a bomb that she carried into the house and stood just feet from when it exploded. No way.

Charles Bennett died in July 2015 after battling Alzheimer's Disease.

THE INJURED BLUE-COLLAR WORKER

Bobby Hudson said he had no idea that Johnny Rauch had been killed in 1998 by a package bomb. In fact, Hudson had no idea who Johnny Rauch was when I contacted him, until I explained when and where he and Rauch had crossed paths.

In December 1984, Hudson worked for the Pulaski County Road and Bridge Department and was riding on one of the county's trucks when another truck, driven by Johnny Rauch, struck him from the rear.

A lawsuit filed by Hudson claimed that he "...sustained severe, permanent, and excruciating injuries to his head, neck, and back, and to his body as a whole." It went on to allege medical expenses, loss of earnings, and mental anguish. All standard legalese, says Hudson now. He collected money from the insurance company and not only had trouble remembering his personal attorney but the accident itself. "I only met John Rauch two times ...once at the wreck and once at the deposition," Hudson told me. "You are the first person who has ever called and asked me about it."

Hudson now says that his injuries weren't nearly as bad as what his lawsuit described, and he certainly had no motive to harm Rauch. But he agrees that ATF agents would have had no way of knowing that unless they had questioned him, which never happened.

THE FUTURE

There were other disputes and lawsuits concerning Johnny Rauch: an excavator in Pine Bluff, a machinery company in Little Rock, and unfinished churches and schools.

It's important to note that although some of the people mentioned thus far were interviewed by ATF agents, no one has been named as a suspect and no one has been charged with a crime. And there were many more people interviewed. Three months into the investigation, 120 people had been questioned. But the tips dried up long ago. The ATF's hotline has gone cold.

"We're reviewing it now and seeing if there is some possible stone that has been left unturned," said Director Crossland in 2011. "We'll revisit every technique that we have available to us. And we will probably go back and, you know, reinterview some people. See if we can get some more information and stimulate some interest in the case. Hopefully, a witness or somebody will come forward and give us some information that can help us."

Glen Cook, Bill Buford, Stuart Lowrey, and Jeff Brzozowski are some of the ATF investigators who have already taken close looks into the case. New agents and leaders must familiarize themselves with the unsolved murder of Johnny Rauch, with all of its twists and turns, assuming they have the time or inclination. Successes involving other cold cases nationwide may provide some hope or inspiration.

For example, Michael Toney was convicted twelve years after three people in Texas were killed by a briefcase bomb.

In Arizona, Pam Phillips and her lover, Ron Young, were also convicted twelve years after they used a bomb to kill Phillips's husband, a wealthy real estate developer. The motive: insurance money.

Theodore Kacyzynski, the Unabomber, killed three people and injured two dozen more over an eighteen-year span before he was caught. His brother turned him in. And it took twenty-two years to crack a bombing murder in West Virginia. Two suspects were convicted. Again, it was the brother of one of the suspects who broke the case.

June 10, 2023, marked the twenty-fifth anniversary of Rauch's murder.

OTHER ARKANSAS UNSOLVED CASES

Longtime law enforcement officers often have unsolved cases that haunt them. For retired Little Rock homicide detective Tommy Hudson, it's the case of Lakesha Chandler. After a strong spring storm knocked out power at Cloverdale Junior High in April 1995, the thirteen-year-old honor-roll student and athlete rode a bus and was home at 11 a.m. Two utility workers found the seventh grader's bound and beaten body the next day in a wooded area of southwest Little Rock.

For retired Arkansas state police criminal investigator Henry La Mar, it's the 1986 murder of twenty-four-year-old Dion Brown. Brown's body was found ten miles south of Conway on Palarm Creek Landing Road. The Heritage Publishing Company employee had been beaten and strangled, most likely in Little Rock, before his body was transported and dumped in Faulkner County.

For retired Little Rock homicide detective Steve Moore, it's the 2004 murders of Francis Hemby (90) and Evelyn Holland (86). The elderly sisters were found inside their Treasure Hills neighborhood home by Howland's fifty-seven-year-old son, Bob Howland, who checked on them daily. The pair had been beaten to death.

Longtime reporters are often haunted by unsolved cases, too. And the one that haunts me the most is the bombing murder of fifty-two-year-old contractor Johnny Rauch.

Linda Rauch eventually remarried and became Linda Sallee. My contact with her and Justin has waned, but I hope justice is served one day. A $20,000 reward remains available for any information that leads to an arrest and conviction. And the number to call remains 1-800-ATF-BOMB. But for now, like the murders of Lakesha Chandler, Dion Brown, and sisters Francis Hemby and Evelyn Holland, the murder of Johnny Rauch remains one of Arkansas' unsolved.

LESSON LEARNED:
Justice on earth is often delayed, denied, or disappointing.

Thankfully, for Christians and those of other faiths, there is a greater Power keeping score and those who escape justice on earth may ultimately endure an eternal consequence.

MORE UNSOLVED
(THE BOYS ON THE TRACKS, JANIE WARD)

Don Henry and Kevin Ives of Benton and
Olivia "Janie" Ward of Marshall

While I have done more reporting than anyone on the murder of Johnny Rauch, there were other cases where I followed in the footsteps of interested, even obsessed, journalists. I always waited until I had a new or different angle before adding to their already extensive coverage.

For example, *Arkansas Times* reporter and author Mara Leverett wrote a book on another Saline County case called *The Boys on the Tracks*. Although Leverett, Mel Hanks, and many other journalists had reported extensively on the 1987 deaths of teenagers Don Henry and Kevin Ives, I, too, was interested in the case but not sure I could add to their coverage. Then, in 2018, a former professional wrestler claimed he had witnessed their deaths. My report on Billy Jack Haynes generated renewed interest, but, unfortunately, no new leads or arrests resulted. Despite her dogged determination and never-ending advocacy, Linda Ives, Kevin's mother, died in 2021 without ever knowing who was responsible for her son's death.

Ron Ward of Marshall is another tortured parent who left this earth (in 2018) without knowing exactly how his daughter died. Oliva Jane Ward, known as "Janie," died in 1989 at the age of sixteen after attending a high school party at a cabin near Marshall in Searcy County. Witnesses say she died as a result of falling backward off of a ten-inch-high porch. *Arkansas Democrat-Gazette* columnist Mike Masterson didn't buy this explanation. Over the years, Masterson has dedicated hundreds of column inches to the case. In 2005, I traveled to the scene and took a "Nestea plunge" off the same cabin porch (onto a couch cushion) to visually demonstrate the seeming absurdity that such a fall alone could result in the death of a healthy teenager. Again, renewed interest did not result in a break in the case.

Since then, podcasts have become a new and effective way to spotlight unsolved crimes, such as Janie Ward's case and other suspicious Arkansas deaths. *Hell and Gone* is a podcast by journalist turned private investigator Catherine Townsend. The first season focused on the 2004 unsolved murder of twenty-two-year-old college student Rebekah Gould near Melbourne, Arkansas. The 2018 podcast was downloaded millions of times, and the attention resulted in an arrest. On Oct. 17, 2022, William Miller pleaded guilty and was sentenced to forty years in prison.

Townsend's second season focused on the death of Janie Ward. Townsend interviewed me about the case for one of the later episodes in the series. Unfortunately, this time the exposure didn't crack the case. Season three took Townsend to California. In 2022, Season four brought her back to Little Rock to take a deep dive into the 2015 disappearance and murder of eighteen-year-old Ebby Steppach. The high school senior's car was found abandoned in park one day after Steppach told her step-father she had been raped at a party. Nearly three years later, her body was recovered from a nearby drainpipe. That case remains unsolved at the time of this book's publication.

True crime and unsolved cases are one of the most popular podcast genres. Episodes usually last from thirty to sixty minutes, and there can be as many episodes as compelling content supports. As a TV reporter, I was always envious of the amount of information that newspaper reporters could include when publishing an investigative or in-depth report. But I still prefer the emotion, sound, and setting that a television story can deliver. Confrontations, excitement, grief, and other elements are much more powerful when shared on air as opposed to on the page. Podcasts seem to offer the best of both worlds.

> **LESSON LEARNED:**
> *Solving crime is a collective effort.*

There are many ways to tell a story. And there are many gifted storytellers. But making a difference all depends on the right people watching, listening, or reading. All of which is out of a reporter's control.

CHAPTER 9

THE IMPACTFUL
(CHILD SUPPORT CHECKS)

ONE QUESTION I AM OFTEN asked after giving a presentation is, "Have you ever been threatened or injured while on a story?" Threatened? Yes. Injured? No. Another popular question: "Which of your reports made the most impact?" The most impactful story I've told happened early in my twenty-year tenure as the 7 On Your Side reporter.

According to the Arkansas Department of Finance and Administration's website, Congress established the Child Support Enforcement Program in 1975 under Title IV-D of the Social Security Act to collect child support. The program's goal is to ensure that all children are supported financially by both parents and to reduce the number of children receiving public assistance.

In 1996, Congress passed a sweeping welfare reform bill that required all states to centralize the collection and distribution of child support payments. This necessary and often thankless job had always been done at the county level, usually by circuit clerks. Congress set the deadline for October 1, 1999, and then extended it for a year. Even then, Arkansas was not ready and requested another extension to July 1, 2001. Despite four years to prepare, Arkansas Governor Mike Huckabee would soon call the state's takeover of the child support collection and distribution system "one massive screw-up."

A few weeks after the deadline to comply, it became clear that thousands of single parents statewide (mostly women) didn't receive their much-needed child support checks. Some of those women began calling, writing, emailing, and even faxing 7 On Your Side out of frustration—and in some cases desperation. The train was off the tracks, and we began telling their stories.

> "I have not received a check since June. This is becoming a real issue for me. I am tired of trying to make my creditors understand that this is not my problem, but the Office of Child Support has made it my problem. I am tired of telling my daughter, no, you can't have something you want or need, because I have not received your child support, nor do I know if and when I will."   —Julie in Pine Bluff.

> "I cannot reach the OSCE Clearinghouse to ask about my child support. If they are not hanging up on me, they make up excuse on top of excuse as to why I am not receiving my child support checks. Their latest? I have to wait 18 days to file a missing check form. They told me this is state law. Is that true? I have to have that money before that time. I count on the child support checks to pay the daycare so I can work."   —A viewer from Marianna.

I have five manila folders full of similar complaints. These calls swamped our volunteers. We developed a system: take down the custodial parent's name, phone number, the number of checks they were behind, and the amount they were owed.

On July 24, the *Arkansas Democrat-Gazette* jumped in and did a story that mirrored exactly what we were seeing. Their headline: "Delay in issuing checks results in call overload." The story began with these two paragraphs:

The toll-free number of the state Office of Child Support Enforcement [OCSE] has been besieged with at least ten times as many phone calls as the staff can answer each day from people upset about delays in processing the child-support checks they needed this month. "The processing of 100,000 payments, some due weekly and some due monthly, worth $20 million to $25 million, has been delayed for periods of up to three weeks," said Dan McDonald, administrator of the agency.

Governor Huckabee set a deadline of August 17 to send checks in the mail. Huckabee hinted that firings could result if his deadline was not met. There were more than 14,000 checks held up because of missing information, or a variety of other reasons. The state pointed the finger at county clerks for providing inaccurate or incomplete information. Legislators pointed fingers at the state for not being prepared. Single parents were less concerned about blame; they just needed their money.

According to the state, on August 14, the number of checks waiting to be processed was down to 2,689 from 11,769 five days earlier. The day before Huckabee's deadline, again, according to the state, the number of unprocessed checks had fallen to 1,324. That was good enough for the governor. The state had met his deadline. McDonald told lawmakers the state had processed all "workable" checks by the deadline.

By September 5, the state reported the number of child-support checks waiting to be processed stood at 119. However, many were skeptical, including 7 On Your Side. We continued to hear from custodial parents who knew noncustodial parents were paying, but they weren't receiving the money. To disprove, or at least call into question, the claims made by the state, we had to give a voice to those parents.

On September 6, 2001, KATV asked custodial parents still missing child support checks to call us. In the first four hours we received nearly a hundred calls. On September 7, I delivered a typed list of 143 Arkansans who were missing payments directly to Governor Huckabee at his Capitol office. We didn't expect to get an audience with the governor, but we wanted the imagery of entering his office and delivering this list to drive home the point that this was a major problem worthy of more attention from our state's top elected leader. It was, for the most part, theater. But it proved effective.

Calls and emails poured into KATV. Three days later, I delivered a second list with another seventy-five names. A third list included 152 names, and a fourth would add another 100. In a very short time, Channel 7 heard from 500 custodial parents who claimed the state had fallen behind on their child support checks, even though a month earlier the OCSE had claimed that number had dropped to 119.

Every list we presented to Governor Huckabee was taken seriously. McDonald hired temporary employees, and Governor Huckabee temporarily transferred employees from other state agencies to the OCSE to help with the backlog. Working Saturdays became mandatory, and McDonald halted any paid time off and vacation time. The office contacted custodial parents, researched each case, and provided help where possible.

The OCSE is tasked with a difficult job. The men and women in that office work to facilitate cooperation and mediate between two parents who oftentimes do not get along. They must try to get money from one parent who oftentimes will do anything possible to avoid paying. The stakes are tremendously high because they involve the basic needs of children.

On October 5, a legislative committee was told that the train was back on the tracks.

"I feel like we're about as good as we're going to get right now," Mc-Donald told lawmakers. That statement motivated a former OCSE employee to contact me and offer his take on how things were really going—or at least had been going up until very recently. He said computer systems failed, machines broke down, cases backed up, and workers were instructed to lie to complaining custodial parents. A state official disputed the claim.

The following day, McDonald's testimony was called into question by Theresa Caldwell, an attorney suing the state in federal court on behalf of nine mothers. Caldwell had a personal interest in the case. A custodial parent herself, she failed to receive a check in July 2001 and then received delayed checks. In October 2003, U.S. District Judge James Moody dismissed the lawsuit. Moody ruled that Arkansas parents who rely on monthly child support checks issued through the state don't have federally enforceable rights to certain collection and distribution procedures.

Complaints to 7 On Your Side about the OCSE tapered off but never completely stopped during the following eighteen years. It takes a special set of circumstances for 7 On Your Side to do a story on matters related to divorce, child custody, and nonpayment of child support. I mentioned this adage in Chapter One: No matter how thin you pour a pancake, it always has two sides. Well, cases involving child custody and child support have more than two sides. They're contentious, potentially libelous, and best left off the television airwaves.

The problems in 2001 did qualify as a special set of circumstances, and many parents told us that our involvement helped prioritize the problem and restore financial stability to their lives more quickly. One awards committee agreed, as our coverage was recognized with a prestigious Edward R. Murrow award.

LESSON LEARNED:
Light generates heat, and heat can produce change.

Shining a light on this problem, and specifically on a person or office with the power to affect change, helped hundreds, if not thousands, of custodial parents (mostly women). It also helped hundreds, if not thousands, of noncustodial parents (mostly men) provide for their children.

MORE IMPACT
(WRONGFULLY JAILED)

Many people will be best remembered for their role in the O.J. Simpson trial. From defense lawyers Johnnie Cochran, F. Lee Bailey, and Robert Shapiro to prosecutors Marcia Clark and Christopher Darden. There were also Judge Lance Ito, police detective Mark Fuhrman, witness Kato Kaelin, and journalists/analysts Dan Abrams and Jack Ford.

Testimony about the handling and testing of evidence was critical in convincing the jury to doubt the validity of the DNA tests. That testimony at the 1995 trial was largely provided by lawyers Barry Scheck and Peter Neufeld. It would be unfortunate, in my opinion, if that is how the pair (especially Scheck) are best remembered.

Three years prior to their involvement in the O.J. Simpson murder trial, Scheck and Neufeld used their interests and intellect not to help the potentially guilty go free but instead to help the provably innocent go free. Founded by Scheck and Neufeld in 1992, The Innocence Project uses DNA evidence to exonerate those wrongfully convicted and to help make reforms in the criminal justice system so that wrongful convictions are less likely. Once their work frees a wrongfully convicted person, The Innocence Project supports that individual to reenter society and rebuild a life.

At the time of this writing, 375 people in the U.S. have been exonerated by DNA testing, including twenty-one who served time on death row. The Innocence Project is willing to use its staff and resources to help anyone who has a reasonable claim of wrongful conviction. According to the organization's website, 225 of those set free have been African American, 117 have been Caucasian, twenty-nine have been Latino, and the remaining handful were Asian, Native American, or "other."

Inmates or members of their family often make claims of wrongful convictions and contact 7 On Your Side for help. We don't have the ability to use DNA testing to help prove such claims. However, there were at least a couple of cases where the information provided to support a wrongful incarceration was enough for us to jump in and help.

In the mid-2000s, our children began attending Otter Creek Elementary in Little Rock, so we got to know much of the staff at the time, including Aaron Withers. When Aaron called to inform me that his brother Deldrick was being wrongfully jailed in Louisiana, it was not just a random viewer calling with a tip.

On the day before Easter in 2012, Deldrick Withers and his wife were traveling through Clark County, Arkansas, when they were pulled over for having a broken license plate light. The deputy's check of Withers' information produced a list of arrest warrants. Unbeknownst to the couple, someone using either a fake ID or Deldrick's actual lost driver's license had been cashing hot checks in states all over the south, including Louisiana. Detectives in DeSoto Parish wanted Withers, and a judge transferred him there to face charges.

Wither's wife, Chequetta, immediately hired an attorney who provided employment and medical records proving that her husband had been in Little Rock on the dates the crimes were committed. The detectives in Louisiana were unmoved; they believed they had the right man in their jail.

To his credit, the Clark County sheriff at the time, Jason Watson, believed in Withers' innocence and called every state where he faced charges. All the states recognized the error except Louisiana. They claimed video surveillance and a photo lineup identification supported Withers' continued incarceration. They also said they had partial fingerprints. Withers' attorney, Damia Rolfe, asked the FBI to fingerprint her client for comparison purposes. But all this was taking time. Soon Withers had been jailed nearly a month. That is when Aaron called me.

We discovered and showed KATV viewers the mug shot of another "Deldrick Withers"—a man arrested for trying to cash bogus checks in Harrison, Arkansas. It was clear the man was NOT Aaron's brother. The media coverage, coupled with the fingerprint results, finally convinced DeSoto Parish to let Deldrick go—but not before he missed Easter, his eighth wedding anniversary, and his son's birthday. We interviewed Deldrick after his release and his return to Little Rock.

"My son's birthday was on Monday the 30th," Withers told me. "So, they came to see me on Sunday the 29th. And I asked him what he wanted for his birthday. And he pointed at the glass and said, 'I want you.' And to know I couldn't give that to him—it really crushed me. When you are put in a situation where you have to sit down and listen to God, read your scriptures, and pray, you can gain strength. Even though it is a time—probably the most trying time in your life—when you see that God will carry you through, that is a lesson in itself."

A viewer saw our coverage and emailed me to say that she knew the identity of the man arrested in Harrison—the man who stole Deldrick Withers' identity and cost him twenty-nine days of freedom. He was the woman's cousin, Douglas Withers (no relation to Deldrick). Douglas Withers has a lengthy criminal history that includes forgeries, assaults, and other crimes. At last check, he was serving a prison sentence in Missouri.

The other wrongfully jailed Arkansan we helped free also involved a Louisiana jail, this time in Morehouse Parish.

The father and sister of Bryant Davis Jr. contacted 7 On Your Side after the 26-year-old had been stopped by an Arkansas State Police trooper. The vehicle Davis drove looked like one that had just been stolen in a carjacking. It was not the same vehicle, but when the trooper entered Davis's information into the database, two active warrants out of Bastrop, Louisiana, popped up; one for bank fraud and the other for conspiracy to commit bank fraud. Davis was held, extradited, and locked up for six weeks by the time I became involved.

"Mentally it is tough for him," explained Bryant Davis Sr. at the time. "I can hear in his voice that it is getting to him. But I assured him that we are doing everything that we can possibly do here in Little Rock for him."

While neither the prosecutor nor public defender would talk with me about Davis Jr.'s claims of innocence, I emailed Davis Jr.'s mug shot to the store manager at Super Foods and asked him to compare it to the video surveillance of the suspects. He did, and quickly reported back that neither man in the video resembled Bryant Davis Jr.

Bryant Davis Jr. had never been to Louisiana prior to this mix-up. One person had the power to immediately set Davis free: Morehouse Parish District Attorney Stephen Sylvester. When I called Sylvester, he said that he was focused on murder and rape cases and that an Arkansas man who may be wrongfully incarcerated in Morehouse Parish was not high on his priority list. Frustrated, I contacted a member of the Arkansas Attorney General's Identity Theft Passport program. A call from that state official convinced Sylvester to rearrange his priorities and compare the surveillance video to Davis's mugshot. Shortly afterward, Stephen Sylvester set Bryant Davis Jr. free.

"It wasn't fun," Davis told me. "It wasn't fun at all. I mean, being in jail for something that you didn't do. And you're trying to explain to everyone that it isn't you."

Davis ultimately spent fifty-five days in jail, sharing a barracks-like room with fifty other men. He witnessed numerous fights, ate horrible food, and read his Bible every day. He also missed his family every day.

"I didn't want my son to know I was in jail," Davis told me. "I told 'em, don't nobody tell him I'm in jail. Just tell him I'm out of town until we get it worked out. I didn't want him to know. And they was asking me . . . do you want us to bring them (Davis's three children) down there to see you? No . . . I don't want them to see me in jail, because I don't want them to grow up and feel that jail is acceptable."

On average, those set free by The Innocence Project spent twelve years wrongfully incarcerated. By comparison, Withers and Davis Jr. got off easy. But to those of us who have never spent a single hour in jail wrongfully accused of a crime, twenty-nine and fifty-five days is an awfully long time. I was thankful to get a small taste of what the members of The Innocence Project get to experience when wrongs are reversed.

> **LESSON LEARNED:**
> *The priorities of others can be changed.*

When it's important, find a way to make others see the urgency in situations.

> **LESSON LEARNED:**
> *When opportunity and ability put you in a position to help, do it.*

My involvement was not the sole reason these men were released from jail, but it played a role. When you can help someone in need, you should.

CHAPTER 10

THE MISTAKES
(#KARMA)

Jason and Mary Carol with his parents Joel and Judy pose for photos at Pirate's Cove mini-golf course in Hot Springs, AR (1996).

HAVE YOU EVER HAD YOUR picture taken after sticking your head and arms hands through the holes of a public stock? Colonial America promoted state-sponsored public shaming in town squares. Today, public shaming is as popular as ever. But it's done mostly online. Social media is our modern-day public stocks. The people dishing it out feel morally justified. But it can be an all-consuming, life-altering experience for the person on the receiving end.

Several years ago, I read a book by British journalist Jon Ronson called *So You've Been Publicly Shamed*. Ronson recounts several examples of ordinary people who said, shared, or posted something extraordinarily dumb. An online tsunami of hatred and judgment swiftly followed, altering their lives in an instant.

One example involved a woman named Justine Sacco, who had fewer than 200 Twitter followers in 2014 when she shared an insensitive, arguably racist tweet just before boarding a plane bound for South Africa. Her tweet found its way to BuzzFeed and went viral. By the time her flight landed, which had no Wi-Fi, she was trending on Twitter, and she'd been fired from her job as senior director of corporate communications for a tech company. Years later, after the online rage had subsided and refocused elsewhere, a spin-off of Sacco's previous employer rehired her.

Early in my career, while at KTVE, I reported on a public shaming of sorts. Municipal Judge Edwin Keaton gave convicted shoplifters in Camden, Arkansas, a choice: eight days in jail or eight hours walking out in front of the store where they had shoplifted wearing a sandwich board sign that read, "I was convicted of shoplifting here. Wearing this sign is part of my punishment." I interviewed one individual who elected to walk back and forth in front of Walmart for eight hours wearing that sign. While embarrassed, he said the alternative was worse. And more than that, he said he would never shoplift again. My story was picked up by CNN, the first time any of my reporting received national exposure. His moment of shame brought me a fleeting moment of fame.

Years later I would have my own brush with public shaming, a mess made by my own thoughtless actions.

It was the third week of the 2013 college football season. The Razorbacks defeated Southern Miss 24–3 earlier in the day in a game that will be remembered for a technical glitch near the end of the first half that turned all the fans, players, and coaches blue. At first,

I thought my television had failed. But Facebook and Twitter soon blue, I mean, blew up with comments from people experiencing a similar color experience. I tweeted out "Bluuuuuue....Pig! Sooie!" A lot of Hog fans liked that and retweeted it.

My next tweet would not be as well received by the Razorback faithful.

It was around 11:00 p.m. I'd filled in on Saturday Daybreak that morning, so I was tired. The best—maybe only—game still being played had Wisconsin leading Arizona State 14–13 at the half. Despite growing up in Wisconsin, I'd never followed the Badgers, so the decision to turn off the TV and go to bed was an easy one. I woke up Sunday morning and found a text on my phone from one of my Wisconsin buddies.

"Did you see how the refs screwed the Badgers last night? It was bad. And to make matters worse, [Arkansas Coach Bret] Bielema's wife tweeted out '#karma' right afterward. No class."

I took to Twitter and found Jen Bielema's tweet. My friend Mike was right. It was one symbol and one word: #karma.

I searched online and found several articles had already been written about how the game ended, her subsequent tweet, and the consternation in Badger Nation. Wisconsin had lost 32–30. With :18 seconds left the Badgers were in field goal range. Wanting to position the ball for a potential game-winning field goal, Wisconsin quarterback Joel Stave took the snap from center, moved the ball to the center of the field, and simulated taking a knee (which is all the rules require). Stave then set the ball down for the refs. Well, an Arizona State player pounced on the ball as if the quarterback had fumbled it. The confused officials didn't set the ball, didn't stop the clock, and time ran out. Game over. Badgers lost. And the wife of the team's former head coach throws salt in the wound by tweeting #karma.

Why? One of the things that Bret Bielema had been criticized for in Madison was his time management at the end of games. Bielema leaves, a new coach replaces him, and what happens? A game is lost due to questionable end-of-game time management. In the quiet of a mid-September morning, with only the sound of my Diet Coke fizzing next to me, I took to Twitter and engaged my thumbs well ahead of my brain.

"Jen Bielema uses one word to describe a controversial Wisconsin loss: karma. Here are a few words: unnecessary, classless, move on. #WPS"

Including that little #WPS (which stands for Woo Pig Sooie) helps ensure a larger number of Razorback fans would see it. Maybe even retweet it. Obviously, I felt my opinion would be widely shared among the fan base. The Bielemas had left Wisconsin for a better job, a better conference, and a lot more money here in Arkansas. It would be best to focus time and energy on moving forward rather than taking shots at the past. Those Wisconsin players had been recruited by Coach Bielema, and they were hurting. It was immature, even embarrassing, for the head coach's wife to behave in such a way. At least in my opinion.

A couple of hours later, at church, I got my first hint of trouble. My news director, Nick Genty, texted me: "Wisconsin fans are retweeting you. Be careful."

Hmmmm. Be careful? I guess it didn't surprise me, but what could I do to stop it? After church, I checked my Twitter feed and could only find a couple examples of Badger fans retweeting my comment. There were many examples of Arkansas fans upset with what I'd tweeted but certainly no hint of a firestorm brewing. Later that afternoon, as I walked the aisles of Bed, Bath & Beyond looking for a product to test for a "We Try It Before You Buy It" segment, I realized Twitter was blowing up. On me.

Somebody, maybe more than one person, in northwest Arkansas had made it their mission to share my morning tweet with the masses. And by masses, I mean Razorback Twitter Nation, that rabid segment of the fan base that publicly rallied to keep Bobby Petrino as head coach AFTER he wrecked his motorcycle while riding with a young blonde mistress, AFTER he lied about it, AFTER we learned he had given that same young blonde mistress a job on his staff over more qualified candidates, and AFTER we learned he also had given her $20,000.

That is NOT the segment of the fan base you want to irritate.

"You realize that ur choice of words r no better than what she said right? You made urself look childish & unprofessional." ShaneLong@WPS_Razorbacks

"When did you start hating the Arkansas Razorbacks? You know exactly what I mean too. You need to remove KATV from your handle." Jesse@WhistlePig11

"Go practice reading ur teleprompter. Obviously not able 2 comprehend where shes been n what crap the wisky fans n AD have given." Jme9@Jayme9Jme9

Seconds later, Jme9 would be the first of many to conclude a tweet with "#boycottKATV."

About that same time, I bumped into Jerry and Pam Digman, a pair of old friends from El Dorado. Jerry retired from the State Police and now the Digmans owned a ranch with horses in central Arkansas. Jerry could see the stress on my face. I told him what had happened, and he started to laugh. "Once upon a time, I worked security detail for the Clintons when Bill was governor. I don't remember what the fuss was, but something was creating negative waves, and I asked Hillary if she was OK. She said, 'Jerry, in three months nobody will remember what this was all about.

All they will remember is Bill and Hillary Clinton. Don't sweat it. Things will be fine.'"

Meanwhile, back in cyberspace, angry fans with Twitter handles like "RazorHog@RazorHogs4Life" were wanting to know more about the TV idiot who tweeted about the coach's wife. One of the smarter ones checked out my bio on the Channel 7 website.

> "Yeah, now we c Jason was raised in New Richmond, Wisconsin, and earned a degree from the University of Wisconsin." #boycottKATV" Nancz@nancz58

Well, as you learned in Chapter Two, I am actually a proud graduate of the University of Wisconsin-River Falls (UWRF), which would be similar to the University of Arkansas-Monticello (UAM). But any link to anything in Wisconsin caused some to start foaming at the mouth.

> "That jack wagon is from Wisconsin...and now it's time for him to go back." Hogfan162@hogfan162

> "Don't forget to wear your STUPID CHEESE HAT on the air tonight! #LOSER #Razorbacks #gohogs #throwtheA" FreedomWarrior@freedomwarrior

> "do you need the address for your local unemployment office yet? #boycottKATV" BenBaker@Thebearjeweler

> "Man, has @KATVJason house burned yet? #Douchebag" PigTrailEric@PigTrailEric

At about 7:00 p.m., my news director, Nick, called. I'd been expecting it, but I'd not been expecting what he'd say.

"Things are getting a little out of hand. Mark [Mark Rose, KATV's general manager] just got a call from Mike Waddell, the Razorbacks Senior Associate Athletic Director, regarding your tweet. Mark said please tell me Jason did not call the wife of the Razorback head coach classless. It appeared to Mark you may have been describing Wisconsin fans, not Jen Bielema. What were you trying to say in your tweet?"

"Um … well … that it was childish and immature for her to tweet #karma after a Wisconsin loss."

"Let's try this again," said Nick. "We have to get on the same page here. It looked like your tweet was aimed at the Wisconsin fans who have been rather ruthless on Twitter toward the coach and his wife for months. Is that right?"

"That sounds about right," I replied.

I'd made a mess. Both my news director and my general manager, on a Sunday, were now involved and looking to me to clean it up. I suggested composing an apology tweet to Jen Bielema and conclude it with #WPS in hopes that it would quell the online assault. It seemed my original tweet had left just enough wiggle room for both truth and escape.

> "@jenbielema The words I used = the way some WI fans have treated you/Coach for months. I apologize & regret any misinterpretations. #WPS"

Both Nick and Mark signed off, and I sent my follow-up tweet into cyberspace. Feedback was instant.

> "Showing class now sir...TY. #forgiveandforget"
> FinisBrewer@FBREWOOO

> "OK you can stay." HogFan@HogNorris

> "Just think you needed to word that tweet differently, easily mistaken for what you were thinking." ChrisRidings@cridings1

But not everyone was willing to accept my "apology."

> "There is no way @KATVJason was talking about how WI fans treated Coach and Jen. No way. I don't buy it. #coverup" ReneeErwin@na_erwin

"It took him 12 hours to "clarify" that? (which I'm not sure he's done...)." Gus@AugustusThe3rd

"I'm not buying JP's tortured interpretation of his own tweet." SharpTuskWilliams@SharpTusk

"Any respect I had for you is out the window. You are a disgrace to the media, and a disgrace to humanity." DancingDonkey@DancingDonkeyAR

Humanity?

Not everyone was hateful and bitter. There were a few who tried to lighten the mood.

"you need to stick to reporting on plumbers who fail to unclog toilets." DavidCouch@arkrzbck

"@KATVJason LOL at you, obviously should've done a little more research on the fanbase you just antagonized. #Notonmyside" BobbytheShill@bobbytheshill

"@KATVJason this guy sounds like a coward! Probably a card-carrying liberal democrat." Moses@MosesMosley

OK ... I found that last one funny.

Nearly 500 Twitter mentions in a twenty-four-hour period. Many of the messages were tweeted by the same two dozen irate people. Some called for my firing, some demanded an on-air apology, others swore never to watch KATV again, and a few came to my defense, but most were satisfied pointing out my poor judgment.

Which is what MY original intent was, to point out what I considered to be Jen Bielema's poor judgment.

#karma?

It wasn't until the end of the day, when things had quieted down, that I filled Mary Carol in on all the drama. She listened to the story, occasionally nodding her head in agreement, and occasionally shaking her head in disapproval. When I finished, she reminded me that the Bible has a lot to say about judging others. Matthew 7:1 is perfect for the brave new world with 140-character limits: "Do not judge, so that you will not be judged."

Did I judge? Yes. Was I judged? Oh yes. Will I judge again? Unfortunately, yes. But there is one person I won't be judging anymore.

> **LESSON LEARNED:**
> *Thou shalt not speak ill of the head coach's spouse.*

I cannot think of an exception to this rule. Just don't do it.

> **LESSON LEARNED:**
> *Keep your opinions to yourself.*

As the fool wisely counseled King Lear: "Have more than you show, speak less than you know." It is so easy to share your opinion about anything, especially in this social media age. In fact, so easy that many fail to think carefully about not only what they're saying but about how it'll be received. The list is long of people who have lost jobs, opportunities, and more following a thoughtless tweet or post. Don't make it longer.

LESSON LEARNED:
Ride out the storm.

If you mess up and find yourself in a social media storm, it can be intense. But it will also likely be brief. The attention span of Twitter is like that of a two-year-old. The next thing for folks to get riled up about is around the corner. It will not be the end of your world. It may nct even last until the end of the week. Don't overreact. It will be OK.

MORE MISTAKES
(CAPITOL BUMP SHOT, ASHLEY COUNTY FATALITIES)

Whoops! The moment I realized that I'd arrived
too early for my live shot on live TV!

I made a colossal mistake tweeting about Jen Bielema. Thankfully, it didn't cost me my job. We all make mistakes; unfortunately, some will inevitably cost people their jobs. Although social media and the internet can still find and amplify mistakes made in smaller markets, the fact that fewer people are watching and reading means less chance of a mistake ending or altering the career path of a young journalist. This is why small markets are still an excellent place to begin a career.

It's preferable to learn from the mistakes of others. My first week at KTVE the bosses fired a reporter for driving his company vehicle (with station logos) through a liquor store drive thru. We also lost a main anchor—our very popular sports guy—after he got upset and made a scene at a local car dealership. The car dealership owner advertised on KTVE, and he gave the station manager an ultimatum: fire him, or we'll spend our money elsewhere. Bye-bye, sports guy.

I've made my share of mistakes. At least one of them was big enough that it could've cost me my job. It was 1993 or early 1994 and cell phones were not yet a thing, but mobile phones—the kind that rested in a bag and you could use in your car—had just been added to our news vehicles. This allowed for instant communication with the newsroom that would've previously required a pit stop to use a pay phone.

KTVE got a call about a fatal wreck on a stretch of Highway 82 between Crossett and Strong in southern Arkansas. This is a long, straight stretch of road built up out of a swamp. There is a steep drop-off on both sides of the two-lane highway, with little shoulder and no guard rails. Any vehicle that goes off the road will likely strike trees and most certainly end up in water.

I arrived at the scene in time to see a wrecker pulling a car out of the water and up the bank. A pair of wet varsity-letter jackets for Crossett High School lay in the road. Some paramedics remained on the scene, and we struck up a conversation. One of the EMTs told me he also worked as an assistant football coach and knew all four of the young men who had died in the accident. I wrote down their names in my reporter's notebook as he shared them with me.

On my drive back to the station, I called the newsroom in Monroe and told them about the video from a four-person fatality wreck that I would send from El Dorado. With four teenagers dead, it would be the top story on the 10:00 p.m. newscast. But I also engaged my mouth before my brain and passed along the names of all four young men killed in the crash. In doing so, I violated one of the cardinal rules of reporting: use multiple sources to verify all information. But a paramedic who was also the boys' assistant football coach saw the bodies. He seemed like a solid source. But he was a single source—and he was wrong (he was also wrong to share the names of the victims before all the next of kin had been notified).

Anchor John Denison read the names of the four victims on air, and we would soon learn that only two of the names were correct. The other two young men we named were alive and well. Thankfully, those teenagers were with their parents and other loved ones as their names were mistakenly broadcast. Imagine the horror and panic families would have felt had they not been able to instantly recognize the information as false. That could have led to lawsuits and, no doubt, my dismissal.

We corrected the error later in the same newscast. My news director and the anchor who had shared the erroneous information reprimanded me for my reckless reporting. Thankfully, I kept my job.

Another news director's reprimand came from Bob Steel at KATV but under very different circumstances.

First, a little TV jargon. A live shot, as you can probably guess, refers to any news team who reports live from a location, usually outside of the TV station. Common live shot locations include along a highway, outside a hospital, or at the state capitol. A bump shot refers to a shot of video from the live location without any reporter or interview subject in the shot. Usually bump shots are used going into a commercial break. For example, at home viewers would see a bump shot of highway traffic as the anchor reads "Coming up, we'll tell you about the Governor's plan to improve Arkansas highways and interstates."

On this particular day, my story involved the state legislature, so I stood outside the capitol for my live shot. The six o'clock producer, Jeff Whatley, would soon be calling for a bump shot of the capitol as anchor Chris May teased my upcoming report, so I said to photojournalist Sandy King, "Hey, let's mess with Whatley." Knowing we were a minute away from the bump shot and that Jeff could see it in his preview monitor, Sandy and I both spontaneously rose up into the camera's frame with goofy looks on our faces, stayed there for a second or two, and then sunk back down out of frame.

But our timing was off! The bump shot was *not* a minute away, it was underway. As May teased my story and Jeff called for the bump shot of the capitol, Sandy and I rose up into view of the entire Channel 7 viewing audience, our heads larger than the capitol dome behind us, and then we receded back out of frame as if we'd cued. It all timed out so perfectly ... and awfully ... for us. Chris May played it like a pro, seeing the two idiots in his monitor and mentioning both of us by name as he read the script, as if we were supposed to be a part of the tease.

Steel, the news director, watched from his office and summoned us upon our return. At the time, the news director's office at Channel 7 had a large window that looked out into the newsroom. Steel shut the blinds covering that window and slammed the door behind us.

"What the hell were you two thinking?" Steel asked.

"We weren't thinking," we replied sheepishly.

"You guys are veterans," Steel continued. "That was a mistake that a rookie ... no, not even a rookie ... would make!"

We both sat there silently. Then Steel surprised us.

"Now, having said that ... man, that was some funny shit!"

Sandy and I looked at each other and smiled. Then we joined in Steel's laughter.

"I want you guys to stay in here for a few minutes, and when you leave, I want you to walk out of here as if you just received the worst ass-chewing of your lives. I don't want any mention that I thought what you did was funny, and you damn sure better never do it again. Idiots."

Under a different boss or on a different day, my career path may have been significantly altered by my juvenile behavior. But again, thankfully, I learned from my mistake without too much consequence.

> **LESSON LEARNED:**
> *Good will can help you survive bad choices.*

I work hard and do good work. I don't think anyone has ever looked for a reason to fire me (other than a couple dozen rabid tweeters, a few scam artists, and an upset advertiser or two). That helps when you screw up. Jerry Mayer and Matt James at KTVE and Bob Steel at KATV liked me and my work and were therefore more forgiving.

> **LESSON LEARNED:**
> *Don't forget the basics.*

No matter your job, there are some basic rules. When you forget those rules, like the journalism rule that requires multiple sources, you run the risk of a bad outcome.

CHAPTER 11

THE VULNERABLE

(WILEY BALLOW)

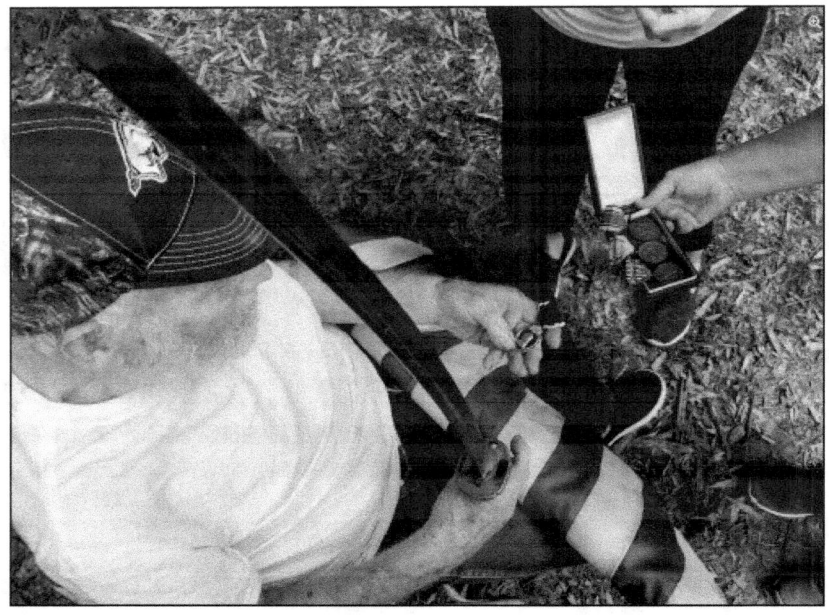

Wiley Ballow of Drew County shows off two prized possessions: his Purple Heart medal and a Japanese sword.

AS A REPORTER, I HAVE had several stories go viral. But my most widely shared story involved a lonely World War II veteran down in southeast Arkansas, sitting on a tract of land that his neighbor across the street desperately wanted for himself. My June 20, 2018, Facebook post about Wiley Ballow has to date been shared over 2,500 times. Usually, a hundred shares of a news story lets you know you hit a nerve.

Wiley Ballow earned a Purple Heart for his bravery while fighting the Japanese on Okinawa in World War II. His hands still bear the scars created when he grabbed the sword of a Japanese soldier intent on killing a fellow American. Ballow still has that sword as a reminder of his victory in that particular battle. The Purple Heart and that sword are his two most prized possessions, along with his land.

An anonymous letter sent to 7 On Your Side with supporting documents brought Mr. Ballow to my attention. The letter contended that the ninety-one-year-old was at risk of losing his land to his neighbor. While hospitalized following a one-car accident, his neighbor from across the road, Jack Bennett, visited Ballow in the hospital. Bennett brought with him a notary public (who was also his niece) and he left with Ballow's signature on a special warranty deed that transferred ownership of the veteran's nearly fifty acres of hardwood to Bennett and his wife, Cindy. The anonymous letter alleged that Ballow was under the influence of pain medication and not of sound mind at the time he signed the document.

The anonymous tipster included the dated and signed deed, a copy of the lawsuit Mr. Ballow filed several months later when he realized he had been tricked, and a classified ad showing a tract of mature hardwood similar in size for sale in southeast Arkansas. This supported the contention that Jack Bennett might have something to gain financially from this transfer of land ownership.

I confirmed that Ballow had been hospitalized following a one-car accident on December 14, 2017. He had signed the warranty deed on December 31 during this hospitalization. The Drew County Circuit Clerk's office recorded the deed on January 5, 2018.

Ballow has no Arkansas relatives. He never married and had no children. His only sibling, a recently deceased brother, also never married and had no children. He does have cousins and other distant relatives in Texas. Ballow also has extremely poor eyesight and requires a jeweler's loop, or a special magnifying eyeglass, to read.

In his response to Ballow's lawsuit to have the warranty deed thrown out, Mr. Bennett's attorney, Charles Clifford "Cliff" Gibson III, argued that it was Wiley Ballow's idea to sign his land over to Jack and Cindy Bennett; that the Bennetts had provided assistance to Ballow over the years, including "… doing work on the homeplace to make same habitable, providing him with water to drink and bath [*sic*], washing his clothes, paying his personal bills from time to time with Defendants' funds, buying and taking him groceries, and so forth and so on. Bennett was further described as having been . . . a supportive friend to him [Mr. Ballow] for decades."

If these claims were true, why was Ballow suing to get his land back? Gibson had an answer for that question too: ". . . others have unjustifiably interfered with their long-standing good and supportive relationship . . . that has existed for many, many years and that they have in effect destroyed that relationship." Gibson referred to these pot stirrers as "intermeddlers" and the Monticello lawyer specifically named one alleged intermeddler, Sherry Knight, in his filing.

Sherry Knight is a middle school art teacher who first met and befriended Wiley Ballow as part of a school project. Her students interviewed Ballow and twenty-seven other veterans as part of a history preservation project. Knight was shocked and saddened when she first visited Ballow's Drew County home. He lived in a rundown camper with "Not to be used for housing" written on its side. These temporary trailers, courtesy of the Federal Emergency Management Agency (FEMA), arrive following natural disasters. It's likely Ballow's camper was sent following Hurricane Katrina. Knight started raising money so that a new "tiny home" could be purchased for Ballow. Her plans to help would be thwarted by a surprising discovery.

A local bank was trusted with the funds raised, and Knight was asked by bank officials if Ballow owned the land where this tiny home would be located. She wasn't positive, so a trip to the Drew County courthouse was in order. In the spring of 2018, Knight discovered the special warranty deed filed by Jack Bennett months earlier. When she asked Ballow about it, he said he remembered

Jack Bennett and a lawyer visiting his hospital room and asking him to sign a document. Ballow said Bennett claimed the document was needed so he could manage Ballow's property during his hospital stay. Knight says when she tried to explain that the document gives Bennett ownership of his land, Ballow kept asking, "Why does Jack Bennett think he owns my land?"

Unable to reach Wiley Ballow by telephone, photojournalist Ray Hamilton and I traveled two hours south to pay him a visit. Not only was he home, but Ballow gave us a spirited interview. He calmly but very defiantly explained that Jack Bennett's claim of ownership of his land was based on deceit and greed. We tried our best to give Bennett a voice, too—visiting his home and place of business, leaving notes at both locations. I also mailed him a section of this chapter prior to publication, hoping he would comment. To this day, he has not spoken or corresponded with me.

Our first report on Wiley Ballow aired on June 19, 2018. Six days later Bennett's attorney, Cliff Gibson, sent a scathing nine-page email to my boss, KATV General Manager Mark Rose. Some of the more colorful terms he used to describe my reporting were "hatchet job," "bald-faced lie," "vicious attack," and "character assassination." Not only was Gibson wanting to bring to light "*... the false and unethical reporting done by Mr. Pederson ... so that KATV may have an opportunity to take appropriate corrective action,*" Gibson himself penned a two-page correction and apology letter that he suggested I sign and widely disseminate.

KATV's legal team in Maryland watched my report, reviewed Mr. Gibson's lengthy email and demands, asked me some questions and, ultimately, did very little. They allowed my reporting on the plight of Wiley Ballow to continue, and they offered to provide more oversight given the irritated and over-the-top reaction of Mr. Gibson.

A little more from Mr. Gibson:

The harm done by Pederson to the Bennetts, Ms. Lemoine [Bennett's niece and the person who served as a notary public when Bennett obtained Ballow's signature], and myself is shown by the fact that as of this writing there have been 2,571 shares and 895 comments on Pederson's Facebook page regarding the matter over the past few days. Pederson's one-sided reporting has so enraged the public that a mob of those posting are asking for criminal charges against the Bennetts, Ms. Lemoine, and myself (I have even received a threatening phone call about the matter, and one of my regular clients asked me with concern whether I was "in trouble"). Just take a look at Pederson's Facebook posts. Also, please be sure to direct Pederson to not delete or edit any of the posts on his Facebook page. Given his reprehensible conduct in this matter, that would not be put past him.

All this just set the table for what really mattered: Wiley Ballow's day in court. He filed the original lawsuit in April 2018 and before the matter went to trial, the Bennetts' attorney, Cliff Gibson, withdrew from the case. A new attorney, Brooks Gill of Dumas, took over. His firm requested extra time to review the case and filed a motion for Judge Quincey Ross to recuse himself. Ballow's attorney, Hani Hashem of Monticello, strongly opposed all the requested delays and changes sought by opposing counsel. Hashem argued in a court filing: "Considering Mr. Ballow's age and infirmities, and the alleged deceitful conduct of Defendants, Defendants should not be allowed to postpone a trial of this matter unreasonably, in an effort to simply outlive 92-year-old Mr. Ballow."

KATV's continuing coverage of the case, specifically the lack of progress, captured the attention of military veterans. Retired Colonel Mike Ross and Purple Heart veteran Mark Diggs with Veterans Villages of America, along with Dwight Witcher, president of the Arkansas Veterans Coalition, mobilized to keep the pressure on to help move Ballow's lawsuit forward. But more importantly, they worked to improve his deplorable living conditions. In August 2018, Ross delivered a new trailer to Ballow, complete with heat and air conditioning, running water, a stove and microwave, and a television. Paul Minton of Little Rock donated the trailer, which came stocked with paper products and other items thanks to the Veterans of Foreign Wars (VFW) Department of Arkansas Auxiliary.

While Ballow's living conditions improved quickly, his efforts to regain his land moved slowly. After several delays, Judge Ross heard the case in September 2019 at the Romanesque-style Desha County courthouse in Arkansas City. The two-and-a-half-story brick structure was built in 1900 and is on the National Register of Historic Places.

The trial's star witnesses turned out to be Jefferson Regional Medical Center employees Nikki Thorton and Meagan Capps. They were part of the team that assessed Ballow's physical and mental condition prior to Jack Bennett's visit to his hospital room. They testified that Ballow was not competent enough to understand and sign legal documents at the time of his hospitalization. Ballow's FIM score (Functional Independence Measure) was eighteen. A score of twenty or below is considered moderately impaired. Plus, they testified that the hospital has policies regarding visitors who present documents to patients for signatures and that Jack Bennett skirted those rules.

Wiley Ballow, now on the verge of turning ninety-three-years-old, also testified. He recalled that Jack Bennett visited him in the hospital with "this lady" and asked him to sign some documents. "I need your signature on these papers so I can look after your place while you're in the hospital," is how Ballow recalled Bennett's description of the need for his signature. When asked how he reacted when later told that he'd signed ownership of his land over to Bennett, Ballow testified that, "It was a shock to me. I couldn't believe it. It was a complete surprise." When asked what he would like to see happen to his land after he dies, Ballow replied, "I want it to go to somebody I want it to go to. And that's not Jack Bennett. I don't want him to have a damn thing of mine."

In the end, Judge Ross set aside the special warranty deed, returning Ballow's property to him. Judge Ross ruled that Ballow trusted the Bennetts and would rely on anything they said to him. He ruled that trust was used to take "unfair advantage of the relationship and Mr. Ballow's physical weakness." The judge noted that Ballow had suffered a laceration to his head and broken ribs during his car accident. Mr. Ballow, in the opinion of the court and medical professionals, was not competent at the time the special warranty deed was signed and even if he was, the hospital's procedure for signing documents, which involves oversight by a physician, were not followed. As to whether Bennett knowingly and willingly committed fraud—Judge Ross refused to go that far.

Due to on-air time constraints, TV reporters always know much more about a story than they can share. Here are a couple of interesting sidebars that I learned while researching and covering this case—and that are being shared here for the first time.

The first witness called to testify was a Drew County man named Roy Huskey. Huskey, from Wilmar, testified that he knew both

Bennett and Ballow and that it was his belief that "Jack Bennett would wind up with his (Ballow's) land."

Well, Huskey and his wife, Rebecca, knew a little something about winding up with a Ballow's land. I mentioned earlier that Wiley Ballow had a brother who'd also never married nor had children. Like his brother, Wiley, George Ballow bought land early in life; in George's case, sixty-three acres off South Allis Road not far from Wiley's land. In 2004, the Huskeys claimed they wrote George Ballow a $40,000 check for sixty of his sixty-three acres. What happened to the sixty acres? In May of 2007, the Huskeys sold the land for $181,000.

George lived on the other three acres until his death and then that land was sold in 2018. George Ballow died penniless, and Wiley alleges that his brother was never paid the $40,000 for his land. Rebecca Huskey told me during a phone conversation on August 28, 2018, that she would share with me the following day the financial records that proved George Ballow had been paid for his land. She never did. I sent the Huskeys a letter and this section of the book prior to publication, giving them another chance to provide the promised proof. There was no response.

The attorney who helped facilitate that land deal was none other than Charles Clifford "Cliff" Gibson III, who was also involved in the estate planning of Bobby Lee Bennett, the father of Jack Bennett and the grandfather of Jack and Cindy Bennett's three children.

In 2002, well in advance of his death in November 2007, Bobby Lee Bennett had Gibson draw up a special warranty deed that would leave his property, after the death of he and his wife, Betty Jo, to their son, Jack Bennett, and upon Jack's death to their three grandchildren due to "the love and affection we have and hold" for all of them. Both Bobby Lee and Betty Jo signed the deed.

In 2008, after her husband's death, Betty Jo Bennett updated the paperwork and still included her son, Jack, and all three grand-children as heirs. In 2016, Gibson prepared a correction deed and presented it to the court. Without explanation, the oldest of his three children, Alex Bennett, had been removed as an heir.

I called Alex Bennett to tell him about the dispute involving Wiley Ballow's land and asked him if he knew there were court filings excluding him from the inheritance that his grandfather had once intended for him. He did not. "Sounds like he took my land the same way," Alex Bennett replied, referring to his father Jack's dealings with Wiley Ballow.

Alex Bennett explained that at the age of seventeen he and his father had a falling out. He told me he received a packet in the mail from Cliff Gibson requesting his signature and asking him to surrender any ownership rights he had to the land once owned by his grandfather. Alex Bennett said he never signed anything and never returned the packet.

Alex Bennett told me that his father had always been interested in not only Ballow's land, but also the veteran's Purple Heart and Japanese sword. Bennett says his father would openly speculate how much he could get on eBay for Ballow's most prized possessions. Bennett says his father would often say, "My best friend is in my back pocket," referring to his wallet.

Jack and Cindy Bennett did not give up their quest to secure the rights to Ballow's land. They appealed Judge Ross's decision. Shortly after their appeal was filed, the pandemic hit, and most court proceedings were significantly delayed. Two years later, on September 7, 2022, the Arkansas Court of Appeals upheld Judge Ross's decision. No appeal was filed, so Ballow, who was now nine-ty-five-years-old, kept his land.

LESSON LEARNED:
The vulnerable need advocates.

Advocates like Sherry Knight, Hani Hashem, Nikki Thorton, Meagan Capps, Mike Ross, Mark Diggs, and Dwight Witcher. They each made a difference. It took all these people and many more to protect and preserve Wiley Ballow's property and possessions from those who wanted to take them and make them their own.

MORE VULNERABLE
(RONALD TODD, NORMAN BUTLER, MIKE HERMAN)

A depiction of a TV news photographer, based on
longtime photojournalist Stephen "Mike" Herman,
by John Deering, *Arkansas Democrat-Gazette*'s
chief political cartoonist and illustrator.

In 2009, a judge sentenced Kristian Nelson to seventy-one months in federal prison for running a real estate scheme. Nelson cheated twenty investors out of over $1 million. He was also convicted of being a felon in possession of multiple firearms.

I knew nothing of that history when 7 On Your Side received complaints against Kristian Nelson in 2015. One woman's plans to open a cosmetology school and a couple's plan to open Pinnacle Valley Restaurant were both seemingly derailed when money was paid to Nelson, and nothing was received in return. Two years later, a new complaint against Nelson was filed by another Arkansas business in Jacksonville. In addition to moonlighting as a non-licensed contractor, Nelson operated Hawgz Blues Cafe in North Little Rock.

About that same time and unbeknownst to me, Nelson's real grift was just getting started. Nelson's mother worked as a housekeeper for a wealthy former real estate investor, and her son had written some hot checks to restaurant employees and was in a tight spot (7 On Your Side heard from some of those employees and reported on the matter in September 2017). Nelson told us in a statement that everyone had been paid what they were owed. He didn't explain where he'd gotten the money.

It turns out that the man Nelson's mother worked for, Richard Toll, gave Nelson a $10,000 loan. Nelson had found the golden goose. Over the course of the next three years, Toll, in his late eighties, loaned Kristian Nelson $4.5 million. Nelson's defense was that he didn't need a defense; there was nothing to see here—just two competent businessmen entering into several business transactions. Toll sued Nelson in July 2020. Nearly two years later, a jury found Kristian Nelson and his subsidiaries guilty of defrauding Richard Toll and awarded Toll more than $43 million in actual and punitive damages. Even if a more reasonable award of actual damages had been awarded, Toll recouping the money is unlikely. Nelson's appeals of the judgment have failed, as have collection efforts by Toll and his attorney.

Matthew House is a Little Rock attorney who dedicates a large part of his practice to the financial exploitation of the elderly. House started a blog, *Arkansas Wealth Wars*, where he writes that "The Baby Boomers are retiring at the rate of 10,000 per day. As they (and their parents) pass away over the next few decades our country will experience the largest transfer of wealth in human history." House says that inheritance-related conflicts are inevitable. House finds these disputes over money and property, which often erupt even before a person's passing, as "...numerous and endlessly fascinating."

I asked House about protections in Arkansas that make the financial exploitation of the vulnerable and elderly a crime. While there are a few statutes that make such activity a crime, he said prosecutions under the statutes are rare. "Prosecuting attorneys seem to be more interested in crimes involving blood, drugs, sex, and money. Fraud-type crimes, where the elderly person may be somewhat incapacitated or where there are questions about the intent to 'give' the alleged wrongdoer the money are often more difficult to prove. Not everything is black and white, and plus many prosecutors are not set up to handle more complex, white-collar crimes. They are harder to prove and frequently the prosecutor will tell the alleged victim to go and try and resolve it in civil court."

House cited a couple of cases where prosecutors took on these egregious acts, including one involving federal charges against a Camden couple who in 2018 pleaded guilty to forging the will of a man who died in a 2015 car accident. That will directed a $1.7 million inheritance to an ex-girlfriend—an inheritance that should have gone to the man's son.

Again and again in Arkansas, I saw first-hand how vulnerable this elder generation is to exploitation. Perhaps one of the more egregious stories was the case involving a Phillips County farm family named Mark and Rosemary Lumpkin.

In 2012, KATV photojournalist Tim Hamilton and I ventured to Phillips County and found hundreds of thousands of dollars' worth of shiny, new farm equipment in the middle of the Arkansas Delta, most of it purchased with Norman Butler's money. Norman Butler didn't live in Arkansas and wasn't a farmer. Butler was a retired optometrist who lived in Washington state. To understand how so much of his money wound up in Arkansas, you need to go back several decades.

In 1987, thirty-seven-year-old Sharon Lumpkin was convicted of stabbing to death a twenty-seven-year-old man. Lumpkin served seven years of a fifteen-year sentence in an Arkansas prison. After her release, Lumpkin changed her name to Shea Saenger and moved west to Washington for a fresh start. There she met eighty-year-old Norman Butler, a retiree with plenty of money. Butler also had Alzheimer's disease. Saenger told Butler she was single, had cancer, and an uncle in trouble. Ultimately, all her lies helped her steal over $2 million from Butler.

Much of that money was sent back to Saenger's relatives in Arkansas, Mississippi, and Louisiana. Mark and Rosemary Lumpkin received the lion's share. They filed for bankruptcy in 2012 despite being given more than $1 million from Mark Lumpkin's out-of-state and out-of-work sister.

A federal judge later convicted Saenger of mail fraud and sentenced her to nearly four years in prison. She served the time and was released from a halfway house in February of 2017. No charges were filed against the Lumpkins or any other relatives who happily received and cashed without question mystery checks from Shea Saenger. However, the court liquidated much of the farm equipment and other property purchased with Butler's money and returned the proceeds to his estate.

As a side note, Hamilton and I won the prestigious Edward R. Murrow Award for our reporting on this case, but it only garnered a third-place award from the Arkansas Associated Press. This is a perfect example of how fickle and random awards can be and why no journalist should put too much stock in them. Your self-image or success should not depend on who is judging your work and what their mood is that day. Do your best every day and awards may follow . . . you just can't predict which ones and when.

Another case of financial exploitation that I investigated involved seventy-five-year-old Ronald Todd. Decades before he contacted me, Todd had been knocked unconscious in a bar in San Antonio in 1955 and suffered slight brain damage. He lived independently in North Little Rock, but not without government assistance and not without the risk of being exploited.

In the mid-90s, Todd and a person whom he trusted entered a partnership to buy, remodel, and sell a home in Sherwood. Todd invested nearly $30,000. Ten years after purchasing the property, Todd had only recouped $1,000, which is why he contacted 7 On Your Side.

I asked a Little Rock attorney, Jason Stuart, to look at the facts of the case. He provided an estimate as to what Todd was now owed. That created a starting point. Ultimately the looming threat of public exposure led to a payment made to Todd in the amount of $42,500.

There were many times in my career where work done behind the scenes resolved an issue without having to put the conflict on TV. Our 7 On Your Side volunteers accomplished this daily. The case of Ronald Todd was one of those cases for me, as was the sad situation involving my longtime colleague photojournalist Mike Herman.

Stephen Michael Herman was born in 1946. His mother listed no father on his birth certificate, and it seemed likely she would have left her own name off had that been an option. She gladly gave him up for adoption when a kindly couple, Ted and Elois Herman, took in the dirty kid who they often saw wandering the streets. While grateful, Mike said the Herman family's biological children never warmed up to him.

In high school, Mike sought out and found his biological mother, Lois Dalka. He visited Dalka at Kavanaugh Pharmacy, where she worked. Mike's mom told him to leave the store and never contact her again. It was another sad rejection. Vietnam was raging at the time, and a young man seeking acceptance was eagerly embraced by the United States armed forces. Mike served in Vietnam and married a woman named Dian Louise Thomas soon after his return. They divorced a short time later without having any children.

Mike worked as a photographer at KATV for more than four decades. He bragged that every Arkansas governor from Bumpers to Beebe could call him by name. Not only that, but Mike also said he was on a first-name basis with most of the Arkansas U.S. senators and one U.S. president, too.

While Mike may have enjoyed familiarity, he lacked family. Over the last couple decades of his life, he lost his adoptive parents, and none of their biological children stayed in touch. Mike had no aunts, uncles, cousins, nieces, nephews, or children to either visit or to visit him. His Channel 7 coworkers were the closest thing he had to family. Former KATV anchor Andy Pearson and KTHV photojournalist Richard Gunter both counted Mike as a good friend.

After Mike retired from KATV, he really didn't have much to do. Pearson, Gunter, and KATV engineer Jim Drew would check on him from time to time at his North Little Rock home. Mike was a big guy, both tall and obese, and inactivity and poor eating habits in retirement didn't help his condition.

He lived modestly his entire life, and near the end of his life he had little debt and quite substantial assets. He owned his home along with three empty lots on a mountain top near Roland (those lots would be sold in 2018 for a collective $202,500). Mike had $144,000 in his 401(k) and a safe in his home that held another $10,000 or so in cash and an extensive gun collection. He had a 1980 Corvette and a 1970 Mustang that he never quite got around to restoring.

After Mike's death in April of 2014, two people who had little contact with him during the previous thirty years would battle for all the money, property, and possessions that Mike had accumulated. Those combatants would be a daughter by marriage, whom Mike never adopted, and a sister by adoption, whom Mike hardly knew.

Here is how it all played out.

Toward the end of 2013, Mike's friend, Jim Drew, noticed Mike's state of physical decline. Both his health and his home seemed to be a mess, and his short-term memory was failing. Mike spent short stints in the hospital in October and November of that year.

Andy Pearson noticed the changes, too. Andy took Mike to the University of Arkansas for Medical Sciences (UAMS) on December 18 out of concern for his mental well-being. Doctors determined that Mike suffered from "moderate to severe dementia with depression, apathy, hypertension and CAD (coronary artery disease)."

Mike asked Jim to check his mail, pay his bills, and watch his home. One day, Jim found a fruit basket on the front porch from someone named Tami Darr. Mike explained to Jim that Tami is the daughter of Dian Thomas, the woman who was Mike's wife for a few years in the early '70s. Mike asked Jim to call Tami and her husband, Andrew Darr, and thank them for the fruit basket. He said their number could be found by the phone at his house. Soon, Andrew and Tami Darr were visiting Mike at the hospital.

Tami would later testify that she and Andrew had seen Mike walking in the Park Hill area of North Little Rock a month earlier and, recognizing him, circled back and stopped to visit with him for a while. That is why Mike had Andrew Darr's business card by his phone.

At first, both Andy and Jim considered the Darrs' willingness to take over and help Mike make medical and financial decisions a godsend. But unbeknownst to them, ten days after visiting Mike in the hospital, Tami asked Mike to sign a document on December

29 that gave her power of attorney over his affairs. On January 14, 2014, Andrew Darr got Mike's signature on another document—a will prepared by attorney Lisa Douglas designating Tami Darr as sole beneficiary of Mike's estate. Douglas, who also drafted the power of attorney document, never met or spoke with Mike.

The Darrs wasted no time exercising their authority over Mike's affairs. They sold his home on February 21 for $52,000 and deposited the money in Mike's account. However, a check for $50,000 was later written on that account to Absolute Construction, Andrew Darr's unregistered construction company. Andrew Darr is not a licensed contractor.

A month later the Darrs bought a house at a HUD foreclosure auction for $28,685, claiming they planned to fix it up and create a more accessible home for Mike to live in. But they purchased the home in their name, not Mike's, and eventually sold it for $109,000 without Mike ever living there. Proceeds from the sale were deposited into Tami Darr's personal account.

The Darrs sold Mike's cars as well as his guns and gun safe. If that wasn't enough, Andrew and Tami Darr used Mike's money to pay themselves over $15,000 for all the "care and services" they were providing him.

Mike, now living at an assisted living facility for seniors, began to question why he was getting his mail but not his bank statements. When Tami Darr refused to provide them, Andy Pearson took Mike to the bank, and they discovered that his accounts had been reduced from $70,000 to less than $1,000. Mike revoked Tami's power of attorney on April 1. Tami and Andrew in turn removed the TV from Mike's room.

On April 17, Mike met with attorney Jack Lassiter to discuss changing his will and removing Tami Darr as sole beneficiary. Andy and I joined Mike at this meeting. Lassiter provided advice, but nothing official was done. The next day, Mike collapsed and died while eating dinner.

Incensed at the thought of Tami and Andrew Darr receiving any more of Mike Herman's money or property, Mike's friends began a quest to find a relative willing to contest the will and stake a claim to the estate. The search led to an eighty-three-year-old woman in Baytown, Texas.

Jean Billeaudeau is the biological daughter of Elois Herman, who along with her husband had adopted Mike. Jean was thirty-years-old when her parents adopted Mike, so although she knew him, she didn't grow up with him. Prior to learning of Mike's death, Billeaudeau hadn't seen Mike since the mid-90s. But Arkansas law recognizes adopted children and siblings as equal to biological children and siblings, which gave Billeaudeau a stronger claim as an heir of Mike Herman than Tami Darr, who was never formally adopted by Mike. But Billeaudeau's attorneys would have to get the will invalidated first.

Tami Darr's attorney, Oscar Hirby, made sure the judge knew about the limited contact between Herman and Billeaudeau over the years:

"She (Ms. Billadeau) had not had any contact with the decedent, who was a half-brother by adoption, for about thirty years. She did not know of his death. A friend of Mr. Herman (Andy Pearson) had called to let her know that he had passed away, and then through that friend, their attorney was hired and we are here today on this will contest."

David Kamps, the attorney representing Jean Billeaudeau, made a similar argument:

"The evidence will show Ms. Darr had little or no contact with Mr. Herman for about thirty years leading up to the relevant time in which the will was executed. This execution was after a period of minimal or no contact, and Ms. Darr appeared at the hospital where Mr. Herman had been receiving treatment, and in a matter of two to three days, Ms. Darr received power of attorney from Mr. Herman. Within a week of getting that power of attorney, she discussed with her husband the execution of a will for Mr. Herman, and within a matter of two weeks Mr. Herman had a new will, and the sole beneficiary of the will was Ms. Darr."

The debate centered on two questions: Was Mike mentally competent at the time he signed the will, and did Tami Darr exercise undue influence during the process?

The medical experts had already determined prior to the will being signed that Mike was likely suffering from moderate to severe dementia. Hirby, the attorney for the Darrs, made the argument that a diagnosis several weeks prior did not apply. "Much of the argument in this case centered on references in medical records to dementia, however, merely because one has a weakened condition due to age does not disallow them to dispose of their property by a testamentary disposition. The issue is not their condition in the past, in any event, as in earlier medical record references, but the question is what was their condition at the time of the execution of the will?"

Circuit Judge Richard Moore didn't agree. He set aside the will, questioning the credibility of Tami and Andrew Darr's testimony on several points, including the following:

- Tami Darr's designation as sole beneficiary in the will;
- Conflicting testimony given by Andrew Darr and Tami Darr;
- Tami Darr's role in obtaining power of attorney prior to the drafting of his will; and
- The flurry of activity by Tami Darr right before Mike removed her as power of attorney.

The Darrs appealed the ruling on several grounds and lost on all of them.

However, by the time concerned parties and the legal process detected and put a stop to what was going on, the Darrs had squandered well over $100,000 of Mike Herman's estate. Billeaudeau could have sued in civil court and attempted to get back some of what was lost, but she did not. As attorney Matt House mentioned previously, prosecutors don't seem to have the time, expertise, or inclination to pursue such matters.

In 2021, the Arkansas legislature enhanced some protections for elderly and vulnerable adults. For example, broker-dealers and investment advisers can now delay a financial transaction if they suspect exploitation. They already had the ability to delay disbursement of funds. A vulnerable or elderly adult is defined as someone sixty-five years of age or older, supervised by adult protective services or thought to be susceptible to financial exploitation. The Arkansas Department of Human Services Adult Protective Services unit must refer cases involving suspected exploitation of elderly or disabled people to the attorney general's office within forty-eight hours of the unit receiving the cases.

Despite these new protections, greed and opportunity will continue to turn helpers into thieves and family into enemies.

"The problem is the same now as it was then," says House, referring to a 2016 blog post he authored on protecting people from financial exploitation. "The elderly are vulnerable, easy targets, often with substantial wealth. The people who take advantage of them often will 'justify,' in their own minds at least, why they are basically defrauding them out of their money."

Who are the perpetrators? House says that perpetrators often include family members who have substance abuse, gambling, or financial problems. They often don't want to wait for an inheritance and feel justified in taking what they believe is "almost" or "rightfully" theirs. Sometimes they fear that if they wait, healthcare costs may use up an older family member's savings (their inheritance). And in many cases, they will profess to love the older person ("sweetheart scams" … as in the case of Norman Butler). Another type of predator I worked to expose and educate about as the 7 On Your Side reporter was the door-to-door scammer (often tree-trimmers, roof-repairers, or those who pave driveways) who target the elderly and overcharge for shoddy work and then use deceptive and unfair business practices (like intimidation) to collect.

Why are the elderly attractive targets? House writes that people over the age of fifty control 70 percent of the nation's wealth. Many seniors do not realize the value of their assets, particularly homes that have appreciated markedly. The elderly are also likely to have disabilities that make them dependent on others for help. These "helpers" may have access to homes and assets and may exercise significant influences over the older person. This is what happened in the case of Mike Herman. It also is the method by which Dara Booth gained access and opportunity (Chapter 5). Severely impaired individuals are less likely to act against their abusers because of illness or embarrassment (Ronald Todd was an exception). Abusers also may assume that frail victims will not survive long enough to follow through on legal interventions or that they will not make convincing witnesses (this may have been a consideration in Wiley Ballow's case).

Why are older individuals more at risk? The elderly are often isolated, lonely, have physical or mental disabilities, a lack of familiarity with financial matters, and have younger family members who are unemployed and/or have substance abuse problems.

What are the signs to watch for? Maybe you have a hunch that someone is being financially targeted. House says things to look for include unpaid bills, an eviction notice, or notices to disconnect utilities. Another warning sign is unusual activity in the older person's bank accounts like unexplained withdrawals, transfers, or ATM visits. If financial statements and cancelled checks stop coming to the elder's home, that may be a red flag. Watch out for new "best friends" or unknown "family" appearing on the scene. A huge red flag involves signed legal documents, such as power of attorney, which the older person may not have understood at the time he or she signed them (courts recognized this problem in both the Wiley Ballow and Mike Herman cases). If you notice missing belongings or property, suspicious signatures on checks or other documents, or if the elder is not aware of or does not understand financial arrangements that have been made for him or her . . . it's probably time to become both a detective and an advocate.

> **LESSON LEARNED:**
> *Be more vigilant, less trusting.*

Andy, Jim, and I all regret not being more skeptical of Andrew and Tami Darr's interest in our friend and the man they referred to as "Daddy Mike." Not only was Mike Herman not Tami's daddy, but he also met many of the criteria laid out by Matt House. He was lonely, wealthy, and dependent on others due to physical and mental issues. We all had busy lives ourselves and willingly gave up control to a pair of people who seemed nice, but who the courts ultimately ruled should not have been trusted.

CHAPTER 12

THE INCREDULOUS
(LYME DISEASE)

Ticks in Arkansas can cause several diseases,
with one exception it seems.

IN 2015 I BECAME INTERESTED in what seemed like a very un-likely claim: Lyme disease does not exist in Arkansas.

That is what the official state statistics at the time showed. While every state around Arkansas had cases of Lyme disease, and while cases were growing nationwide, Arkansas seemed to be in a pro-tective bubble.

Here is the news script of what we reported on November 12, 2015:

(Scott Inman): Modern gun hunting season opens in Ar-kansas this weekend. Waiting in the woods for all those hunters will be millions of ticks. While the Centers for Disease Control says tick-borne Lyme Disease is a growing epidemic in this country, state statistics indicate Arkansas hunters need not worry. Seven On Your Side's Jason Peder-son joins us to try to answer: is Lyme Disease here?

(Jason): Twenty years ago, Arkansas saw a couple dozen Lyme Disease cases pop up each year. But while the num-ber of Lyme Disease cases nationwide has been increasing, the number of recognized cases in Arkansas has dropped. To zero.

(NEWS STORY)

Abby Shrewsberry of Benton says she lost most of her senior year of high school to Lyme Disease. "I've had quite a few tick bites before. But there was one that was painful, that was big and red."

Christy Davis of White Hall says her Lyme Disease has progressed to the point where she can't help her kids with their homework. "Mine is neurological so it has my brain all jumbled up."

If either one of them has Lyme Disease, it's news to the Arkansas Department of Health.

"Different states interpret the CDC guidance a little bit differently in terms of diagnosing cases," says Dr. Dirk Haselow with the Arkansas Department of Health. "We interpret it very strictly."

Lyme Disease has become an epidemic in the United States, with the CDC acknowledging 300,000 new cases each year. Most of those cases are concentrated in the Northeast and upper Midwest. Lyme in the South is extremely rare. Since 2007, statistics show it is more than rare in Arkansas – it is non-existent. While all the states around Arkansas have reported cases, Arkansas has none.

If you are bitten by a black-legged tick with Lyme it sometimes, but not always, leaves a slowly expanding, circular red rash (or "bulls-eye rash"). This can be followed by mild headaches, a stiff neck, fatigue, low fever, and migrating muscle and joint pain. Lyme Disease is easily beaten by antibiotics if caught early, but catching it early is unlikely in Arkansas.

A clinical review of Lyme Disease published in the Journal of Arkansas Medical Society advises that testing for Lyme Disease "...can lead to clinical confusion, unnecessary treatment, and excess cost." The Arkansas Foundation for Medical Care get more to the point: "Lyme Disease is not acquired in Arkansas."

"They refused to test," says John Shrewsberry, Abby's father. "They said it wasn't called for and it would be a waste of time and money. And that it just didn't exist. And that was the end of it."

I asked Dr. Haselow if doctors are discouraged from considering Lyme as a possible diagnosis in Arkansas. "We would discourage them from thinking of it as the first cause."

Lyme left untreated leads to chronic and severe conditions so serious they are often mistaken for other ailments like multiple sclerosis, Alzheimer's, Parkinson's, fibromyalgia, meningitis, chronic fatigue syndrome, severe depression, or lupus. And when doctors can't figure out what is wrong, sometimes the patient is blamed.

"Because there was no proof...it was all in my head," recalls Abby Shrewsberry.

In his book *Why can't I get better*, Dr. David Horowitz writes that the CDC's Lyme Disease "...definition is narrow" and that "...the magnitude of real Lyme patients eluding the standard tests could be vast."

Could some of these patients be here in Arkansas?

"We look at every lab report that gets reported to us," says Dr. Haselow. "And we haven't had anyone in years meet the criteria that the Infectious Disease Society of America uses to diagnose Lyme disease."

"She was suffering, she was treated for Lyme disease, and she got better," says John Shrewsberry about his daughter Abby. "And to me that is enough to go OK...there is an issue here."

"I think they just need to acknowledge that Lyme disease is here, and we should be able to get the treatment we need here instead of having to go somewhere else," says Christy Davis.

And for Christy, somewhere else is Washington, D.C. She was told her Lyme Disease has progressed to the point where she needs a port, or PICC line, so she can receive antibiotics through an I.V. She says that kind of treatment isn't available in Arkansas, and even if it was, she can't afford the $46,000 price tag. Her insurance won't cover it.

This was one of those "sweeps" reports—highly promoted and highly viewed. Not surprisingly, it generated a lot of viewer response.

From Dorothy Leland with LymeDisease.org: "Thank you for your excellent coverage of the Lyme disease conundrum in which so many people in Arkansas and other states often find themselves. They are suffering terribly from Lyme disease symptoms, yet the health officials who are supposed to help them instead deny their illness and make it well-nigh impossible for them to get appropriately treated. One point your reporter might be interested to know: even though Arkansas' state health leaders refuse to acknowledge the existence of Lyme within your borders, the scientists at IDEXX labs (who make veterinary tests) evidently believe otherwise. If you look at their interactive map at www.dogsandticks.com, you will see that 158 Arkansas dogs have tested positive for Lyme disease within the past five years. Presumably their vets don't say the dogs are making it all up."

From Amber Cochran: "Thank you for the Channel 7 special on Lyme disease in Arkansas. It was an interesting, yet infuriating, piece. Lyme disease DOES exist in Arkansas. I contracted it in Arkansas. I was tested CDC positive in Arkansas. I have Chronic Late Stage Lyme Disease due to years of misdiagnosis and mistreatments (for the last 26 years) because doctors in Arkansas are discouraged and told not to test for Lyme disease. I am now NOT a fully functioning person due to years of non-treatment."

From Capri Dillon: "Thank you for the report on Lyme disease! Lyme disease absolutely does exist in Arkansas and it is time the medical establishment starts admitting it and addressing it!!!! My husband went to several specialists over a two-year period, and all agreed something was wrong but couldn't figure out what it was. I mentioned my frustration to a friend in Texas and when I told her his symptoms, she said "sounds like Lyme disease." Her son was dating a girl who went undiagnosed for five years and finally found a doctor in Houston who knew how to treat it. My husband (who is a dental professional) and has been using Buhner's Protocol now for two months is a changed man. Over the last two years he had progressed to not being able to walk at times and too fatigued to get out of bed and now he is almost completely back to his former, energetic self. Please do another more extensive report on this! You have just touched the tip of the iceberg of Lyme disease in Arkansas!"

From Jeanne Murphy: "Glad you have the courage to cast suspicion on the ADH's contention that Lyme disease is not endemic in Arkansas. It was until 2004, but as you've noted, zero cases have been reported since then, which is absurd. It's highly political, but now that it is a national epidemic of huge proportions, the ADH and infectious disease "experts" at UAMS [University of Arkansas for Medical Sciences] will have to eat their words. As a physician, I thank you for doing a great service to the health of all Arkansans by finally getting this ball rolling in the statewide media."

It certainly wasn't immediate, but in February of 2017 a pair of preteen sisters in Springdale, Arkansas, were diagnosed with Lyme disease. They were the first such diagnoses recognized by the Arkansas Department of Health in a decade.

While sharing this news with KATV viewers, I also revisited Christy Davis. Her health was improving after finding a more affordable doctor in Louisiana who put her on antibiotics for Lyme disease. In the same follow-up report, I shared that the Arkansas Department of Health had recently sent a tick found in Saline County to a California lab for testing, and it was found to be positive for Lyme disease and that UAMS was about to begin more such testing.

In fact, KATV partnered with UAMS in this effort and encouraged our viewers to send ticks in for testing. The goal was to obtain ticks from all seventy-five counties. We interviewed Dr. Jon Blevins, who encouraged people to send in ticks of all sizes, dead or alive, for testing. In the first two months, over 1,000 ticks were collected and sent in from fifty-two different counties.

I checked back with UAMS four years later to learn what the tick study had found. Has Lyme disease been detected in Arkansas? Dr. Jon Blevins replied that he didn't have an update. He said the work had been stalled by COVID and funding restrictions.

According to the CDC, there were five cases of confirmed Lyme disease in Arkansas in 2019 (the most recent year data was available at the time this was written). There were an additional thirteen probable cases of Lyme disease that year. Only Hawaii and Oklahoma reported zero cases of Lyme disease in 2019.

LESSON LEARNED:
Just because a government agency says so, that doesn't make it true.

President Biden stated in the summer of 2021 that "You're not going to get COVID if you have these vaccinations. If you're vaccinated, you're not going to be hospitalized . . . and you're not going to die." Well, as much as we wish that were true, it just isn't. When information defies common sense, take the time to study the matter and question authority, if necessary. I truly wish that Arkansas was an oasis of nonactivity when it comes to Lyme Disease. But that's not the case.

MORE INCREDULOUS STORIES
(BIG FISH FROM VOWS TO VICTORIES)

Rodney Fly holds a mount of his "should
be a record" striped bass.

On any given day in the 7 On Your Side office, you have no idea
what kind of issues will be brought to your attention. But the five-
page letter received in the spring of 2012 was a complaint like no
other.

Rodney Ply of Diamond City, Arkansas, pulled an enormous
striped bass out of Bull Shoals Lake on February 18. Ply and his
fishing partner immediately called the owner of 125 Marina in
Peel, Arkansas. Farris Brotherton agreed to meet them at his marina to weigh this potential state-record catch.

The trio weighed the fish multiple times. Each time it weighed
just over sixty-eight pounds. The state record at the time for a
striped bass was sixty-four pounds, eight ounces. The world record

for a freshwater striped bass was then sixty-seven pounds, eight ounces. Ply's catch beat them both. The scale at the marina was later certified to be accurate, but it had not been certified prior to this weigh-in.

The informal Arkansas Game and Fish Commission's (AGFC) policy at the time required any state-record fish to be weighed on a certified scale and in the presence of an AGFC or U.S. Fish and Wildlife Service employee. Unable to get such a witness with a certified scale to join them in Peel, Ply filled up a tank in the back of a pickup and drove his fish all over northern Arkansas in search of a location with both a certified witness and a certified scale. The effort proved to be frustrating and ultimately unsuccessful.

Ply was determined to get his fish certified as a state record, maybe even a world record. Ply's determination was fueled by both pride and money. Several weeks before landing his huge fish, Ply registered for Mustad Hook's "Hook a Million" contest. Anyone who caught and registered a state-record fish using a Mustad hook had a chance to win $100,000. Anyone who caught and registered a world record fish had a chance to win $1,000,000.

Although the state of Arkansas raised concerns over the scale and the witnesses present at the time the fish was weighed, these issues did not concern the International Game Fish Association (IGFA). But the IGFA did have an issue with the bait Ply used—a patent-pending lure he had designed himself called a "bass-tricker" lure. The IGFA calls such baits multi-arm spinner baits, umbrella lures, or Alabama rigs.

When moving through water, these lures create the illusion of a school of bait fish swimming. Sometimes an angler can catch more than one fish at a time, since there's more than one hook being used. The lures are popular but controversial. Some bass fishing tournaments have banned such lures.

Ply drove to Florida to meet with IGFA officials to convince them that his lure was different from the ones that had earned the scorn of many fishing purists. He had to wait a few months for a ruling, and it was more bad news for Ply. The IGFA decided that lures like the one Ply used, when the line is not attached to the bait's snap or other release device, are illegal. Ply appealed the ruling, and later sued unsuccessfully to get his catch certified as a world record.

But Ply still thought he had a shot at convincing AG&F officials that his big catch should count. That's because the requirements of having an official witness and a certified scale had not always been enforced in the past. Ply used the Arkansas Freedom of Information Act to get the documentation submitted by all past state record holders. Here is how I summarized that information in our first of many reports on Ply's predicament:

> With bragging rights and big money on the line, Ply took his case all the way to the top – to Arkansas Game and Fish Director Loren Hitchcock. Hitchcock's emailed response reads in part "You seem to think I personally certified all previous records and it is my decision to vary from standards. It doesn't work that way on my watch. You are misinformed. I'm not going to vary from the written guidelines."

> Well, three of the most recent records certified on Hitchcock's watch seem to have varied from the written guidelines.

> A tilapia caught in November was weighed in without a qualified witness present, but the fish's weight of three pounds, eight ounces is in the record book.

> A state record yellow bullhead was weighed in at the Lonoke post office on June 6th. The

> scale was certified on June 7th...after the fact.

And on June 6th, a ten-year-old who caught a black crappie beat a thirty-five-year-old state record, even though there is no record of the scale used to weigh the fish and the witness to the weigh in was a store owner and not a Game and Fish or Wildlife Service employee.

In reviewing the applications for state record fish, we found some that lack official witnesses, some that lack scale certification information, and many that show fishes were weighed on scales that had not been certified in years.

"We're going to try and figure out if some weren't done correctly … as best we can," said Mark Oliver, AG&F's Chief of Fisheries. "Some of them date way back. And if we do find ones that weren't done correctly, those fish would be decertified."

"I don't want to take anything away from anybody," said Ply. "That is not what this is about. It's just being treated fair. If you hold us to a standard different from everybody else—that's not fair. They've took the fun plum out of it. I never dreamed of a fish that size at Bull Shoals Lake to begin with. But I never dreamt of catching a record fish and not getting to say you caught the record fish. I mean … I just don't understand that whatsoever."

Sometimes when the media casts its spotlight on a problem, those involved rethink their position and things change. Other times, those involved dig in their heels and change becomes impossible. In the end, all Rodney Ply was left with was something that all anglers value and can appreciate: a really good fish tale.

As of 2023, Jeff Fletcher of Golden, Missouri, still holds the Arkansas record for striped bass at sixty-four pounds, eight ounces. Fletcher caught that fish out of Beaver Lake on April 28, 2000.

> **LESSON LEARNED:**
> *Greater attention does not always result in greater justice.*

It seems likely that Ply's persistence and the media attention it generated caused some to oppose, rather than champion, his cause.

Another story that raised eyebrows involved not catching fish but catching footballs.

From big cities and higher classifications to small cities and lower classifications, high school football is a *very* big deal across Arkansas. It has the power to unite, divide, inspire, and enrage. A winning season can lift the spirits of an entire community.

In the tiny town of Mountain Pine, winning seasons had become rare. In 2017, when a KATV viewer alerted me to a unique situation in Garland County, Mountain Pine High School (MPHS) was in the middle of its first winning season since 2009. Actually, let's be clear: the Red Devils had only won three games since 2011, a stretch that included a thirty-one game losing streak and a forfeited season (2016). This was a community that had experienced back-to-back state championships in the late '70s.

The star of the team was a running back who'd transferred from Lake Hamilton, where he'd played football and basketball the year before. In fact, on November 13, 2016, the young man practiced with the Wolves' basketball team. According to Lake Hamilton Superintendent Steve Anderson, the next day, "Poof! He was gone."

Soon, Anderson learned that the student was now playing ball for the Mountain Pine High School's Red Devils. So, Hamilton wrote Mountain Pine Superintendent Bobby Applegate a letter:

> …Unless he and his Mom have made a complete and bona fide move of his residency, it appears that this would be a desegregation violation. I would hate to see MPHS have to forfeit games for having an ineligible player on the team. Obviously we have some folks over here that don't want to lose him. He is a good kid and a good athlete that can help our program or yours. If he is legal to enroll there and legal to play, more power to him.

The student was forced to reenroll at Lake Hamilton until his grandmother, who lives in Mountain Pine, could get a court order that gave her legal guardianship. That happened in January 2017, so it was back to Mountain Pine. But a move into a new school district requires a one-year pause from any participation in athletics. A week later, Superintendent Applegate applied for a hardship exception with the Arkansas Activities Association (AAA) so that the young man would be immediately eligible to play sports at Mountain Pine. The exception was denied. Applegate requested an oral appeal hearing but later withdrew the request.

In late August, on the eve of a new football season, Applegate tried another approach: he asked the AAA what information is needed for a married student to gain athletic eligibility.

AAA Executive Director Lance Taylor quickly emailed a response: "1. Hardship forms filled out; 2. Transcript; 3. Letter from you detailing the hardship; 4. Letter from Mother detailing the hardship; 5. Marriage license; and 6. Proof that the student has a parent with a domicile in the district or a spouse who had an established domicile in the district one year prior to the marriage."

Later that same day, August 31, Applegate applied once again for a hardship exception, citing Rule 16, subsection A, exception #6, which allows for a hardship exception if "The student is married and living with a spouse, has a parent with domicile in the school district, or a spouse who has an established domicile in the district one year prior to the marriage."

Applegate's application did not include a marriage license. That wasn't available until September 7. That's when two seventeen-year-olds visited the Garland County courthouse on a Thursday afternoon (one day before Mountain Pine's next game) and were joined in holy matrimony by Reverend John Vise. I later asked Rev. Vise if he had any misgivings about marrying the young students. "I'm not the moral compass as far as who is getting married or why," Rev. Vise told me. "It is not within my purview to ask a lot of questions. All I do is make sure that they have a proper license. I did ask them what they were going to do for the rest of the day. They told me they were going back to school."

The following Friday night the young groom starred in the Red Devils' second game of the season, a victory over Cutter–Morning Star, starting a seven-game winning streak in which he would rush for over a hundred yards in every game and score eleven touchdowns. A special season ended in the playoffs—a place Mountain Pine football had not been in a very long time. And the success would continue. Mountain Pine won a state championship in eight-man football in 2020 and finished as state runner-up in 2021.

I visited the home where the young couple reportedly lived. The father of the bride declined an on-camera interview, stating only that the primary reason for the marriage did not involve sports or eligibility. Superintendent Applegate refused all requests for an interview.

Years later, I decided to look into whatever happened to the young couple. It appeared to me that the adults in their lives had thrust them into a sham marriage. How did things work out? Not surprisingly, the answer is—not well.

The union lasted an unhappy twenty months. The bride secured a no contact order in April 2019, preventing her husband from coming within a hundred yards. She filed for divorce the following month, explaining to the court, "I was only seventeen when we got married. We lived together for two months after our marriage, and then we lived with our parents. When we were together, he was verbally abusive on a regular basis. He was physically abusive once, and that's when I filed for divorce."

I did not name the young people involved (or their parents, as that would have been the equivalent of naming them), because it seemed clear to me that the adults in their lives—from the school officials to the pastor to their parents—were complicit in a scheme that placed football victories over marital vows. I did not want this period of their lives to come up whenever a potential employer or anybody else searched their names online.

> **LESSON LEARNED:**
> *Marriage is not designed to be convenient, temporary, disposable, or replaceable.*

Marriage was God's idea, and when you don't follow the design, you should not be surprised by the results.

CHAPTER 13

THE HEARTBREAK
(PAUL EELLS/ANNE PRESSLY)

KATV Sports Director Paul Eells and KATV
Reporter/Anchor Anne Pressly.

EVERY WORKPLACE EXPERIENCES HEARTBREAK. YOU and your coworkers will experience loss and suffering from deaths, divorce, disease, and other disappointments. You come together and console one another following everything life throws at you.

Being a member of a television family is no different, except that some of the losses and our collective grieving can be more public. Two obvious examples are the death of Paul Eells in July 2006 and the murder of Anne Pressly in October 2008—a one-two punch that thankfully not many workplace families will ever endure.

Both Paul and Anne were shining lights in our newsroom. If every KATV employee had been asked in early 2006 to list their five favorite coworkers, I believe both Paul and Anne would've been on every single list. They were positive, strong Christians who loved people and who smiled and laughed constantly.

By the time I arrived at KATV in 1995, Paul Eells had almost finished his second decade at Channel 7. He was an institution as

"The Voice of the Razorbacks," Arkansas' football team, a.k.a, the Hogs, and he was a legend who was able to replace Bud Campbell, another legend. By age seventy, Eells joked that he was "in the twilight of a mediocre career." Mediocre? Hardly. The longtime KATV sports director was as respected and revered as any man in the state. Still, he had hinted that the 2006 football season would be his last as play-by-play broadcaster on the radio for the Hogs and that his TV days would also be coming to an end.

Anne Pressly arrived at KATV in 2004, right out of college. I was wrapping up my first decade at Channel 7. She worked as both producer and reporter, but soon her talent elevated her to full-time reporter status. I got to know her because she did live reports for Saturday Daybreak, which I hosted with Renee Shapiro. At twenty-six, Pressly seemed to be at the beginning of a possibly meteoric rise in broadcasting. By sheer force of personality, she had earned a small role in Oliver Stone's film *W.* While she was an excellent reporter and morning show anchor/news reader, her real interest was in entertainment reporting. I could easily envision her rising quickly in that arena. Anne hosted "Friday Night Touchdowns" pep rallies, flying into small cities aboard Chopper 7, and firing up local crowds with her infectious spirit and enthusiasm.

Before serving as "Voice of the Razorbacks" for twenty-eight years, Eells was the "Voice of the Iowa Hawkeyes" for five years shortly after graduating from the University of Iowa. In 1967, Eells moved to Nashville where he worked for ten years at WSMV-TV as the play-by-play announcer for the Vanderbilt Commodores. In Tennessee, Eells' trademark call was "Holy smokes!" After arriving in Arkansas in 1978, Paul changed things up and became known for his excited and often delivered "Oh my!"

Each year, thirty-two young students in the United States are selected as Rhodes Scholars and attend the University of Oxford in England. Pressly, a native of South Carolina, was a graduate of

Rhodes College in Memphis and as such liked to inform people, accurately but with a wink, that she was a Rhodes Scholar. Pressly moved to Little Rock during her junior year of high school and quickly formed friendships that would help keep her close to the area for the rest of her young life.

Eells was driving back to Little Rock from a Fayetteville golf tournament on July 31, 2006, when his eastbound vehicle crossed the Interstate 40 median at Russellville and crashed into another vehicle traveling westbound. Both Eells and the other driver, forty-year-old B.J. Burton of Dover, were killed instantly. Eells had done live shots for KATV during the 5 p.m. and 6 p.m. newscasts during a scorching hot day prior to driving home. During the day, he'd mentioned to a few people that he felt unwell. Police believe he suffered a massive health event while driving— possibly a heart attack or stroke—causing the accident.

On the evening of October 19, 2008, Anne Pressly had enjoyed a surprise thirtieth birthday dinner for a colleague before returning home to her two cocker spaniels and turning in for the night. Pressly worked the Daybreak shift, so every morning her mom Patti or stepdad Guy would give her a wake-up call around 3 a.m. Patti happened to be in Little Rock visiting the morning of October 20, so when Anne failed to answer multiple wake-up calls, Patti hustled over to check on her daughter. What she found is every parent's nightmare. Anne had been beaten almost to the point where she was unrecognizable. Her injuries were severe, and she never recovered. She died at St. Vincent Medical Center five days later.

While all of the TV stations were aware of Paul's death prior to the ten o'clock news, and while any one of our competitors could have led their programs with this shocking news, they all waited for Channel 7 to share the news first. It was a kind and classy gesture by our competitors to hold off on reporting this big news. Anchor

Scott Inman broke into regular programming around 11:30 p.m., after we were sure Paul's wife, Vicki, and other family had been notified. Scott got his start working in the sports department with Paul. Paul was one of the nicest men I've ever known, and there are many who would agree, including Scott. He got through it, but it wasn't easy.

The first opportunity to share news about Anne would come about ten hours after the attack, during a short newsbreak at the end of Good Morning Arkansas. The news reader that day, Beth Hunt, had been crying all morning. I offered to take her place, and she readily agreed. At that time, Anne was in the hospital and while we knew she was in bad shape, the extent of her injuries were not fully understood. I announced her attack, but I didn't have to deal with the finality that Scott had to process. That would come days later, on the weekend, when Pamela Smith shared the news that Anne had died. Pam considered herself a mother hen to all the young female reporters in the Channel 7 newsroom and like Scott, Pam exuded the perfect combination of professionalism and heartbreak under ridiculously difficult circumstances.

When things happen beyond the scope of my understanding, my impulse is to get busy and do something. The night Paul died, I went up to the station and started searching the Channel 7 archives for great Paul moments. I found a half-dozen clips and wrote accompanying scripts so Daybreak could begin memorializing our suddenly departed friend. Steve Sullivan and I also traveled that week to Dover to attend the funeral of B.J. Burton. We both felt that Paul would've preferred Burton receive all the attention and spotlight that Paul was understandably getting. We learned at her service that Burton and her husband, Gary, loved listening to Paul call Razorback games on the radio. Like much of the state, she was a big Paul Eells' fan.

After Anne's murder, I kept busy by trying to help Little Rock detectives solve her case. I submitted a Freedom of Information Act (FOIA) request to the Arkansas prison system for a list of all violent inmates paroled to Pulaski County during the two months prior to her murder. I then cross-referenced that list with all the stories Anne had reported, searching for any men she had done stories on in the past who were living in Little Rock. I found several possibilities and shared them with homicide detective Tommy Hudson.

Hudson assured me that once the DNA from the crime scene was back from the lab, he would cross-reference it with all the names I provided. In the end, DNA did help Hudson and his colleagues catch Anne's killer, but it wasn't a name that I or anyone else had provided. The DNA matched a sample from a rape that had occurred in Marianna earlier that year. Marianna is about a hundred miles east of Little Rock, and Little Rock police detectives worked with law enforcement in Lee County to develop a list of possible suspects whose DNA could be secured and matched against the DNA found at Anne's crime scene. Curtis Vance matched. A jury convicted Vance of capital murder, and he will live out his days inside Tucker Maximum Security Prison. As the 7 On Your Side reporter, I didn't have to cover Vance's trial. It was well attended by many of Anne's friends and colleagues. Impartiality and objectivity were elusive that week.

Prior to his death, Paul was invited to speak to the Capital Chapter of the University of Arkansas Alumni Association. Following his death, I was asked to speak in his place. Here is part of what I shared:

> "How many people do you know who you have never heard swear?
>
> How many people do you know who you have never heard speak bad about someone else?

How many people do you know who you have never heard anyone say anything bad about?

How many people leave you feeling better after every meeting or every conversation?

Paul was Mr. Positive. Mr. Popular. A man loved by the people because he loved the people. At a restaurant, Paul's food would get cold while he visited with the admirer who would inevitably approach. He told his pastor that his life could be summed up this way: He loved the Lord, he loved people, and he loved life.

Six years ago, Paul discovered a church and a pastor in his hometown of Maumelle with whom he really connected. Soon word was out that Paul Eells was willing to speak to groups about his faith and his testimony as well as his career and the Razorbacks. Paul was recently featured in *The Spirit* magazine and interviewed about his faith. Here is an excerpt:

Eells' faith has also helped him in the workplace. "It's given me patience. There are a lot of things that could make you impatient in a newsroom."

Eells feels that demonstrating Christ's love by example will touch someone's life. "I've never taken someone aside and said 'Hey, do you have Jesus in your life?' I think people who know me and who are around me see the peace in my life," said Eells. "I try to treat others the way I want to be treated. With respect."

Eells takes time to talk with anyone who wants to chat, ranging from players and coaches to die-hard sports fans, and from long-time friends and coworkers to strangers on the street. "I want people to know that there is more to me than just what they see on television," said Eells.

Eells says he is not sure how long he will remain 'The Voice of the Razorbacks.'

"At least another year," said Eells. "Next year I will take a look at it and evaluate if I am still doing a good job." In the meantime, he knows it is all in God's timing.

I share this with you because although Paul was known as a sports broadcaster, I think he would want to be remembered as a follower of Christ and would like for his life to make a difference beyond sports. The scholarship you are donating in his name is another way to honor his memory. I told Vickie about it and asked her what Paul would think about it. She told me Paul would be embarrassed. "He would be overwhelmed and feel unworthy of such an honor. But he would accept the honor gratefully as a blessing...a way God was using his life and his celebrity to benefit a fellow human being."

I had speaking opportunities of a different variety following Anne Pressly's death. Anne's death left a hole in the Daybreak team, and I was asked to fill in for three months. Back then, Daybreak aired for two hours (5:00–7:00 a.m.) and included news, weather, sports, and reporter live shots. Saturday Daybreak was another two-hour show (7:00–9:00 a.m.) that included all the same elements but added movie reviews, animal adoption opportunities, and live guests. Both shows, because of their length, also had time and opportunities for the hosts to chit-chat.

After Anne's attack and murder, I was uncommonly bold in discussing her life, her death, her funeral, and especially her faith. I wasn't the only one. Viewers noticed and responded. Here is some of that feedback:

"I am proud of you, Beth, and Melinda this morning. I know it was difficult to be at work and do the news. I am even more proud of the fact that you let the viewers know

God is your strength. There are so many television personalities who will "skate around" the issue of faith and God.
He is truly the only One that can see friends and family
through a time like this."   — Penny in Star City

"It was so nice to see you on Daybreak with Melinda and
Beth, talking about your faith and helping each other
through this terrible time. I am stunned and horrified as
much as anyone over Anne's attack and death. But as seemingly senseless as all this is, if she truly knew Jesus, and
it seems she did, then we know God has a purpose, even
though we may not understand it. I pray for her family and
you and your KATV family as well."   —Kerri in Marvell

I also had the opportunity to speak about Anne to a small group
of her colleagues, media members of a Christian organization
started by former KATV Morning Meteorologist Matt Mosler. The
group was called Little Rock Media Fellowship. We met in a room
at Dickey Stephens Park and listened to guest speakers, many of
them members, share their faith journeys.

In my talk, I examined Romans 8:28 in the aftermath of Anne's
murder: "And we know that in all things God works for the good
of those who love Him, who have been called according to His purpose." Anne loved the Lord. What good resulted from her death?
What purpose was served?

She was young, in excellent health, and didn't smoke or drink. Six
people received her organs. Her funeral was a packed house, and a
pastor delivered a very clear presentation of the Gospel. The pastor also asked those in attendance, "If you were to die today, do
you know where you're going?" I am confident seeds were planted
and souls were saved. But the truth is, the truth and totality of Romans 8:28 in this instance (or any instance) won't be fully known
this side of Heaven.

Following Anne's death, Mosler arranged for Gray LeMaster, a former LRPD detective who was now director of Napa Valley Counseling Services, to lead two sessions of Little Rock Media Fellowship for women journalists only. Several other counselors and clergy also took part and worked to help Anne's female friends and colleagues process her murder. Remember, at this time there was a lot of fear and anxiety about why Anne was targeted, and her killer remained at large. Only later would we learn that her attack was a crime of opportunity. Vance likely had no idea that Anne was on television.

The following are some thoughts shared by Mosler following Pressly's murder. "(Anne) had only been on the air in Little Rock for a few years, but she owned this town just like she owned every room into which she walked. It didn't hurt that she was 6 feet tall and stunningly beautiful. I mean, that's why she could walk onto a movie set and get offered a role in that movie before she left!

Anne was special that way. She had a sparkle about her. I've heard from other anchors and reporters in this market that they were a bit jealous of Anne—not her talent or looks as much as her spirit. I've heard them say, "I wish I could be more like her." I wish I were more like her too. Sure, we're all unique. But it seemed to me that Anne lived her "uniqueness" out loud. She held nothing back. She personified the abundant life that Jesus promises (John 10:10).

Why then did someone so young, so talented, so beautiful, so full of life, leave this world in such a violent way? Where was God in those early morning hours? Why didn't He intervene?

Those same questions are the central theme in what had become Anne's favorite book, *The Shack* by William Paul Young. Earlier in 2008, Anne received a copy from the author who spoke at the first-ever meeting of Little Rock Media Fellowship. Anne attended nearly every meeting.

In his book, author Young tells the tale of Mack, whose daughter, Missy, is murdered in a particularly brutal manner. Mack has a hard time dealing with the loss and how a loving God could have allowed it to happen. In the novel, Mack is told, "He doesn't stop a lot of things that cause Him pain. Your world is severely broken. You demanded your independence, and now you are angry with the one who loved you enough to give it to you ... Right now, your world is lost in darkness and chaos, and horrible things happen to those He is especially fond of.

Then why doesn't He do something about it? Mack asks and is told about Jesus on the cross.

He already has ..."

Later in the book, Jesus talks to Mack about his daughter's murder: "I don't think you want to know all the details. I'm sure they won't help you. But I can tell you there was not a moment that we were not with her. She knew my peace, and you would have been proud of her. She was so brave!"

The wisest man on earth once wrote, "The day of one's death is better than the day of one's birth" (Eccl 7:1). I'm not sure what that means other than Anne is now seeing God face to face. But maybe it also means that while our birth is out of our control, the way we live our life is not. Our legacy will be fully considered after our death. Anne's legacy is more than just images on film and videotape. Those things will fade. Her true legacy is the impact she made on the lives of others.

> **LESSONS LEARNED:**
> *All lives are equal in the eyes of God but rarely in the eyes of man.*

The family of B.J. Burton would admit to me later that while it was totally understandable that Paul Eells would get the lion's share of the attention on the anniversary of the crash, they lost a wonderful person that day, too. And a few days after Anne's death, thirty-two-year-old Sonya Ratliff, a mother of three, was murdered in Little Rock by her ex-boyfriend. In sharing that news on Daybreak, I added, "And to the family of Ms. Ratliff, please do not compare the size of the reward funds or the amount of flowers received on behalf of our Anne and your Sonya. Sonya's life was just as important. We are all grieving."

MORE HEARTBREAK
(BLACK FRIDAY)

One of the other difficult days at KATV occurred on January 23, 2009, a day commonly referred to as "Black Friday" among those who worked at Channel 7 at that time. Allbritton Communications, the company that owned KATV and several other TV stations around the country, had a massive round of layoffs that day as part of a company-wide downsizing.

My good friend Christina Munoz was on maternity leave with her first child Sydney (also Mary Carol's and my godchild), so I kept her up to date on every move via email.

At 11:04 a.m., I sent Christina this message:

"Layoffs hitting today. So far, I have heard …

Fred Anderson

Fred English

David Jones

James Tidwell

Newsroom not affected yet. Those guys were called in at 9:00 a.m. this morning and given the news. That's all so far."

Often with layoffs, it's "last hired, first fired." But not in this case. Those four men had decades of experience and seniority at KATV. If they weren't safe from the chopping block, neither were the rest of us.

At 11:12 a.m.:

"Billy Cannon

Michelle Duvall

Dale Butler

Steve Powell"

Steve Powell probably had more Emmy awards than anyone in Little Rock television history. His wife, Amanda, was an account executive with Channel 7. Again, if he wasn't safe, I certainly wasn't. The mood in the newsroom was somber, with a healthy dose of paranoia.

11:31 a.m.:

"Two editors. One is Jason Poss.

Robyn.

Clement.

Dan Weathersby is out on the parking deck. Not sure.

At least I am still typing. All the photogs are huddled together back in the edit hallway. Not much noise here in the newsroom. Just a lot of uneasiness. In fact, I think I'm going up to the 7OYS office."

12:11 p.m.:

> "Anthony Eckert
>
> Mike Moravec
>
> Maybe more . . . I was out of the newsroom for 30 minutes.
>
> I'll call when I find my cell."

1:38 p.m.:

> "Richard Farrester
>
> Aaron Malyk
>
> Joyce up in traffic
>
> There may be others. I don't know."

By day's end, over twenty of our friends and colleagues were out of a job.

I sent handwritten notes of sympathy and encouragement to many who were affected. Some wrote back and said thanks. Others were probably too busy job hunting to have time to respond, or they were still in shock and didn't quite know what to say.

Job loss and career loss lack the finality of death, but they're still devastating. For many people, their job is their identity, especially in TV. When it's ripped away without notice, the loss can be disorienting and devastating.

Of those who lost their job that day, a couple of people retired. Most moved on to better jobs and greater opportunities. One person spiraled into alcoholism, while another stopped working and is now homeless.

> **LESSON LEARNED:**
> *Anchor your identity in something other than your work.*

Even if you own your own business, your business can be lost. One day, Lord willing, you will get old and retire. Build your identity and reputation around things with more permanency: your love of others, your kindness toward others, your generosity, your faith. Those are things that people, circumstances, or an economic downturn cannot take away from you.

CHAPTER 14

THE RANDOM
(DO IT YOURSELF DIVORCE)

TELEVISION REVENUE IS BASED ON eyeballs; the more people you have watching, the more money you can charge for a commercial.

During almost the entirety of my career in television, the number of people watching was measured only four times a year: in February, May, July, and November. These months are known as "sweeps," or ratings periods. They're also called "books," as in the "May book" or the "November book." Nielsen Media Research pays participating viewers a small stipend to record their viewing habits in a book (or diary) sent to them (all of this is now done digitally) and TV stations pay Nielson for the all-important ratings information.

To charge a premium for commercials, you need to get a lot of people to watch. To get a lot of people to watch, you need compelling stories. Weeks prior to the start of any ratings month, there's a large meeting of newsroom staff where story ideas are pitched. This is a free-for-all, where dozens of ideas are discussed and debated before the news director ultimately picks the handful that seem best. Sometimes a reporter gets to pursue the idea that he or she proposes. Other times, a reporter is assigned someone else's idea. It's then the job of the reporter/photographer/editor team to put together a highly engaging, promotable story.

It's essential for reporters to get these stories completed well in advance so the promotions department has time to develop and broadcast teases designed to attract the largest audience possible. To help accomplish this, sweeps stories are given extra time. A typical news story is given two minutes, sometimes less, and is done in a day. A sweeps story is given four or five minutes, sometimes more, and a reporter can spend weeks working on it.

The following are some examples of "sweeps stories" that I did over the years spotlighting emerging technologies: "Spying on your Babysitter" (1996), "Modern Day Dating" (1998), "Cell Phone Safety" (2000), "Getting Prescription Drugs Online" (2003), "Hybrid Cars" (2005), "Tracking Your Teen" (2005), "Illegal Downloads" (2005), and "Digital vs. Film Cameras" (2006).

I did highly promoted special reports on mysterious deaths like "The Boys on the Tracks" in Saline County, Janie Ward's death in Searcy County, and the package bombing that killed Johnny Rauch near the Saline/Pulaski County line (all discussed in Chapter 8).

Would you tune in to watch a report on Arkansas' dumbest crooks? How about school lunches vs. jail lunches? Dangerous driveways? What about a profile on a bad landlord? How about a special report on prison inmate deaths linked to the synthetic drug known as K2? I packaged all of those ideas and presented them as sweeps reports.

In 1998, I journeyed to Haiti with photojournalist Scott Munsell to create a three-part series on the work being done in the village of Pignon by a group of Arkansans. Munsell and I later traveled to California, where we did another three-part series on a leadership-training boot camp.

Following the big sweeps meeting in January 2007, the news director assigned me to do three special reports for the February ratings period: "50 Ways to Cut your Electric Bill," "Buyer Beware: Hurricane Damaged Cars for Sale in Arkansas," and "Do-It-Yourself Divorce Kits." All three definitely had appeal and benefit to consumers. And I had no problem with the first two. As for the third story, I was and remain happily married. I am a big fan of marriage. My personal belief is that marriage is a godly rather than earthly institution, and divorce, while common, is often disruptive and damaging.

I could not refuse the "Do-It-Yourself Divorce Kits" story because the idea came from my boss, News Director Randy Dixon. This is how he pitched it: "There are websites out there that claim you can order a divorce kit for $39.95 that is custom to Arkansas law. 7 On Your Side's Jason Pederson checks them out with lawyers to see if they're for real." Dixon wanted me to determine whether such divorce kits were legitimate, or if saving money on a divorce attorney could cost you more in the long run. However, I thought I could take the story beyond a likely debunking of the divorce kits and into other possible solutions for those in a troubled marriage. I didn't share my intentions with Dixon because I didn't want to be discouraged or even denied the chance to tell the story my way. Here is the report that aired at 10:00 p.m. on February 6, 2006:

The story lasted three minutes and thirty-four seconds. It took less time than that for my home phone to ring. Soon, an angry boss was yelling into my ear.

Dixon told me he was "shocked" and questioned my news judgment. He said it "was supposed to be a story about $40 dollar divorce kits, not a debate over marriage and divorce." Dixon compared it to turning a story about an execution into a debate over the death penalty. I pointed out that we always include groups who are for/against the death penalty in such coverage. He countered that we don't promote such groups by putting links on our website.

"You were wrong," he insisted. "It was inappropriate to open and close the piece with comments from FamilyLife." My wife, Mary Carol, worked at FamilyLife at the time, which Dixon knew and said he didn't have a problem with. But he said it wasn't supposed to be a Christian story or anything like that. FamilyLife is a Christian nonprofit dedicated to improving marriages and families. At the time of my report, FamilyLife was headquartered in Little Rock.

"This is not up for debate," declared Dixon. "Your job is consumer education. It is not your job to save marriages."

I didn't record our conversation. But I was so shocked by Dixon's response that I immediately wrote down some of his comments. When I went to work the next day, he called me into his office, shut the door and the blinds, and ranted some more. He had removed the story from the KATV website and ordered Daybreak not to rerun the story.

The news director made his opinion known but so did many KATV viewers. I received more emails following that story than almost any other story I'd done at Channel 7. Here are a few examples:

> "Awesome job on the Divorce Kit story! I was VERY encouraged to see one of our local news stations placing a high value on marriage, knowing that it's a hot topic in our culture, by showing a "product" isn't always what it appears to be. Your story was also objective. It didn't have the slant that is so often attached to what's being reported, and

it didn't feel like it was coming from the "religious right" either. Way to go Channel 7!"

"I would like to thank Jason Pederson for bringing this subject to light. He did a masterful job with a sensitive subject. It is far too easy to get a divorce now. Every couple goes through hard times, they don't need to throw in the towel too quickly. Given time they would cool down and see it can be worked through. Thanks again Jason!"

"You did a great job of showing what a waste of time and money do-it-yourself divorce kits are. I also very much appreciated the info about the marriage conferences. Because of your story, my husband and I hope to attend the one next week. Thanks for showing that the family is "the most important unit in society." Please make sure that Jason Peterson and the station manager both know how thankful I am for this story."

And then there were plenty of emails from viewers looking for the story online:

"Could you please tell me how to locate on your web site the article your station did last night on 02-06-07 on getting a divorce for $40? I looked in the Seven-On-Your-Side site and was unable to find it anywhere. I appreciate all your help."

"On last night's show I had seen the 40$ divorce and at the end there were 2 weekend workshops could you please send me the info?"

"I work for Chief Justice Hannah. He was out of state on Tuesday and did not see the news that aired the Seven-On-Your-Side story that included his son, Judge Craig Hannah, being interviewed. I copied the link for that day and emailed it to him. When we opened that link, it went to the February 7th story. Would you mind sending me a copy of the February 6th story to show the Chief?"

Here in Arkansas, people love to get married—and divorced. According to the Center for Disease Control and Prevention (CDC), in 2019 only two states had a higher marriage rate than Arkansas and those states were the wedding destinations of Hawaii and Nevada (Las Vegas). Also, in 2019, only one state, Nevada, barely had a higher divorce rate than Arkansas.

I believe marriage is foundational to society. Cheap and easy divorces run counter to that belief. But my news director was right: what a reporter believes is not foundational to what they report. It should be irrelevant—and it would be if reporters were robots.

A story debunking divorce kits as a risky proposition would have been acceptable, but I took it a step further and advocated for saving and strengthening marriages. Right or wrong, advocacy and activism in journalism have become more commonplace. The acceptance and tolerance of such activist journalism varies greatly. Factors include the network, the size of the market, the history of the station involved, the region of the country, and where the journalists at that station were educated. A viewer's acceptance or objection to activist journalism is usually dependent upon one thing: whether or not they agree with the position being promoted or highlighted. With rare exceptions (and this was one of those exceptions), I worked hard to hide my personal beliefs and biases from the viewers.

Journalists make decisions daily involving both story structure and facts that reveal personal opinions. For example, let's say a dog attacks and kills a child. The dog is a pit bull mix. Here is a list of possible people to interview:

- Someone who knew the child (parents/relatives/ neighbors/teachers/friends)
- An eyewitness to the attack

- The public information officer for the agency investigating the death
- The owner of the dog
- The owner of the dog's neighbors
- The president of a property owners association who has been pushing for a pit bull ban in that neighborhood
- The CEO of Best Friends Animal Society, a group that lobbies against breed specific legislation and laws
- The executive director of Animals 24-7, a nonprofit that tracks dog attacks and links them to specific breeds

It's television news, so time constraints won't allow *all* of these potential voices to be heard. A reporter must choose who to include AND, just as importantly, in what order to include them. For example, if a reporter interviews someone who thinks certain dog breeds are inherently dangerous and someone who believes the problem lies with dog owners and that breed bans are discriminatory, whichever voice the reporter chooses to air first in the story likely reveals that reporter's bias. The first voice sets an idea in the mind of a viewer that the second voice must then combat while also trying to persuade.

Reporters don't usually flat-out lie. But the way they structure a story or what they choose to leave in or leave out can reveal bias. Good reporters are aware of their biases and will try hard to report the facts only, allowing viewers to make up their own minds. But even good reporters occasionally fall into the allure of activism journalism.

LESSON LEARNED:
Rather than risk being told "no," act and accept the consequences.

There will be times when you feel compelled to do something you suspect your boss will not appreciate. Weigh the risks and potential costs, carefully consider why you feel the way you do, and move forward with a decision you can live with. You can and probably will have other bosses. But you're stuck with your choices and the reputation they create. Because of my report, I was chewed out and lost some trust with my boss. I could've been fired, and I would've been OK with that. Remember: you can't shave with your back to the mirror.

MORE RANDOMNESS
(PONTIAC PARISIENNE, BLACK FARMERS, MEDICAL MARIJUANA, HALEY ZEGA)

I have never purchased a vehicle made during the decade in which I lived. I just can't bring myself to spend big money on a new vehicle when I view cars and trucks as a necessary evil—a way to get from Point A to Point B. In the mid-1980s my first car—a 1972 Kingswood Estate station wagon—was purchased by my parents and given to me and my brother, Eric, who is one year younger than me. My next car was a '78 Dodge Diplomat. Then in 1991, I bought an '85 Pontiac Parisienne with 65,000 miles on it.

Pontiac only made the Parisienne for three years (1984–1986) and my two-tone blue bomber served me well. It was a smooth ride with a plush interior. You may notice that all of these vehicles put a lot of metal around the occupants. My dad found all of them. He believed that saving lives in case of an accident mattered more than saving money on fuel. When the time came, I also put my children in used, larger vehicles. Thankfully, they were both grateful, both safer, and maybe both a tad embarrassed as they compared their vehicles to the ones driven by their fellow students. That's OK. It was character-building transportation for me and for them. And they still love me.

The Parisienne got me to Arkansas, carried me to Little Rock, and traveled my paper route every night when the kids were young. But when I started getting headaches and suspected they were caused by fumes somehow leaking into the cabin, Mary Carol said, "Enough!" The odometer was approaching 250,000 miles; it was time to retire Big Blue. Rather than sell it, I donated it to charity, fully disclosing all its problems.

And that was the end of that—or so I thought.

Several months later, while sitting at my desk in the KATV newsroom, reporter Michelle Rupp and photojournalist Ray Hamilton came in from the parking garage and told me they'd just seen my old car. "Really, where?" I asked with a hint of longing, as I'd loved that car. "It's upside down on Interstate 30 near the UALR law school," Ray said. They both laughed as I followed them back to an edit bay where I could see the visual evidence for myself.

The hubcaps were gone but it looked like my old car. Apparently, the driver had been fleeing police when he lost control on a curve and flipped it. The suspect wasn't seriously hurt (just like Dad had planned!) and he briefly ran away on foot before being caught. Pontiac Parisiennes weren't all that common in September 2003. Although I felt sure the car on video had once belonged to me, I had no proof—until a Little Rock police officer knocked on the newsroom door.

"Is Jason Pederson here?" I walked over and introduced myself and asked what was up? "We were involved in a police pursuit, and the suspect crashed his car on the interstate. We searched that car and found crack cocaine, marijuana, and one of your business cards."

Thankfully the officer believed my explanation and never seriously entertained the notion of me as a suspect or coconspirator. The next day my old car made the front page of the Arkansas section of the *Democrat-Gazette*, and a week later columnist Michael Storey interviewed me and had some fun with the situation. The title of his September 2003 column: "Reporter's old cruiser takes a bruisin' on I-30." He refers to Big Blue as a land yacht, "...a prodigious four-door display of iron and steel."

For the record, the current Pederson vehicle fleet (2023) includes a 2004 Honda CRV, a 2005 Toyota Camry, a 2007 Ford Freestar, and a 2008 Dodge Grand Caravan.

> **LESSON LEARNED:**
> *Thoroughly clean out your vehicle before you sell or give it away.*

My journalism professor once gave me this advice: be well-rounded and well-read. He suggested that every reporter read their local newspaper and a national newspaper every day along with a national news magazine every week. So for much of my career, I read the *Arkansas Democrat-Gazette, The Wall Street Journal,* and *U.S. News and World Report.* This helped me keep up with the goings-on in my city, state, nation, and the world, but they also provided me with story ideas.

I was able to localize one story from *The Wall Street Journal.* Black farmers had filed two class action lawsuits in 1997 and 1998 against the United States Department of Agriculture (USDA), alleging discrimination in loan distribution. Several of the plaintiffs were from Arkansas, and I interviewed them for a special report.

A judge combined the two lawsuits, and a year later, the farmers and government leaders reached a settlement, the largest civil rights settlement in U.S. history: over one billion dollars for cash relief, tax payments, and debt relief (*Pigford v. Glickman*). Black farmers in some rural areas were unaware of, or missed, a filing deadline, so in 2010 Congress allocated an additional $1.25 billion to help pay their claims.

LESSON LEARNED:
Never stop learning.

A reporter has to be curious and inquisitive, which means reading, watching, and listening closely to what's happening in your surroundings.

It is essential for reporters to learn all sides of an issue, and in 2012 there was an issue that piqued my curiosity that had plenty of sides to it. Arkansas citizens were preparing to vote on whether to allow the sale and use of marijuana for medicinal purposes. As a consumer reporter, I wanted to help educate the public on the pros and cons of the proposal.

My bosses and I decided I'd go to Colorado where marijuana had been legally available for medical use for over a decade. In Colorado Springs, for example, there were four cannabis dispensaries for every one Starbucks. What impact was the easy availability of marijuana having on the Centennial State?

This trip, more than any other for KATV, required a great deal of preparation and research. Photojournalist Chato Wilson and I would only have a couple of days to schedule and shoot video and interviews from multiple cities and from all sides of the issue. We would have to work fast and efficiently, and we did. The trip resulted in a two-part series, set to air during our November ratings period. The reports aired one week before voters narrowly rejected the initiative that sought to make Arkansas the first southern state to legalize marijuana as medicine.

All reporters have personal opinions, and I have a strong personal opinion about this subject. When reporting on any topic, the goal is to make sure viewers or readers cannot detect your opinion. Hopefully, if you choose to watch my two reports, you will not be able to tell which side of the fence I'm on.

Four years later, supporters successfully got the measure on the ballot again and this time it narrowly passed. At the time this book went to press, efforts to legalize marijuana in Arkansas for recreational use have failed.

LESSON LEARNED:
Politics and popular opinion can change quickly.

In 2012, Democrats dominated Arkansas politics, and a slight majority of voters—51.4 percent—did not believe treating pain and other ailments with marijuana was a good idea. Four years later, Republicans dominated Arkansas politics and a measure to legalize medicinal marijuana passed with 53 percent in favor. So don't get too discouraged or celebratory about the way things are because they can change quickly.

In addition to keeping our opinions in check, journalists also must work to keep their emotions in check. Whether it's a case of giggles, anger over a mistake, or sadness over a news story, the pursuit of professionalism is a valued trait.

Only once in my career do I recall becoming emotional on air. In the spring of 2001, a six-year-old girl named Haley Zega was missing. Haley had been walking a trail with her grandparents in the forest above the Buffalo National River when she fell behind and then wandered off alone.

By the time KATV sent our satellite truck to the area, Haley had already spent two nights in the wilderness and anxiety was running high. Six years earlier another six-year-old, Morgan Nick, had been abducted from a ballpark in Alma and she remains missing. Although the circumstances here were different, Morgan's mother, Colleen, came to the command site to comfort Haley's parents while search teams continued to comb the woods.

Two locals on mules suspected that the search teams might be looking in the wrong area, and they found Haley—dirty, dehydrated, and tired but safe—fifty-two hours after her solo adventure began. I'd spent the afternoon listening to people at a press conference, trying to remain positive in the face of dimming prospects. Now, about an hour before news time, everything changed. I had some amazing, positive news to share. This is, sadly, far too rare in our business.

This story coincided with the fact that I was a new parent, with an eighteen-month-old son and a daughter due in six months. As I shared the news of the joyous reunion that would be occurring soon (Haley was still being carried out of the woods to her parents), I let myself "go there" and put myself in Haley's parents' shoes. If you watch the video, my voice catches for a moment, and anyone paying close attention can tell I was moved by the news. There's certainly no need to apologize for displaying a normal human emotion. It's rare because journalists are trained and try hard to keep their emotions under wraps.

LESSON LEARNED:
Be real. Be sincere. People appreciate it.

I received a few comments from people who noticed. They loved the emotion displayed, even if it made me uncomfortable. In a world of social media where everyone tries to look and seem as close to perfect as possible, being honest and genuine is much needed and more relatable than ever.

CHAPTER 15

THE ENTERTAINING

(SPENCER AND SHELBY VISIT SAT. DB, WTIBYBI)

Perfect Smile Veneers promise big smile
confidence. Hmmm. What do you think?

MY JOURNALISM PROFESSOR, RAY NIEKAMP, gave me a lot of practical advice that no textbook ever covered, including something along the lines of, "Don't worry about becoming a news anchor. Concentrate on being the best reporter you can be. News directors want reporters who want to report, not reporters who want to anchor. If someone sees anchor potential in you, then you'll get a shot. But it's not up to you. Worry about things you can control."

It's not difficult to figure out why reporters want to anchor. It's more money and more prestige. But I knew early on that anchoring was not for me. The main reason? The hours. Anchors generally work a 1:30 p.m. to 10:30 p.m. shift. They may have time to go home for dinner between the 6 p.m. and 10 p.m. newscasts but only for sixty to ninety minutes. If you have school-aged children, they're gone when you go to work, and they're asleep when your workday ends. While you can provide more money, it comes at a price: less time. I've seen many colleagues struggle with work-life balance. If they leave the business, this is often the number one reason.

For most of my career, I enjoyed weekends off. But there was a stretch where I cohosted Saturday Daybreak with Renee Shapiro. The weekend weather people rotated in and out (most often Todd Yakoubian or Devon Lucie), as would the news readers and reporters (Anne Pressly, Christina Munoz, Janelle Lilley, and others). The show aired from 7:00 a.m. until 9 a.m., so I was home before our children, Spencer and Shelby, had time to miss me. But there were rare occasions when Mary Carol had to be out of town for the weekend and I would have to figure out what to do with the kids.

With grandparents either two hours away or out-of-state, we didn't have many early morning childcare options. So, on occasion, I had to bring them to work with me, settle them down in the break room, and check on them periodically during the show. They could sleep, watch cartoons, eat donuts or chips—anything, but come down to the studio, unless it was an emergency.

Like Adam and Eve in the garden, it's often difficult to abstain from doing the ONE thing you're not allowed to do. So, one Saturday morning the little darlings made an unexpected appearance on Saturday Daybreak during Renee's movie review segment.

I was mortified at the time but later comforted by viewers who emailed how much they enjoyed seeing our kids and how it reminded them of working days past when they also had to work and manage their kids.

Not all of Spencer's and Shelby's TV appearances were unintentional. They both served as occasional helpers on a weekly segment I did on another Channel 7 morning show.

In the year 2000, right at the start of a new century, KATV launched a new program called Good Morning Arkansas. News director Bob Steel approached me as the newly minted 7 On Your Side reporter and challenged me to come up with an idea for a weekly segment on the new one-hour show, which would start every weekday morning at nine o'clock. Since I was now earning more money than a regular reporter, it seemed logical that I should have more responsibility. Steel gave me the freedom to come up with my own ideas, so I proposed product testing, or specifically "As seen on TV" product testing.

Grill Daddy, Scrub Daddy, Dust Daddy, Angry Mama Microwave Cleaner.

Walmart, Walgreens, Bed Bath and Beyond, and other stores have sections and shelves dedicated to these often goofy and seemingly gimmicky gadgets.

One-Second Slicer, Three-Second Brow, Five-Second Fix, 30-Second Smile.

Some malls and outlets have entire stores that sell nothing but "As Seen on TV" products.

Hurricane Spin Mop, Tornado Can Opener, Fitness Twister, Cyclone Power Mixer.

I often wondered if any of these products worked, and I imagined a lot of other people wondered as well.

Insta Grip, Insta Fix, Insta Hang, Insta Slim.

So why not find out by spending the company's money and test the stuff myself?

My Pillow, Miracle Bamboo Pillow, Chillow, Pillow Pad.

The segment would be called, "We Try It Before You Buy It."

Wonder Wax, Wonder Snake, Wonder Hanger, Wonder Bible.

Right from the start the segments were wildly popular, in large part due to the chemistry that I enjoyed with show-host Steve Powell. While we both wanted to provide viewer benefit and determine the usefulness or uselessness of the products we featured, we also recognized the opportunity to entertain and have some fun. Self-cleaning litter boxes, The Water Bra, Toma's Tan Perfect, a body fat percentage scale, Lip-ink, a radar baseball, D-Snore, and the Peace of Mind alcohol detector are just some of the products we tested in those first few years.

KATV General Manager Dale Nicholson also liked the segment. He emailed Steel after the first "We Try it Before You Buy It" segment aired: "Good segment on GMA this a.m. . . . this is perfect for this show." —Dale

Sometimes we enlisted the help of volunteer viewers to try products like Nu-Bust, a pill for women claiming that it could increase cup size. On occasion we would enlist the help of a professional, like when we tested Lo-Bak Trax, a device designed to alleviate back pain. And, when we had a product designed for kids that needed to be tested, well, I knew where to find a pair.

One of my favorite product tests involving Spencer and Shelby was the TravelJohn Jr. Disposable Urinal. As one of those fathers who loves to make good time on a trip, I really wanted to know if this product could help reduce all of those "emergency" bathroom stops. The TravelJohn Jr. works like a portable potty. It's a bag full of diaper-like absorbent crystals attached to a form-fitting plastic oval-shaped rim. All I had to do to test the TravelJohn Jr. was to load the kids up with juice and water and then wait . . . as well as figure out a tasteful way to videotape them using the product. They were young enough to be unaware, unashamed, and unafraid. I intentionally did not tell Steve exactly how we tested the product. As I explained things to him live on the air while we watched the video we had recorded of the kids the day before, he was beside himself with laughter.

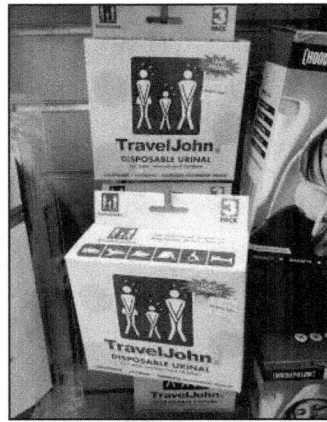

This test and others can be seen as part of a compilation of the early years of "We Try It Before You Buy It."

After I'd been doing the segment for about twelve or thirteen years, it got tougher to find new products to test. I asked news director Randy Dixon about the possibility of phasing out "We Try It Before You Buy It" and allowing me to come up with a new segment. I was unprepared for his reply. Not only would Channel 7 *not* be ending "We Try It Before You Buy It," because of its popularity it would now be featured weekly on *both* Daybreak and the 5:00 p.m. newscast. These were more lucrative shows for our sales staff and anything that might help improve the ratings of these shows, which were already very good, would be beneficial for KATV, if not for me. Jason Harper, Chris Kane, Scott Inman, Chris May, Erin Hawley, and many other anchors and hosts would now help me test products, many of them suggested by viewers. The dual goal never changed: to inform and entertain.

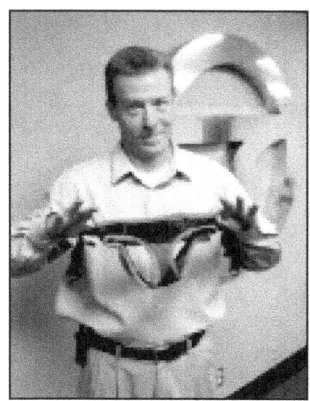 

A pet harness and "3-Second Brow" were two
of many products tested over the years (with
daughter Shelby pictured on the right).

Other stations tried to do similar product-testing segments. One that I remember was called "Deal or Dud." But without the commitment and consistency of one primary person to test a product each week, those attempts never lasted long. From 2000 to 2019, I tested in the neighborhood of 800 products. In mid-November of each year, we would auction off the products to our viewers. We gave the money raised (usually between $1,000 and $2,000) to the Salvation Army to help buy toys and gifts for any children on the Angel Trees who had not been adopted.

> **LESSON LEARNED:**
> *If it looks too good to be true, it probably is.*

A lot of talented people make commercials and infomercials that make "As Seen On TV" products look like must-have items. Save your money. Close to 90 percent of them don't live up to the hype, and the other 10 percent probably aren't needed.

MORE ENTERTAINMENT
(CHRISTMAS CELEBRITY KARAOKE)

Celebrating a 2012 Christmas Celebrity Karaoke victory with
KATV colleagues.   (Photo courtesy: DeWaine Duncan)

People who watch television news are usually doing other things at the same time. They're scrolling their phone, cooking dinner, visiting, reading, or doing laundry. Undivided attention is hard to get, which helps explain why, when I'm recognized in public, people often call me by the wrong name (typically Justin, Scott, or Chris). Many times, I'm not called by a name at all. I instead hear "Hey, Mr. 7 On Your Side" or "Channel Seven!" or "Newsman!" or "News Scene 7." I love the last one because it lets me know that person is a longtime viewer since KATV hasn't been known as News Scene 7 for many decades.

But even with less-than-attentive viewers, it's surprising how recognizable you are if you spend enough time reporting for the same TV station. Channel 7 viewers have approached me at Disney World, on the beaches of Gulf Shores, Alabama, and even at a small lakeside resort in northwestern Wisconsin. I was surprised and grateful each time.

Outside of my news persona, I was commonly recognized for two other contributions to central Arkansas culture: the "We Try It Before You Buy It" segments and Christmas Celebrity Karaoke.

In 2005, a local sports-talk radio station, 103.7 "The Buzz," hosted a Christmas Celebrity Karaoke event to help raise money for Youth Home, Inc. Located several miles west of Little Rock, Youth Home is a residential psychiatric treatment center for youths aged twelve to seventeen with underlying mental health diagnoses. The private nonprofit has operated since 1966. While in treatment, the teens at Youth Home live on campus, attend school, and receive counseling. Professionals work with both the kids and their families. It is a worthy cause, as more youth than ever struggle with mental health issues post-pandemic.

Christmas Celebrity Karaoke was the idea of morning radio host Tommy Smith, but it was Promotions and Marketing Director Lindy Blackstone-Lanford who cultivated that idea. "Philip Jonsson (the owner of the station group) was amazing, and he just wanted us to do whatever we thought would be successful," says Blackstone-Lanford. "We decided to make it a thing. Let's find a venue, partner with a charity, invite some local celebrities, charge $10 at the door, get some sponsors, and see what happens. And then it was insanity. Insanity!"

Blackstone-Lanford describes the venue chosen for the inaugural event, Hog Wild, as a typical dive-bar. Chrissy Jennings, Special Events Coordinator with Youth Home at the time, was collecting money at the door. "So many people handed me $20 bills and told me to keep the change," recalls Jennings. "The whole place was absolutely electric!"

"Chrissy had buckets of money," recalls Blackstone-Lanford. "She had to keep going to her car to dump money because people were just flooding in. I was freaking out. 'We don't have enough room!' The staff was overwhelmed. They were in tears. My boyfriend at the time was a bartender. He jumped over the bar and started schlepping drinks. It was incredible! It's a big blur now, but I remember thinking...wow. People really had fun. After that I knew and Tommy knew that...OK, this is something we can grow."

I did not attend the first event. A former Razorback football player, Anthony Lucas, won. He was joined in the competition by, among others, KTHV anchor Anne Jansen (who sang "Hit Me with Your Best Shot") and KATV anchor Beth Hunt (who sat on the lap of Arkansas Democrat-Gazette sportswriter Wally Hall and sang "Santa Baby").

When did the organizers know that this event, in the words of movie anchorman Ron Burgundy, was 'kind of a big deal?' "I would have to say first...when Anne Jansen sang and brought the house down," says Jennings. "But then the next morning when we talked about the event on the radio...the singers, the crowded room, the money raised, and the energy that was still surrounding all of us. We knew we wanted to do it again. I just hoped it would benefit Youth Home again!"

"The local celebrities were great, and the event wouldn't have been possible without them," says Blackstone-Lanford. "But it was Governor Beebe. Every year he would be like 'Hell yeah, I'm in.' And Justin Moore. I remember the first time he did it and I thought we literally have a big-time celebrity coming in. And Daly. John Daly!"

The second year, Christmas Celebrity Karaoke moved to Sticky Fingerz in Little Rock's River Market district. It was another packed house. Media personalities from both television and radio, newspaper columnists, politicians, former athletes, and coaches all came out to support the cause. I arrived dressed in a purple shirt borrowed from colleague Jason Harper and prepared to perform a song by Prince called "Kiss." Expectations for me were nonexistent since no one knew I could sing. The crowd liked it from the first note, and I fed off their energy.

I won, so the following year the element of surprise was gone. While I am an OK singer, there are many who are much better. I knew I would have to get creative if I were to defend my Christmas Celebrity Karaoke crown. The radio station hosts and their listeners primarily talk about the Razorbacks, so the crowds at these events were made up of sports fans, specifically Razorback fans, more specifically Razorback football fans.

In 2007, A LOT was going on with the football program. The Razorbacks had high expectations under head coach Houston Nutt after going 10–4 the previous year, rising to as high as #5 in the country and winning the western division of the Southeastern Conference (SEC). An easy opening win against Troy sent the #16 ranked Razorbacks to Tuscaloosa, where Alabama won a close game 41–38. But the fan base grew restless after two home losses to Kentucky and Auburn. Before the season was over, there were Freedom of Information Act requests for Nutt's state-issued phone, and planes flew over stadiums calling for his firing. An epic late-season 50–48 win over #1 LSU in Baton Rouge wasn't enough to save him. Before the bowl game, Nutt left the program and landed at rival Ole Miss.

The gasoline on this fire was social media. In 2007, Facebook was starting to explode, and talk radio and message boards gave voice to discontents and malcontents like never before. This toxic brew inspired me to rework the "The Grinch" lyrics, adding a little Christmas humor to Christmas Celebrity Karaoke. "The Grinch" would represent the rabid fans who are seemingly always unhappy. Here's the opening line that I sang in a deep bass voice, which was vastly different from my falsetto Prince imitation the year before:

> *You're always a critic ... Mr. Grinch*
> *You're neeeeh-ver saaaa-tis-fied*
> *If the Hogs were ten and two, it's the two that*
> *bother you*
> *Mr. Grriiii-inch. You are the dark side!*

The event was held at the old Cinema 150 at Asher and University in Little Rock. My good friend and colleague Matt DeCample helped my performance greatly by suggesting that I rent a Grinch costume and allow one of his improvisation buddies to silently perform alongside me. It would not be the last time Matt would lend his creativity to help me win.

The following year, I went political and lost. I was inspired by the election of Barack Obama and what it might mean for a country with a troubled racial past. I've always loved the song "Shed a Little Light" by James Taylor. It's a tribute to Martin Luther King, Jr. and a plea for "hope and love, sister and brotherhood." I was joined on stage at the Wildwood Performing Arts Center by members of the Arkansas Baptist College Choir, and I created a video featuring positive images that played on the big screen behind us as we sang. It was good, but it just wasn't what most people wanted. Years later, a woman came up to me and said she loved my karaoke performances but was disappointed that the only time she went to the event in person was the year I "went all serious." The performance was a favorite of my friend KATV meteorologist Melinda Mayo, but she's in the minority. I wasn't going to win in 2008 no matter what I did because the KATV women performed "Dancing Queen" in memory of Anne Pressly, who'd been murdered less than two months earlier. It was emotional. It was perfect— and it was unbeatable.

The KATV ladies would again take home the top trophy the following year as they danced and sang to Beyoncé's "Single Ladies (Put a Ring on It)." Their performance included a powerful solo by KATV Weekend Anchor Pamela Smith and a jaw-dropping appearance by KATV Sports Director Steve Sullivan, who pranced about the stage clad in a leotard. My performance as Weird Al Yankovic imitating Michael Jackson singing "Tweet It" was only good enough for second place.

With Steve Sullivan at the 2009 Karaoke event.

In 2010, Christmas Celebrity Karaoke was held for the third straight year west of Little Rock at Wildwood Performing Arts Center. I don't recall what inspired me, but I decided to sing "Endless Love," performing simultaneously as Lionel Richie and Diana Ross. There was panic in the days leading up to the show when the costume I'd ordered online didn't match the male/female wig I'd found. With the costume, the red dress was on the right side and the black and white tuxedo was on the left. But the flowing blonde hair of the wig was also on the left side. I had to wear the wig backward. After A LOT of work and hairspray it looked passable. The entire concept was somewhat ridiculous, so why shouldn't my appearance be ridiculous as well?

That victory was the first of five straight wins. In 2011, I partnered with Frankie Clay, a.k.a. "Sweet 'n Low," a man with dwarfism who lived up the street from Channel 7 at the old Albert Pike Hotel, a historic property built in 1929 and converted into income-restricted housing for seniors and people who are disabled. Frankie was often seen with a broom sweeping the sidewalk in front of the apartments, and over the years I would stop and visit with him. When I got the idea to turn "Just the Two of Us" by Grover Washington into a song about Santa and his favorite elf taking to the skies on Christmas Eve, Frankie was all in. He already had his costume since he would go to elementary schools during the Christmas season dressed as an elf. I wrote the lyrics and sang as Santa, while he voiced a rap and danced as Santa's little helper. I let Sweet 'n Low keep the trophy, which was slightly taller than him. At some point, Frankie moved to Jonesboro, and we lost touch. He died in November of 2022, a month shy of his seventy-seventh birthday. While writing this book, I contacted Frankie's daughter, Tammy Prince, and asked her if dwarf and/or dwarfism were the proper terms to describe her dad. She said yes, dwarf is the term he always used. She added that he read his Bible daily and preferred to be called "Sweet 'n Low" over anything else.

Frankie "Sweet 'n Low" Clay stands next to his
2011 Christmas Celebrity Karaoke trophy.

In 2012, the venue moved to the Jack Stephens Center on the campus of the University of Arkansas at Little Rock. After another tumultuous season and off-season for the Arkansas Razorbacks football team, I decided to sing Atlantic Starr's hit "Secret Lovers." I crossed the gender divide again; half of me was (former) Coach Bobby Petrino, and the other half was his twenty-five-year-old mistress, whom Petrino also employed. On April 1 of that year, the pair had an infamous motorcycle accident. I won't recount all the lurid details and fallout that followed, but the story was familiar to The Buzz listeners in the audience that evening. And they were ready to laugh about it.

In 2013, Celebrity Christmas Karaoke hit the big-time: it would be held at Verizon Arena (now Simmons Bank Arena), the same venue that hosted Taylor Swift, Bruno Mars, and George Strait! But what to perform? That year, the top trending video on YouTube was an electronic novelty dance song by a Norwegian duo called Ylvis. The song "The Fox (What Does the Fox Say?)" was a top 10 hit in the U.S., around the time of Christmas Celebrity Karaoke. I reworked the lyrics and made the song into an Arkansas original—but making it work on stage would require a bunch of help from many mascots.

While Ylvis may have wondered what the fox says, I was more concerned about what sound the weevil makes, as in the cotton-munching boll weevil. The boll weevil is a pest worthy of insecticide but also worthy of the title of mascot at the University of Arkansas at Monticello (UAM). If I could recruit the boll weevil mascot to be a part of my act, then I could work on finding other state mascots to join in the performance. Thankfully, UAM's boll weevil said yes.

Next, I started with the top targets: the University of Arkansas (U of A), Arkansas State University (ASU), and the University of Arkansas at Pine Bluff (UAPB). The U of A's Big Red, Sue E, and Pork Chop all had prior commitments. So did the inflatable Boss Hog. As for ASU, the Red Wolf wanted to be reimbursed for travel and put up at a Little Rock hotel the night of the performance. These were reasonable requests, I suppose, but there's no prize money for winning this charity event, just bragging rights, and I couldn't bankroll his demands. I couldn't reach UAPB's Golden Lion, so I set my sights on other colleges and high schools. Amazingly, Southern Arkansas University (SAU)'s Mule Rider was willing to travel from Magnolia to North Little Rock for the show. On cue during the performance, she rode her mule onto the arena floor to the delight of the crowd. The other mascots who agreed to join me on stage included the University of Arkansas at Little Rock (UALR)

Trojan, the Lake Hamilton Wolf, the Bryant Hornet, the Benton Panther, and the Tiger of Little Rock Central.

If you watch the video by Ylvis, you'll see a lot of craziness and hear a lot of gibberish. I captured the craziness with all the mascots, but I needed to add gibberish. So, I once again turned to Matt DeCample for help, this time utilizing his vocal and improvisational skills. Matt and I had worked together as reporters at KATV for many years before he became spokesperson for Mike Beebe, first in Beebe's role as Arkansas' attorney general and then as Arkansas' governor. Matt did everything he could to support his boss and set him up for victories, and he would do the same for his friends. That quality or ability is ingrained in improv performers, and it was in Matt's DNA, too. Mike Beebe benefited, I benefited, and so did many others fortunate enough to call Matt a friend. Matt left this earth way too soon in 2019 at the age of forty-four. He battled a rare form of liver cancer and humorously blogged about it ("Mattie D vs. The Evil C") for three years and lived longer than predicted. In addition to his mother, father, sister, and beloved niece, the worlds of Arkansas journalism, politics, and theater all mourned his loss.

Matt DeCample and I celebrate a 2015 Karaoke
victory backstage with a few of our closest
friends. (Photo courtesy: DeWain Duncan)

Here's the story behind the story of that 2015 Karaoke win.

Matt, the mascots, and I almost never hit the stage. One of the people who meant the most to me died the morning of the event. Robert "Pappaw" Chowning was my wife's grandfather, but he called me his grandson and treated me like blood. Pappaw and Paul Eells were the two kindest men I have ever known. It was truly a blow, but with all those mascots coming to Little Rock to join me, I decided the show must go on. It turned out to be a welcome distraction from the grief that Mary Carol and I were processing. Had he been alive to watch my performance, Pappaw would have smiled and chuckled and privately wondered what in the world he was viewing. But as a champion of me and everyone he loved, Pappaw would've said it was "Outstanding!" It's hard to say goodbye to someone who was always happy to see you.

In 2014, event emcee and morning radio host David "Baz" Bazzel was certain my winning streak was about to end. I picked the song, "Nobody" by Keith Sweat, which David had never heard.

My inspiration was born out of the Channel 7 edit bays, where at times electric fans were needed to help keep the small rooms cooler in the summer. I would sing into the fans to amuse photojournalists Richard Newman, Tony Ranchino, and others. As a huge Keith Sweat fan, Ranchino especially enjoyed this. But the Keith Sweat song is a duet, so I needed a partner. I posted a two-part question on Facebook to help find the right person. It read: 1. If you know who Athena Cage is, continue. 2. If you can sing like her or know someone who can, continue. 3. If you have a lot of entertainer in you, continue. 4. Inbox me. Fortunately, Tiffany Lowrey of White Hall replied.

The day before the performance, which I intended to sing without altering the lyrics, our daughter Shelby questioned the wisdom of that decision. "Does Mom know?" she asked me after listening to the song. I said, "Yes, why?" "Well, it's kind of a romantic song and you are singing it with another woman." I agreed that it might come off as a bit odd, and although it seemed crazy to make a major change on such short notice, I reworked the lyrics and turned it into a 7 On Your Side jam:

> *I'm here to help you*
> *If somebodys hurt you.*
> *If there's a scam going on*
> *I want to alert you.*
>
> *And if there's a product*
> *That you see on TV*
> *Please wait til I try it*
> *You might save some money.*
>
> *Who can help you like me? Nobody.*
> *Who will help you for free? Nobody.*
> *Who puts crooks on TV? Nobody.*
> *Nobody baby.*

I wore a silk shirt borrowed from colleague Tyrone McIntosh that waved in the wind, a breeze created by the fan I used to manufacture an amusing vibrato every time I sang the word "nobody." Then, after two refrains, Tiffany walked on stage and blew the crowd away with her soaring, impassioned vocals ... playing a poor scam victim who called 7 On Your Side and got the help she desperately needed. Much to the surprise of Baz, the audience loved it, and Tiffany got to sing both at Verizon Arena and take home trophy #7.

Even before that win, there'd been grumblings about my success. Baz told me it was getting harder to recruit performers because "You always win." Some felt I unfairly benefited because I performed near the end. Others felt the judges were biased, or the competition was somehow rigged. Many talented people from other media outlets and other areas of public life put serious effort and money into their entertaining acts. The public was willing to pay good money to attend the event during a busy month not only because it supported Youth Home, but because the talent level on display was genuinely top-notch. Baz was trying to keep a lot of people happy, so it was decided that my days of winning were over. The trophy would be named for me, and I would still perform at night's end, while the judges tabulated their scorecards. But I was no longer eligible to win.

In 2015, the event was once again held at Verizon Arena. I had some fun with the new dynamic, coming out following a humble introduction dressed like a king and singing reworked lyrics to Taylor Swift's "Blank Space."

> *Kara-oke ... I'm the King*
> *Seven times I've worn this crown*
> *But this year, here's the thing*
> *They all think I should step down*
> *Because ... it's not fair*

Other acts . . . don't have a prayer
All this glory I should shaaaaare. Oh no.

When Joe Montana won his third,
No one told him he couldn't win four
When Jimmie Johnson won his sixth,
No one told him he couldn't win more
Because . . . that's what makes
The good 'ol USA so great
You work hard, do what it takes
And then they tell you, you can't win
It kind of sounds like socialism!

Stuck on seven wins forever
No chance for victory
For me the competition's over
My performance now is honorary

There's a long list of ex-losers
For someone that's about to change
The trophy's got a blank space, baby
It should have my name.

Mary Carol and her sweet aunts, Mary Depper
and Margaret Pierce, visit with the "Karaoke King"
backstage at Christmas Celebrity Karaoke 2015.

In 2016, Christmas Celebrity Karaoke moved to the Statehouse Convention Center. Matt DeCample and I collaborated on an act set to the song "Hey There, Delilah" by the Plain White T's. We dressed like redneck Razorback fans and sang "Hey There, Bielema," as in Razorback football coach Bret Bielema. After an up-and-down season, the Hogs went from 5–3 in SEC play the year before to 3–5, ending with two bad losses. The fan base was split; some loved Coach B, and others were ready for a change. So, we presented both sides of the debate. With a country twang, I sang about Bielema's positives, and Matt did the same with the negatives. We had a lot of fun with it. And Matt was right—things got worse the next year, and Coach B was history.

Matt DeCample and me at Christmas Celebrity Karaoke 2016.

The following year, the event was back at Verizon Arena. I sang "Body Like a Back Road" by Sam Hunt, a hot hit at the time. My creative twist: I did impressions with a video on the big screen to help the audience recognize who I was trying to imitate. The impressions included Kermit the Frog, Sean Connery, Porky Pig,

Patrick Star, Prince, Barry White, Hermey the Elf from *Rudolph the Red-Nosed Reindeer*, and even Drive Time Sports Radio Host Randy Rainwater!

By 2018, Christmas Celebrity Karaoke began losing steam. Make no mistake, 2005 to 2018 was an incredibly successful run, but all events have a shelf life. So, the 2018 event was billed as the "last hurrah" as well as a tribute to longtime radio host Tommy Smith. Blackstone-Lanford, who stopped organizing the event when she left the radio station in 2011, was brought back to plan this special finale...and to keep it a secret from both Tommy and Baz. It was held at The Rep, a downtown Little Rock theater. I dressed up as Johnny Cash and instead of "Because you're mine, I walk the line," I sang "Before you buy, first let me try."

It was a special night for me because my mother-in-law, Diane, joined Mary Carol and attended the show. Although her intentions were always to join in, the reality at that point in her life was she often needed or chose to stay home instead. It was wonderful to have her there and watch her have such a good time. Her health would decline, and she passed away about a year later. But on that night, she laughed a lot—and for that, I am grateful for Christmas Celebrity Karaoke.

Performing as Johnny Cash in 2018.
(photo courtesy: DeWaine Duncan)

Central Arkansas car dealer Frank Fletcher would donate $10,000 to Youth Home at most of these events. Youth Home COO Larry Betz says that Fletcher's generosity, coupled with the $5,000–$6,000 that each Christmas Celebrity Karaoke event raised, was used to pay for Youth Home's "Christmas for Kids" campaign. Betz says the gifts and goodies help to brighten the holidays for the seventy or so kids who spend Christmas on the Youth Home campus each year.

Youth Home volunteers helped make each event run smoothly. Betz says that while other events may have raised more money for Youth Home, the media attention and publicity that Christmas Celebrity Karaoke generated for the nonprofit was hard to beat. Betz was given opportunities to talk about what Youth Home does and the young people it serves, which he says generated more supporters, volunteers, and donations. According to Betz, "The Buzz" events attracted a different crowd than those who attended glitzy galas or golf scrambles. Betz adds, "Talking on the air and on stage about mental illness ten to fifteen years ago still carried a stigma.

This event helped normalize the important conversations that needed and continue to need to happen in order to help individuals and families find help."

The first event in which Betz participated was in 2010. He said he had doubts when event organizer Lindy Blackstone told him that tickets would sell out on the first day. But she was right, which is when Betz realized what a big deal Christmas Celebrity Karaoke was to the nonprofit he had just joined. "The professional and personal relationships it helped create and strengthen over the years, not only for Youth Home but for me personally, are precious." Betz adds that after each event there was an after-party at Cajun's Wharf in Little Rock, but he says those recollections are best left off the printed page.

Christmas Celebrity Karaoke has continued...just in a manner more like the original event at that west Little Rock dive bar as opposed to the extravagance of later events when the competition was at its peak. "Honestly, I think, Channel 7 during that time and The Buzz during that time will never be recreated," says Blackstone-Lanford. "Your group during that time and our group was so special. You just can't...I don't think it could ever be...you can't get that back. We were a family. We did so much together."

For readers who are interested, some of the Christmas Celebrity Karaoke performances described on these pages can be found by searching my name on YouTube. I hope you enjoy them and remember it was all for the kids.

> **LESSON LEARNED:**
> *Give 100 percent and have an ace up your sleeve in case that's not enough.*

I learned this lesson in college when I entered and won a "hot buns" contest at The Rendezvous Bar in Somerset, Wisconsin. Did I have the best buns? Absolutely not. In fact, I had entered on previous nights and not won. But I was the only contestant at the club that night who dropped his pants to reveal a straw-hat-wearing-stork G-string (sorry, no QR code). The crowd loved it, so I won the $100 bar tab and bought most of my fellow patrons a drink. Although I can sing and have a decent voice, there were always Christmas Celebrity Karaoke contestants who had better voices and who could sing better. But while people appreciate talent, they really appreciate being entertained by someone who goes "all in." If it's worth your time, do it to the best of your ability. "Seven-time Christmas Celebrity Karaoke champion" might merit a line in my obituary one day.

EPILOGUE

THE GOODBYE

(UNDELIVERED)

UNLESS YOU'RE A MAIN ANCHOR who is leaving central Arkansas or retiring, most television personalities don't get to say goodbye to the public. One day you see us; the next day, we're gone without explanation (although the *Arkansas Democrat-Gazette* and other publications noted my departure). It's just the way management prefers to do things. The public doesn't like it, but I don't have a problem with it. How many other jobs allow for public farewells? Not many. I did write a goodbye speech for my newsroom colleagues and planned to share it at a Christmas luncheon to which I was graciously invited, despite having left KATV for a job at the Arkansas Department of Human Services a month earlier. Time didn't allow for me to share it that day, so I'll share it here:

> I stopped off at the post office on my way to this staff luncheon today and the woman working the counter congratulated me on my new job. Then she asked a question that I've been getting a lot lately: "So who is going to replace you?" I told her that I didn't know and that they were working on it. She replied, "Well, I hope so. We have got to keep that thing going."
>
> Note her use of the word "we." After over thirty years, people in Arkansas feel a sense of ownership of our 7 On Your Side franchise. So does KATV, as evidenced by the recent branding of the station as "On Your Side."
>
> What you all hopefully know is that even though I've left, 7 On Your Side continues. Dan and his team of volunteers are here with us today, and they show up every Tuesday, Wednesday, and Thursday morning to help Arkansans with their problems. That is important to know because anyone who has worked at KATV for a while—I don't care on what floor or in what department—has probably heard the following: "Hey, you work for Channel 7. I need to contact 7 On Your Side." It feels good to be able to give them

the number 501-324-HELP. More than that, it feels good to give them some hope.

A lot changed during my twenty-four years with KATV. We had a change in ownership, a change in general manager, and several different news directors. We lost a legendary sports anchor and celebrated a legendary meteorologist when he retired. But two things remained unchanged: Channel 7 is the only station in central Arkansas serving the public with a full-time consumer reporter, and Channel 7 is a popular ratings leader.

When 7 On Your Side was launched in 1987, KATV was not a dominant #1. Channel 4 [KARK] was often the ratings leader. Things started to change in the early '90s. Dewayne Graham's arrival as the 7 On Your Side reporter was a huge part of that change. Then News Director Bob Steel left KARK and joined KATV and convinced some big-time talent like Steve Sullivan, Melinda Mayo, and Barry Brandt to join him. The leadership at KARK also made some poor decisions that alienated loyal viewers. By the time I arrived in 1995, KATV was on top and has with rare exception stayed there.

In 1999, Dewayne decided to run for Congress. I took over his duties and inherited a healthy franchise ... I just needed to listen to Donna (Nunn, longtime 7 On Your Side producer) and avoid screwing things up. We added some new stuff like product testing and a partnership with the Arkansas Better Business Bureau, but for the most part, the mission remained the same: help, educate, alert, and listen to our viewers.

KATV is currently posting an opening for an investigative reporter. I was not an investigative reporter; I was a consumer reporter who worked on investigations when time allowed. I won a few awards for investigative work, but for the most part my job was assisting Arkansans. It was rewarding work and greatly valued by the public. Look at past internal surveys if you need proof.

If the public loves 7 On Your Side so much, why haven't other stations developed their own brand? "Here 4 You" seems logical. Good question. I believe there are several reasons. Having a consumer reporter can be a pain in the butt for management. We expose scammers and scoundrels and sometimes they threaten to sue us. We also can irritate advertisers when we call asking about a complaint. I know one car dealer who will never send me a Christmas card. Plus, it takes office space, infrastructure, and a producer and a team of great volunteers to make things work. Those are probably the reasons why no other station has added a consumer reporter to their news team.

7 On Your Side is the biggest thing that separates us from our competition and the biggest reason why I believe KATV has remained a solid #1 for over a quarter century.

Every station has investigative reporters. My hope ... and the hope of the postal worker I visited with this morning ... is that we keep 7 On Your Side going; that Channel 7 will continue to dedicate a consumer reporter to serve Arkansans. It's also my hope that in doing so, Channel 7 maintains a bond with our viewers, allowing all of you, my friends and colleagues, to continue to enjoy ratings success and the stability that comes with it."

And it has kept going, with Marine Glisovic becoming the first female 7 On Your Side reporter. Keeping the franchise going is good news because, as evidenced by the scam letter I discovered from 1860, scoundrels aren't new and aren't going away.

ACKNOWLEDGMENTS

IN 2002, THE CITY OF Conway, Arkansas, experienced its first double murder—the execution-style killing of businessman Carter Elliott and his young protégé, Timothy Wayne Robertson. Without that sordid story, you might not be reading this book.

That's because Carter Elliott's daughter, Ashley Elliott, wrote a book about her father's murder. She was twenty-five when her father was murdered and thirty-five before anyone was charged. In 2013, Richard Conte was sentenced to life in prison without parole, where he died in 2018. In 2021, after many years of research and assistance, Ashley published *The Demon in Disguise*. Her book recounts the story of her father's murder, her mother's kidnapping, and the long, winding road to justice.

I was at Barnes and Noble looking at books by Arkansas authors and specifically who published those books, when I saw Elliott's book. I bought a copy, read it, and liked it. Elliott utilized the services of a ghostwriter, Michael Coffino. I wondered what that process was like. What services did her ghostwriter provide? What did it cost to publish her book? How did she find a publisher and a printer? In March of 2022, I contacted her. Ashley was gracious enough to answer my questions and put me in touch with Coffino in California, who in turn was gracious enough to put me in touch with others who were helpful in moving my manuscript toward publication.

The first of these was Carolyn Schurr Levin, a New York attorney. Levin reviewed my contract with KATV and offered advice on how to approach my former employer and request permission to use video clips of my work. Over the years, I saved clips of some of my stories and performances. I had clips on a hard drive, DVDs, thumb drives, VHS, and half-inch and three-quarter-inch video-tapes. Getting those clips organized and usable for you, the reader, required help from my former KATV colleague Kenny Reynolds. I can't thank him enough.

Next, Coffino put me in touch with David Wogahn in California. Wogahn has written five publishing how-to books and is founder of AuthorImprints, a professional self-publishing services com-pany. We entered a partnership that was instrumental in getting my book into your hands.

Wogahn's first order of business was to refer me to a professional editor, Paula Fitzgerald (also in California). I did not hand her a raw manuscript in need of a ton of work. A former *Arkansas Democrat-Gazette* reporter and now Department of Human Ser-vices (DHS) colleague, Amy Webb, had already applied her gram-mar-policing skills to it. My late father-in-law, Jim Spencer, a prac-ticing attorney for over fifty years, also read it with potential legal pitfalls in mind. And my wife, Mary Carol, offered some very wise edits and revisions that helped make it a better read by the time I sent it to Fitzgerald.

As good as I thought it was, Fitzgerald applied her expertise and keen eye to what I had written and made it much, much better. She helped weave a thread of consistency throughout this book. And her attention went beyond spelling, punctuation, and verb tense consistency. Fitzgerald added comments, telling me what she liked, what she didn't like, and why. Many things I changed, a few I left the same, but regardless this book is a much more enjoyable read for you because of her involvement.

Two other DHS colleagues helped with key elements. Ben Mathews worked to develop a website to accompany the book and Ben created the QR codes, or flow codes, that will allow you to watch many of the stories and events. I've decided it is pointless to try and convince people to put down their smart phones. In fact, I don't want you to! Keep your phone handy while you read. I hope you find the ability to watch the dozens of related video clips as cool as I do! And if you like this book's killer cover, much of that credit goes to photographer Kaitlin Davidson. The lens, location, lighting . . . she made me look like . . . somebody knocking!

David Wogahn and his daughter, Manon, took things from there. From book cover design, formatting, copyright, and ISBN numbers to printing decisions and marketing advice . . . the Wogahn clan was helpful and available throughout the process. They offered great guidance and supported my decisions on the rare occasions when our opinions differed.

All this assistance costs money, and I am deeply grateful to have a wife who supported me through the process. Contrary to public perception, being on TV does not necessarily mean you're rich. As Ashley Elliott informed me, getting a book from your mind onto the page and ultimately into the hands of readers—when done right—is an expensive process. Mary Carol never blinked; she is an invaluable source of encouragement for which I am truly grateful. Thank you, Sweet.

I wouldn't have these stories to tell and these lessons to share if it weren't for KATV. Channel 7 provided me with a career I enjoyed and a salary with which I could support my family for nearly twenty-five years. That made me a much happier husband and father. I am thankful to have worked with so many fun and talented people over the years, many of whom (but nowhere near all of them) are mentioned throughout this book. One who deserves special mention here: longtime 7 On Your Side producer Donna Nunn. Donna's oversight, attention to detail, organizational skills, and sharp mind are major reasons why, despite wading into contentious disputes weekly, 7 On Your Side never settled a lawsuit and was never sued successfully. Donna and the dedicated volunteers she trained and supervised were the backbone of the franchise. Plus, she is a fun-loving, warm, and wonderful person!

And, of course, KATV wouldn't have been such a great place to work had it not been for many of you, our loyal Channel 7 viewers. I still enjoy being approached by many of you, and if I'm ever going to get back some of the family finances that I put into this book, I'm going to need your help! If you like what you read, tell a friend. Share about the book on social media. Invite me to speak and sign books at your book club, church, civic group, or library. Visit Amazon or www.jasonpedersonbook.com and buy a copy or two. Thank you in advance.

I would also like to acknowledge the foundational influences of my parents, Joel and Judy Pederson, as well as our church, Fellowship Bible Church, and specifically the teachings of Dr. Robert Lewis. My work ethic and desire to provide for all the needs of my family were instilled by these people. They also helped mold a man who strived to bring a sense of justice and fairness to the role of consumer reporter. I tried hard not to prejudge anyone or any situation, and I brought peace and joy to an oftentimes difficult job that in many cases surpassed all understanding, including my own.

ABOUT THE AUTHOR

JASON PEDERSON IS A WISCONSINITE by birth, an Arkansan by choice, saved by grace, and for nearly twenty-five years employed as a television reporter by KATV Channel 7, the ABC affiliate in Little Rock.

During his time in Arkansas television, Jason earned one Regional Emmy award, two Regional Edward R. Murrow awards, and a host of Arkansas Associated Press awards. In 2002, Pederson was named Citizen of the Year by the Arkansas Trial Lawyers Association, and in 2018 he was presented with the Liberty Bell Award by the Pulaski County Bar Association. Jason's talents earned recognition outside the field of journalism, too. For example, he owns several Arkansas State Fair Celebrity Cow Chip Toss titles, and Jason was crowned Christmas Celebrity Karaoke King seven times.

Pederson has served on the board of Soaring Wings Ranch in Faulkner County for over fifteen years, and he recently joined the board of the Salvation Army's Central Arkansas Area Command. He has mentored young men for more than twenty-five years via his church, the Little Rock School District's Volunteers in Public Schools (VIFS) program, CityChurch Network, and STEP Ministries.

As for family life, Jason married Mary Carol Spencer of El Dorado, Arkansas, in 1995, and they began attending Fellowship Bible Church in Little Rock that same year. The Pedersons are proud parents of two biological adult children, Spencer and Shelby, as well as an adult "bonus-son," J.B., and his wife, Terra, and son, Eli. It is a beautiful family that only God could have assembled.

Jason left television and took a job with the Arkansas Department of Human Services in 2019, only months before the pandemic would change so much for so many. At the time of this book's publication, he was serving as Deputy Chief of Community Engagement for the Arkansas Department of Human Services.